University Textbook Series

June, 1987

Especially Designed for Collateral Reading

HARRY W. JONES
Directing Editor
Professor of Law, Columbia University

ADMINISTRATIVE LAW AND PROCESS (1985)
Richard J. Pierce, Jr., Dean and Professor of Law, University of Pittsburgh.
Sidney A. Shapiro, Professor of Law, University of Kansas.
Paul R. Verkuil, President and Professor of Law, College of William and Mary.

ADMIRALTY, Second Edition (1975)
Grant Gilmore, Professor of Law, Yale University.
Charles L. Black, Jr., Professor of Law, Yale University.

ADMIRALTY AND FEDERALISM (1970)
David W. Robertson, Professor of Law, University of Texas.

AGENCY (1975)
W. Edward Sell, Dean of the School of Law, University of Pittsburgh.

BUSINESS ORGANIZATION AND FINANCE, Second Edition (1986)
William A. Klein, Professor of Law, University of California, Los Angeles.
John C. Coffee, Jr., Professor of Law, Columbia University.

CIVIL PROCEDURE, BASIC, Second Edition (1979)
Milton D. Green, Professor of Law Emeritus, University of California, Hastings College of the Law.

COMMERCIAL TRANSACTIONS, INTRODUCTION TO (1977)
Hon. Robert Braucher, Associate Justice, Supreme Judicial Court of Massachusetts.
Robert A. Riegert, Professor of Law, Cumberland School of Law.

CONFLICT OF LAWS, COMMENTARY ON THE, Third Edition (1986)
Russell J. Weintraub, Professor of Law, University of Texas.

CONSTITUTIONAL LAW, AMERICAN (A TREATISE ON) (1978) with 1979 Supplement
Laurence H. Tribe, Professor of Law, Harvard University.

CONTRACT LAW, THE CAPABILITY PROBLEM IN (1978)
Richard Danzig.

CORPORATE TAXATION (1987)
Howard E. Abrams, Professor of Law, Emory University.
Richard L. Doernberg, Professor of Law, Emory University.

CORPORATIONS, Second Edition (1971)
Norman D. Lattin, Professor of Law, University of California, Hastings College of the Law.

i

UNIVERSITY TEXTBOOK SERIES—Continued

CORPORATIONS IN PERSPECTIVE (1976)
Alfred F. Conard, Professor of Law, University of Michigan.

CRIMINAL LAW, Third Edition (1982)
Rollin M. Perkins, Professor of Law, University of California, Hastings College of the Law.
Ronald N. Boyce, Professor of Law, University of Utah College of Law.

CRIMINAL PROCEDURE, Second Edition (1986)
Charles H. Whitebread, II, Professor of Law, University of Southern California.
Christopher Slobogin, Associate Professor of Law, University of Florida.

ESTATES IN LAND & FUTURE INTERESTS, PREFACE TO, Second Edition (1984)
Thomas F. Bergin, Professor of Law, University of Virginia.
Paul G. Haskell, Professor of Law, University of North Carolina.

EVIDENCE: COMMON SENSE AND COMMON LAW (1947)
John M. Maguire, Professor of Law, Harvard University.

EVIDENCE, STUDENTS' TEXT ON THE LAW OF (1935)
The late John Henry Wigmore, Northwestern University.

JURISPRUDENCE: MEN AND IDEAS OF THE LAW (1953)
The late Edwin W. Patterson, Cardozo Professor of Jurisprudence, Columbia University.

LEGAL CAPITAL, Second Edition (1981)
Bayless Manning.

LEGAL RESEARCH ILLUSTRATED, 1987 Edition with 1985 Assignments Supplement
J. Myron Jacobstein, Professor of Law, Law Librarian, Stanford University.
Roy M. Mersky, Professor of Law, Director of Research, University of Texas.

LEGAL RESEARCH, FUNDAMENTALS OF, 1987 Edition with 1985 Assignments Supplement
J. Myron Jacobstein, Professor of Law, Law Librarian, Stanford University.
Roy M. Mersky, Professor of Law, Director of Research, University of Texas.

PROCEDURE, THE STRUCTURE OF (1979)
Robert M. Cover, Professor of Law, Yale University.
Owen M. Fiss, Professor of Law, Yale University.

PROPERTY, Second Edition (1975)
John E. Cribbet, Dean of the Law School, University of Illinois.

TAXATION, FEDERAL INCOME, Fourth Edition (1985)
Marvin A. Chirelstein, Professor of Law, Columbia University.

TORTS, Second Edition (1980)
Clarence Morris, Professor of Law, University of Pennsylvania.
C. Robert Morris, Professor of Law, University of Minnesota.

TRUSTS, PREFACE TO THE LAW OF (1975)
Paul G. Haskell, Professor of Law, University of North Carolina.

WILLS AND TRUSTS, THE PLANNING AND DRAFTING OF, Second Edition (1979) with 1982 Supplement
Thomas L. Shaffer, Professor of Law, University of Notre Dame.

WILLS, TRUSTS AND ADMINISTRATION, PREFACE TO (1987)
Paul G. Haskell, Professor of Law, University of North Carolina.

PREFACE TO ESTATES IN LAND AND FUTURE INTERESTS

By

THOMAS F. BERGIN
William Minor Lile Professor of Law
University of Virginia School of Law

and

PAUL G. HASKELL
Graham Kenan Professor of Law
University of North Carolina School of Law

SECOND EDITION

Mineola, New York
THE FOUNDATION PRESS, INC.
1984

Library of Congress Cataloging in Publication Data

Bergin, Thomas F. (Thomas Francis), 1924–
  Preface to estates in land & future interests.

  (University textbook series)
  Includes index.
  1. Estates (Law)—United States. 2. Future interests—United States. I. Haskell, Paul G. II. Title. III. Series.
KF577.B4 1984   346.7304'2   84–13695
ISBN 0-88277-184-1 347.30642

Bergin & Haskell 2nd Ed. UTB

2nd Reprint—1987

PREFACE

The purpose of this book is to enable students to master a good deal of doctrinal material on their own, and to provide the teacher with more class time to deal with cases, problems, and policy considerations. Part I defines the several estates and future interests and traces their historical development—common components of the first-year Property course. Part II deals with matters treated in the Trusts and Estates course: conditions of survivorship, class gifts, powers of appointment, and the rule against perpetuities.

Estates and future interests is a complex, highly-technical body of material, foreign to most students' experience, and difficult to grasp. If there is any law school subject that calls for supplemental textual material, this is it. We have attempted to present this subject in readable style; but we must caution our student readers to beware of the tidiness, the consoling symmetry, of the rule system we present. Rules are important, but they are only part of "the law." In the judicial resolution of disputes, rules are sometimes determinative, but often they are used to rationalize results arrived at on other grounds. In out-of-court resolution of disputes, rules may, once again, be determinative, but frequently they are only one factor among several that affect the course of the negotiations.

This second edition maintains the organization and basic content of the first edition. Why, then, a second edition? First, we have reworked the presentation in a number of places to make the book a better self-teaching device. Secondly, although future interests is not one of the more dynamic areas of the law, there have been a good number of changes in the almost two decades since the first edition was published. There has been new legislation on powers of appointment and perpetuities and in several constructional areas, and the Uniform Probate Code has been adopted in whole or in part in a number of states. The Restatement (Second) of Property, Donative Transfers, dealing with perpetuities and powers of appointment, has come into being. There have also been many new judicial decisions. Future interests requires a new edition every eighteen years.

We wish to acknowledge with gratitude the fine help given us in the preparation of this edition by our student assistants. Therese Michaels, Debra Whited, and Carolyn Wood, all of the class of 1983, University of North Carolina School of Law, provided valuable research assistance, as did Anthony Valente of the University of Virginia School of Law, class of 1983. The improvements in

PREFACE

Part I owe so substantially to the professional editing and writing abilities of Amy Moore, also of Virginia's law class of 1983, that we note here with special gratitude her important contribution to this edition.

THOMAS F. BERGIN
PAUL G. HASKELL

July 1984

SUMMARY OF CONTENTS

*

TABLE OF CONTENTS

*

PREFACE TO ESTATES IN LAND AND FUTURE INTERESTS

*

Part I

THE TRADITIONAL CLASSIFICATIONS OF ESTATES AND FUTURE INTERESTS

Chapter 1

THE FEUDAL BEGINNINGS

SECTION 1. INTRODUCTION

Property students in the United States are likely to have ambivalent feelings about the Battle of Hastings. As pure history, the story of the Norman Conquest of England is as colorful as the Bayeux Tapestry, bringing to mind knights in armor and kingly combat. But for the student of American property law, the pleasure of reading about Duke William's glorious expedition against King Harold is likely to be tinctured by the memory that it was this same William the Bastard who set in motion the forces that would make American property law the monstrously complex and mysterious body of law that it is.

The English law student may think more kindly of the Conqueror; for the enactment, in 1925, of wide-sweeping statutory reforms wiped away in England much of the ancient dogma that the American law student must still learn.[1] It is a strange twist of history that at almost the same time the 1925 reforms were becoming effective in England, the American Law Institute was embarking on its massive *Restatement of the Law of Property*, which would, when published in 1936, give new life to the old learning.[2] The blunt fact is that the English can celebrate their Hastings; we Americans must live with it.

We do not propose to present in this text even a concise history of English feudalism. "Concise" histories have a way of becom-

---

1. The vehicles of reform were the Law of Property Act, 1925, 15 & 16 Geo. 5, c. 20, and its two predecessor and six companion acts. See generally Cheshire's Modern Law of Real Property, E. H. Burn, ed., 8–9, 82–112 (12th ed. 1976) [hereinafter cited as Cheshire].

2. See Restatement, Property (1936, 1940, 1944) (5 vols.). For criticism of the Restatement, see Clark, Real Covenants and Other Interests Which "Run With Land" (2d ed. 1947); McDougal, Future Interests Restated: Tradition Versus Clarification and Reform, 55 Harv.L.Rev. 1077 (1942).

ing 700-page books.[3]   Nor do we propose even to present the standard catalogue of labels that distinguish the various forms of feudal land-holding.[4]   Our purpose is to present just enough of the feudal background to make intelligible to the law student some of the more important doctrines and concepts of our modern law of property.   Many of those doctrines and concepts trace their beginnings to the institution of *tenure by knight service*. In this chapter we shall attempt to show how that most feudal of feudal institutions contributed to the development of three of our modern property notions: potentially infinite ownership through inheritability;   free alienability;   and independent ownership.

SECTION 2.   FEUDAL LAND-HOLDING: TRANSFER BY INFEUDATION AND SUBINFEUDATION

It was one thing for William to win his crown, but it was something else again for him to hold it.   Had it been a twentieth-century England he had conquered, his task would have been an easier one.   He should not have found it difficult to establish adequate control over a country that had an established system of transportation and communication, a monetary system controlled through an existing central bank, a population largely dependent for its survival on the continuance of major industrial enterprise, an organized tax collection process, and a single defeated national military force.   But the England of 1066 did not lend itself to such easy domination.   Its political power was scattered among the great land owners with their private armies; its economy was tied directly to the produce of its soil;   its royal treasure was, to use Plucknett's word, a "casual" one.[5]   The challenge to William was to secure his throne by maintaining a military capability superior not only to that of the land owners but also to that of potential foreign invaders, and at the same time to gain political and economic control of the land.

The challenge was not a new one to William.   During the 31 years of his dukeship of Normandy, he had faced similar challenges to his power and had met them successfully.   But the conquest of England gave William an opportunity to impose royal

---

3.   See, e.g., Plucknett, A Concise History of the Common Law (5th ed. 1956) [hereinafter cited as Plucknett], which is a mere 746 pages long.   This is an exceedingly difficult book for the first-year student because it assumes conversancy with law and history.

4.   Specifically, we will not examine the intricacies of the tenures of serjeanty (ceremonial services), frankalmoin (spiritual services), and copyhold (unfree tenure). Excellent discussions of these tenures appear in Simpson, An Introduction to the History of the Land Law 1–14 (1961) [hereinafter cited as Simpson] and in Holdsworth, An Historical Introduction to the Land Law 16–29, 39–48 (2d ed. 1935) [hereinafter cited as Holdsworth].

5.   Plucknett, 11.

control on the land to an extent not possible on the Continent. Because the English land owners had forced him to fight for his crown, he was able to assert his absolute right to all the land of England as spoils of war.   Much of this land he redistributed to the Norman barons who had supported the expedition against England.   But it would not do, of course, simply to hand out the land as rewards for services rendered; for how could William be sure that among the recipients would not be men whose ambitions might later prove threatening?   It made sense to keep some strings attached to the land.

One string, conceptual in nature but of enormous practical significance, was the retention in William of ultimate legal ownership of the land that he granted.   The grantees were permitted to enjoy many of the benefits that we normally associate with full ownership today, but in many important respects they more resembled tenants than owners.   As tenants holding *of the king*,[6] their chief obligation was to render loyal service to him, service that usually took the form of specific duties assigned at the time the land was granted.   Failure to perform the required service, or any other act of disloyalty to the king, might result in the loss of the tenant's holdings.[7]   So thorough was the process by which the land of England became subject to fixed obligations to the king—the process generally referred to today as the *infeudation* of England—that by the time of the famous Domesday survey,[8] a scant twenty years after Hastings, it was possible to assign to almost every rock and stone of English soil its precise duty to the Crown.[9]

6. This phrase is the traditional description that implies the tenurial or feudal relationship between the king and his vassal. Any land could be located in the feudal structure by similar language: "A holds of B, who holds of C, who holds of . . . who holds of the King."   The last name in the series was always the king's.

7. Originally, the feudal relationship was a personal one.   Fidelity and loyalty were its necessary attributes.   "[T]his was felt to be a solemn and sacred bond. . . . The obligations of mutual aid and support which grew out of it may perhaps owe their sacred character to the fact that they were so absolutely necessary to the preservation of society."   Plucknett, 507.   Any great breach of the relationship would result in a forfeiture of the holding; such a breach was originally described by the word "felony."   The term came, of course, to describe all heinous crimes.   Cheshire, 20.   In time, the refusal to perform services ceased to be a felony; but the Statute of Gloucester, 6 Edw. 1, c. 4 (1278), again gave the lord a right to claim a forfeiture.   Plucknett, 31, 536.   It was usually easier to seize some of the tenant's chattels to make him perform or pay up. This procedure was called "distraint of chattels."   Painter, Studies in the History of the English Feudal Barony 106–09 (1943) [hereinafter cited as Painter].

8. This survey, recorded in Domesday Book (which is still extant), described every parcel of land in the domain "with a view to settling clearly the rights of the Crown and the taxable resources of the country." Plucknett, 12.   Overseeing this great task took up the last two years of the reign of William the Conqueror.   At his death in 1087 the feudal relationships were solidly, because indelibly, established.

9. It should be mentioned, though it would not serve our purpose to explore the

Although the services required of each tenant varied—some highly personal in nature, such as tending the king's bedchamber; others ecclesiastical in character, such as praying for the king's soul—the most important from a purely practical point of view was the obligation to provide a fixed number of knights annually for service in the king's host.[10] Historians speculate why William did not choose to establish a mercenary standing army rather than to rely on knights supplied by the barons.[11] It seems probable that the shortage of money in circulation played a role; but it is entirely possible that William and his barons merely followed the Norman fuedal traditions to which they had become accustomed on the Continent. Whatever the reason, there can be no doubt that the holding of land in knight service—that is, subject to the obligation to provide the agreed number of knights—was to become one of the most important elements in shaping the legal institutions of land-holding for centuries to come.

The basic idea of feudal land "ownership," then, was that it was *tenurial* in character—more a *holding* of land on good behavior than ownership as we think of it today. For the barons to be able to perform the services assigned to their land, it would obviously be necessary to put the land to productive use. The ultimate value of the land lay in the timber and agricultural produce it would yield. The problem for the barons was to translate this real value into the knight-value assigned to it by William. One method of securing the necessary number of knights was simply to invite the young men of knightly ambition to become part of the baronial household.[12] A baron could feed, clothe, and arm his knights out of the productive labors of the lowly villeins who tilled the soil in exchange for the privilege of continuing to occupy the land they had occupied before the Conquest. But a more common method of obtaining the annual quota of knights was to *subinfeudate* portions of the baronial lands to individual knights in exchange for their obligations to spend a fixed portion of time anually in the king's or baron's service. A knight who so received a portion of a baron's land would hold *of* his baron in much the same way as the baron held *of* the king.

matter in detail, that not all the land of England was redistributed to the Norman barons. Much of it was left in the hands of those who had held it before the Conquest and who had not opposed William's claim to the throne. But the legal theory that the king was ultimate owner of all the land applied equally to land left with its former owners. For such an owner to continue his control, he would have to redeem the land with a money payment and, of course, subject it to the same obligations of service that had been exacted from the Norman barons. See Cheshire, 13–14.

10.   For the best description of the economics of knight service, see Painter.

11.   See Painter, 20; Stenton, William the Conqueror 444–46 (1925).

12.   See Painter, 20–21.

The transfer of land from baron to knight did not, of course, discharge obligations that had attached to it when first granted by William. Thus, if a baron, having transferred portions of his lands to individual knights, committed an act of disloyalty to the king—perhaps merely the refusal to perform the required services—the king would not be barred from taking back even the lands now held by the knights. In a practical as well as a legal sense, therefore, a knight who received his land from a baron by subinfeudation held both of his baron and of the king—*immediately* of the former and *mediately* of the latter. It is not possible to say how much bargaining went into the transactions between baron and knight; but it is reasonable to suspect that they were negotiated with care.[13]

To complicate matters a bit more, the subinfeudation process did not end with the knights. They would often grant portions of their holdings to still others, exacting from their transferees fixed obligations of service measured in terms of labor in the fields, of agricultural produce, or simply of money payments.[14] A transferee from a knight would receive his land subject to the risk that his chattels would be taken, and in some cases his land actually lost, if the knight or baron above him committed a serious enough breach of his feudal obligations.[15]

Although it grossly oversimplifies matters to do so, we can for our purposes imagine the structure of feudal land-holding as fundamentally pyramidal in shape. From the king at the apex, the pyramid is built downward: first with grants to the barons, then with grants from the barons to the knights, and lastly (though the process sometimes went much further) with grants from the knights to those who actually occupy and farm the land. In each instance of transfer, the transferor and transferee agree on a fixed service that remains with the land no matter how much further it is transferred. From the base of the pyramid, services flow upward, changing perhaps in kind and quantity from tier to

13. We do know that in many cases the number of knights yielded was greater (and in a few cases, smaller) than the number actually owed by individual barons to the king. See Painter, 24–27.

14. At first all "free" tenures that did not come within the categories of military, spiritual, or ceremonial tenures were grouped under the heading "socage" tenure. Socage tenure was free from many of the feudal burdens accompanying tenure by knight service. Gradually, socage tenure spread up the feudal ladder. Services were generally "commuted" to money payments. See Cheshire, 22–23. Almost all the other free tenures were transformed into socage tenure in 1660 by the Tenures Abolition Act, 12 Car. 2, c. 24. All tenure not previously converted into socage tenure was so converted in 1925 by the Law of Property Act, 15 & 16 Geo. 5, c. 20. Tenure between ordinary persons may still exist, but only if the relationship was created before 1290; most "tenure" now involves only a relationship between subject and Crown. See Cheshire, 84–88.

15. See note 7, supra.

tier, but ultimately arriving at the king in the form of fully-armed knights.   Holding the structure together is the mortar of personal loyalty—loyalty downward in the form of assurances of military protection, and loyalty upward expressed in the ceremonial pledge of fealty given to each grantor by his grantee.[16]

SECTION 3.   TECHNICAL TERMINOLOGY

To facilitate further discussion, we will now need to use the traditional terminology to describe the relations and positions of persons on the pyramid.   In each instance of transfer, the grantor exacts obligations of service from his grantee.   In a sense, then, the transferor can still be said to "own" the transferred land much the way a modern landlord "owns" the land that he has leased.   Both have merely translated their possessory rights into service obligations.   In the feudal system, this retained right to receive services (and other important benefits that we shall describe later) is called a *seignory*.   Land held in the form of a seignory is described as held *in service*.   Land held in possession is held *in demesne*.   A tenant who holds a seignory is called a *tenant in service*, and a tenant who actually possesses the land is called a *tenant in demesne*.   The king, of course, is *lord* of all the land.   The barons, referred to as *tenants in chief* or *tenants in capite*, are *mesne lords* (middle lords) to the knights.   The knights, in turn, are mesne lords to the tenants in demesne.

SECTION 4.   RESTRICTIONS ON ALIENABILITY

As we have performed the architectural feat of building a pyramid from the apex down, we have assumed that each successive transferee was free to subinfeudate his lands.   It is difficult to imagine a mesne lord's objecting to this sort of transfer.   In the first place, subinfeudation would leave intact the services personally owed by each transferor.   In the second place, it was subinfeudation that made performance of the services possible.   But the lord might well object if his tenant wished to transfer by *substitution*—that is, by conveying his interest to a replacement and dropping off the pyramid entirely.   Such a transfer, if freely permitted, might easily result in a baron's or knight's discovering that someone he did not know and could not trust— perhaps even his worst enemy—had become his immediate tenant.   It would be reasonable to suppose, then, that substitution was barred unless the mesne lord permitted it.

But land law was no more governed by reason in the twelfth century than it is in the twentieth.   The truth seems to be that the tenant could alienate his land either by subinfeudation or by

---

16. See Plucknett, 507.

substitution, and the lord was powerless to prevent the transfer unless it would seriously injure his own interests.[17]   The question whether a transfer was sufficiently damaging to be forbidden was decided in the lord's court, where the tenant was entitled to a judgment of his peers.[18]   In order to understand why the lords should have tolerated a rule so favorable to tenants, it is helpful to remember that every feudal landlord, with the sole exception of the king, was himself the tenant of someone higher on the feudal pyramid.   And in some cases, at least, the lord was able to reap some benefit from the conveyance by extracting a fee from his tenant at the time the transfer was made.

SECTION 5.   GROWTH OF THE CONCEPT OF INHERITABILITY;   PRIMOGENITURE

Still to be answered is the question of how much of an interest each transferee by subinfeudation or substitution would receive. We must retreat to surmise for part of our answer.   Today, when we think of someone's owning a parcel of land outright, we think of the ownership as implying the right of the owner's heirs to have the land if the owner has not transferred it during his life or by his will.   So deeply imbedded in our law is the idea of inheritability of land that it is difficult to imagine that ownership could ever have meant anything else.

It seems quite clear that inheritability of land had been known in England before the Conquest.[19]   But it is also clear that lands held in feudal knight service immediately after the Conquest were not freely inheritable.   A transferee would receive from his transferor simply the right to enjoy the land for life.   Upon the transferee's death (and sometimes upon the transferor's death as well), the transferee's ownership would wholly terminate, and the right of enjoyment would move back up the pyramid to the

---

17.   The Great Charter of 1217 loosely defined the lord's right by providing that no man could transfer so much of his land that he could not perform the feudal services out of the remainder.   That this provision was not of much practical help to lords who wished to prevent undesirable substitutions is evident from the statement of the thirteenth-century justice Bracton: "[A]lbeit the tenant has done homage, he may put a new tenant in his place, and the lord must accept him, will he, nill he."   Bracton, f. 81, quoted in 1 Pollock & Maitland, The History of English Law 345 (1968) [hereinafter cited as Pollock & Maitland].

The extent of feudal restrictions on alienation has been a matter of controversy since the days of Coke and Blackstone. Although most historians now agree that the tenant could, at least by the end of the twelfth century, transfer by substitution without the lord's consent, several authors and casebook editors have taken the opposite view.   See, e.g., Casner & Leach, Cases and Text on Property 233–34 (1969); Dukeminier & Krier, Property 357 (1981); Bergin & Haskell, Preface to Estates in Land and Future Interests 8 (1st ed. 1966).

18.   1 Pollock & Maitland 343.

19.   See Plucknett, 524–25.

next tier of ownership.   A mesne lord could, upon the death of his tenant, accept the tenant's heir as tenant;   but he was not required to do so.   When he did accept his deceased tenant's heir as tenant, it was typically because the heir had paid the mesne lord a substantial sum (known as a *relief*) for the re-grant of the tenancy.

Even in the retrospect of 900 years, it seems obvious that such a system could not long survive.   Life was certainly a more precarious business in those days, and it is not difficult to understand why a proposed transferee, knowing that his death in battle would leave his family landless, might dare to request, or even to insist, that his transferor commit himself *at the time of transfer* to accept his heir as substitute for him in the tenancy upon his death.   For a time this commitment extended no farther than the transferee's immediate *eldest surviving son*.   A son would be able to perform the knight service.   Moreover, if the land passed to only one son, rather than to all the surviving sons of the deceased tenant, the administration of the tenancy would be more efficient.

Although this preference for the single male heir would remain a fixture of English property law for centuries to come,[20] the lord's commitment to accept his tenant's heir in the tenancy soon came to include not only daughters of the tenant (who took as a group, and then only when there was no son to take) but also, when there were no *lineal* heirs to take, brothers and sisters of the deceased tenant and even more distant *collateral* relatives. Moreover, the commitment extended not only to the tenant's immediate heir but also to the potentially infinite succession of heirs that followed.

To express this full commitment to accept as substitutes in the tenancy this potentially infinite succession of both lineal and collateral heirs, with preference to eldest surviving sons in single file down the years, the transferor would simply add the words *"and his heirs"* to the words of grant at the time of transfer. Naturally, a transferor would not make such a commitment unless *his* transferor had earlier made it to him.   Thus the custom of giving the commitment moved first from the king to the barons, then from the barons to the knights, and ultimately down through all the layers of the pyramid.[21]

---

20. Primogeniture was not abolished in England until the Administration of Estates Act, 1925, 15 & 16 Geo. 5, c. 23.   See Cheshire, 868, 871.

It must be noted that just after the Norman invasion there seems to have been a period of uncertainty, during which the principle of primogeniture struggled with that of giving an equal share to each son. See Plucknett, 527–28.

21. See Plucknett, 523, 524.

primogeniture

We might note here, parenthetically, that the English preference for single-file male descent—that is, the system of descent known as *primogeniture*—was never cordially received in this country. Our statutes of descent and distribution uniformly provide for sons' and daughters' sharing the inheritance equally. Although this seems a fairer method than primogeniture, which was finally abolished in Britain with the 1925 reforms,[22] the descent of property to an ever-expanding group of heirs can seriously complicate the clearing of old titles.

SECTION 6. LAYERS OF POTENTIALLY INFINITE OWNERSHIP CLAIMS

What we see emerging, then, is a concept of potentially infinite land ownership or tenancy. As long as there is an heir to claim the inheritance, the tenancy will go on and on, subject only to the continued performance of the required services and the occasional payment of other feudal dues. These "other feudal dues" will have to occupy our attention shortly. They will include, not so surprisingly, the *relief*, which, by this time, is no longer a matter of bargain between lord and heir, but a fixed legal obligation. But let us look further at this notion of potentially infinite ownership. Let us assume that A, the king if you like, infeudates "B and his heirs." B then subinfeudates "C and his heirs." Who has what? A and B both have seignories. A's seignory is potentially infinite as a matter of royal right. B's seignory is also potentially infinite since A used the appropriate "and-his-heirs" formula. C's tenancy in demesne is potentially infinite in duration for the same reason B's seignory is.

We have three layers of ownership, all potentially infinite. What happens if C dies without any heirs surviving him? Since C held of B, C's right of possession would pass back to B. This passage of ownership back to the mesne lord upon the death of his immediate tenant without heirs was called *escheat*. To complicate our example very slightly, let us assume that by the time of C's death without heirs, B's eldest son had succeeded to his father's seignory. Did B's son get C's land by escheat? Certainly. By inheriting the seignory, B's son also inherited the right of escheat. Now let us alter the model more seriously. Instead of C's dying without heirs, let us assume that B dies without heirs. The question is, what happens to C? Since C held of B, and since it seems obvious that B could not have transferred to C more than B had, we are forced to the conclusion that B's death without heirs cut off C's ownership claim. *But that is not what happened!* C's interest was left undisturbed.

escheat

---

22. See note 20, supra.

Only B's seignory escheated to A! [23]   Thus, C would now hold of A, owing to A the same services that he had formerly owed to *B.*   Although it is easy to imagine why the courts took this position (Who would pay for a potentially infinite interest in land if it might be cut short by the expiration of the *grantor's* line of heirs?), its consequences to the feudal system were immense. We shall see why in a few pages.

Summing up the two preceding paragraphs, the use of the "and-his-heirs" formula came automatically to imply lineal and collateral inheritability (in short, *general inheritability*) of the transferred interest—hence, potentially infinite duration. Whenever a potentially infinite interest, whether a seignory or a tenancy in demesne, expired by reason of the running out of the line of heirs, the interest would escheat to the lord of whom the interest had been immediately held.   The escheat of seignories left interests below them undisturbed; but the rule that the grantee's interest could continue after the grantor's interest had expired applied only to situations where the grantor had had a potentially infinite interest to start with.   Thus, if all the grantor had was a life-enjoyment interest (which would be the case if the "and-his-heirs" formula had not been used when he got his interest), he could *lawfully* transfer no interest that would outlast his own life. [24]

Let us pose, but leave temporarily unanswered, two questions about these potentially infinite interests.   *Question one:* When the "and-his-heirs" formula was used, did that mean that the transferee's heirs actually got ownership rights *at the moment the transfer was effected?*   We have already impliedly answered this question, but we will answer it more fully in the next chapter. *Question two:* When the owner of a potentially infinite interest transferred a clearly *finite* interest, such as a life-enjoyment interest, what did the transferor keep?   We shall answer that question partly in the next chapter and partly in Chapter Three.

SECTION 7. TRANSFER BY FEOFFMENT WITH LIVERY OF SEISIN

To add to our vocabulary, we may now pause to wonder how transfer of these potentially infinite interests was accomplished. Without a modern system of land records, it would be desirable that the transfer be effected with sufficient ceremony not only

---

23. Plucknett, 539; 1 Pollock & Maitland, 330–31; Simpson, 50.

24. This is still the law today.   Of course, one could *unlawfully* try to sell more than he had.   This was called, in the case of one who possessed a life interest but tried to sell more, a "tortious feoffment"; it operated to create an interest in the innocent transferee that might legally outlast the lifetime of the tortious feoffor or transferor.   See Simpson, 113. For the definitions of the terms "feoffor" and "feoffment," see Section 7, *infra.*

to mark itself indelibly in the memories of the participants, but also to give notice to interested persons such as the mesne lord above the transferor.   The central idea was to make ritual *livery* (meaning "delivery," from the Old French *livrer*) of *seisin* (meaning, roughly, "possession," from the Old French *saisir* or *seisir*). The transferor and transferee would go to the land to be transferred, and the transferor would then hand to the transferee a lump of soil or a twig from a tree—all the while intoning the appropriate words of grant, together with the magical words "and his heirs" if the interest transferred was to be a potentially infinite one.

The entire ceremony of transfer was called *feoffment with livery of seisin*.   To *enfeoff* someone was to transfer to him an interest in land called a *fief*—or, if you prefer, a *feoff, feod,* or *feud*.   Our modern word *fee,* a direct lineal descendant of *fief*, implies the characteristic of potentially infinite duration when used to describe an interest in land today;   but in the earliest part of the feudal period, a *fief* might have been as small as a life interest.   We shall see later that feoffment was *not* used to transfer interests "smaller" than life interests—e.g., so-called *terms for years*—but for our purposes now we may simply note that transfers of interests for life or "larger" were accomplished by livery of seisin.   Although the ceremony of livery of seisin was often noted in writing, the writings, or "charters," were not the operative elements of transfer;   they were merely evidence of transfer.

To sum up, then, we have a land transfer system based on transfer of physical possession.   Each *feoffee* (recipient of a fief), having received the seisin from his *feoffor*, would be said to be *seised*, or possessed of an interest in the land.   The importance of possession, or *seisin*, in the feudal scheme of things will occupy our attention fully in pages to come.   As we explore the concept of seisin more thoroughly, we will see that it means something more than physical occupancy of land;   but it is too early in our discussion to attempt a refinement of its meaning now.   Transfer by feoffment with livery of seisin will be the dominant method of transfer until 1536 and will continue to be used in England until 1845.[25]

SECTION 8.   THE FEUDAL INCIDENTS

As we have seen, the ownership of a seignory carried with it benefits in addition to the right to receive the annual fixed ser-

---

25.   The Real Property Act, 1845, 8 & 9 Vict., c. 106, did not really abolish livery of seisin;   but it allowed free use of the deed as a granting device, which had the same effect.   The Law of Property Act, 1925, 15 & 16 Geo. 5, c. 20, finally got around to abolishing the old feudal device. See Cheshire, 752–53.

vices. Two of these benefits, or *incidents*, as they were called, we have already mentioned: the right to receive a money payment, called a *relief*, when one's immediate tenant's heir succeeded to the tenancy, and the right to get one's immediate tenant's interest back by *escheat* when the tenancy became vacant for lack of heirs.[26] We shall now have to examine these, and two other feudal incidents, more carefully.

Let us stay, for a moment, with relief and escheat. What kind of economic benefits did these incidents bring to the mesne lord? Looking first at relief, we have seen that the amount payable by an heir to the mesne lord upon the heir's succeeding to his ancestor's interest was originally strictly a matter of bargain. If the tenancy was a profitable one—that is, one that generated more income than the amount of annual services owed—the mesne lord might demand and get a substantial sum as a relief. An heir probably computed the amount he would be willing to pay for a re-grant of the tenancy much the way an investor today might compute the value of a rental building—by *capitalizing* its profit yield.[27] Thus, the amount of the relief would move upward as the value of the land itself moved upward. Unfortunately for the mesne lords, this common-stock characteristic of reliefs did not continue after inheritability became a standard fixture of land ownership. The relief became, like the services, a fixed sum, sustained by custom and regulated by law.[28] It would remain a benefit to the mesne lord and a burden to the heir, but it would no longer accurately reflect the real value of the tenancy.

Escheat, on the other hand, would continue, at least where tenancies in demesne were involved, to reflect real value. When a tenant in demesne died without heirs, his mesne lord would get the land itself back. He could either keep it and enjoy its profits or transfer it again at a price reflecting its full value. Even escheat of seignories would, of course, produce profits in cases where the deceased mesne lord had been receiving more services than he owed to *his* mesne lord. Thus, if A had subinfeudated B and his heirs at an annual service of five knights,

26. This was technically called escheat *propter defectum sanguinis*, to distinguish it from the situation whereby the tenancy escheated because of felony, which was called escheat *propter delictum tenentis.* See Cheshire, 20, 28.

27. The "capitalized value" of an income-producing property or enterprise is the amount a reasonable investor, taking into account possible alternative uses of money, would pay for the right to the projected income.

28. Chapters 2 and 3 of Magna Carta fixed ceilings on relief payments made by the barons to the king. See Howard, Magna Carta: Text and Commentary 10 (1964). The idea that relief was a fixed payment probably worked its way down the feudal ladder as a matter of course. See Painter, 56–64, 146–47.

and B had transferred separate portions of his demesne by sub-infeudation to C, D, and E and their respective heirs at an aggregate annual service of eight knights, the death of B without heirs would entitle A, by escheat, to B's seignories worth eight knights a year—netting A the tidy profit of three knights a year.[29]

Two other incidents with this common-stock characteristic must be mentioned. One was *wardship*, the right of the feudal lord to guardianship of a deceased tenant's infant heir until the heir reached his majority. In feudal days, guardianship was not the paternalistic trusteeship we associate with the word "guardian" today. It was money, pure and simple. By becoming guardian, the mesne lord become entitled to treat the heir's lands for all practical purposes as his own, enjoying fully their use and whatever profits they yielded. At the end of the period of wardship, no accounting was owed by the mesne lord. If the heir's lands were demesne lands, the profits enjoyed by the mesne lord might be very considerable. If, however, all the heir had was a seignory yielding modest annual services, the wardship might be of little or no benefit.

Another important tenurial incident was *marriage*, the right of the mesne lord to pick the marriage partner of a female heir (and sometimes a male heir as well) of his deceased tenant. Since becoming the husband of an heiress meant for all practical purposes becoming the owner of her lands,[30] a wealthy young suitor might be willing to pay the lord a substantial sum in order to be picked for the honor. Here, again, the amount paid would undoubtedly vary depending on the value of the inheritance, seignories probably yielding less than lands in demesne.

SECTION 9. PRE-1290 TECHNIQUES OF "TAX AVOIDANCE"

We have now set the scene for some fancy feudal skulduggery—or, if you prefer euphemism, tax avoidance. The year, let us say, is 1268. C is tenant in demesne, and his interest is a generally inheritable one—that is, one originally created by the "and-his-heirs" formula. The knight service that was fixed to C's land at the time his great-grandfather first got it probably originally represented a fair return to the grantor, but it no longer reflects the much-increased value of the land. Perhaps

---

29. See note 13, supra.

30. At common law, a husband was often entitled during the marriage to exclusive possession or to the entire rents and profits of all the inheritable estates of which his wife was seised. We will not attempt a lengthy treatment in this text of the niceties of the common-law claims of spouses to each other's lands. A brief discussion appears in Section 5 of Chapter Two, infra.

it has now become a relatively modest annual money payment.[31]
The relief, too, has become fixed in amount, somewhat burden-
some but not onerous.   But the incidents of escheat, wardship
and marriage still reflect real value.   Surely it would be absurd
for C to allow B, the mesne lord, to have the benefits of these
incidents if there were any way of avoiding it.   Let us try to
devise some avoidance techniques.

To put our problem in a real environment, let us assume that
C has reached an advanced age, and that he has one son, S, who
is six years old.   Wardship, therefore, is our most serious problem.   We first note that the incident of wardship attaches *only
upon inheritance—the automatic* passage of ownership from father
to eldest surviving son.   If there were any way we could get
the tenancy to S other than by inheritance, our problem would
be solved.   The obvious solution is for C to leave the tenancy
to S by will.   In that way, S will get the tenancy not as an *heir*
but as a "purchaser"—a term that is usually applied today only
to one who "buys" something, but that meant in feudal law one
who acquired ownership of a tenancy *other than by inheritance.*[32]
Unfortunately for C and S, transfers of interests in *land* by will
are not yet recognized by the law courts.[33]   Well, then, why not
have C transfer the tenancy to S right now—that is, by *inter
vivos* transfer.   That will certainly make S a purchaser; and
even though S may later turn against C, that risk seems pref-
erable to letting B have wardship.   But here again we are blocked;
for last year, 1267, a statute was passed that makes transfer to
one's eldest son fraudulent.[34]

[in left margin: rule]

[in left margin: purchaser]

---

31. With the introduction of the cross-
bow and the shift in focus of English war-
making from the consolidation and coast-
defending of the period 1066–1155 to the
active continental campaigning of Henry
II (1154–1189), Richard the Lionhearted
(1189–1199), and John (1199–1216), the king
became less interested in cumbersome
knights who had to be transported across
the channel and more interested in being
able to pay mercenaries.   Thus a money
payment, called *scutage*, was substituted
for the levy of all or a part of the knights
to be supplied by a baron, at least as early
as the time of Henry II, who levied five
such scutages during the first eleven years
of his reign.   Painter, 34.   After the scutage became a fixed and expectable tax,
e.g., 20 shillings per fief, the number of
knights each vassal was expected actually
to produce became much smaller.   Id. at
38–39; see generally id., 30–45.

32. The feudal definition of "purchaser" is given fresh currency by the Uniform Commercial Code's use of the term
to apply to one who takes by "sale, dis-
count, negotiation, mortgage, pledge, lien,
issue or re-issue, gift or any other voluntary transaction creating an interest in
property."   See U.C.C. § 1–201(32) and
(33).

Laymen—and sometimes first-year law
students taking exams—wrongly assume
that one who receives real property by will
is an heir.   Technically, the word "heir"
is reserved for one who receives real property by action of the laws of intestacy, which
operate today only in the absence of a valid
will.

We shall have a good deal more to say
of the distinction between heirs and purchasers in later chapters.

33. They will not be recognized until
the Statute of Wills, 32 Hen. 8, c. 1 (1540),
except for some local customs.

34. The Statute of Marlborough, 52
Hen. 3, c. 6 (1267).   See Plucknett, Legislation of Edward I, 79–80 (1949).

Those of you who have read ahead may be suggesting the "use" as a technique for avoiding wardship—that is, transferring the tenancy now to a trustee with instructions to transfer it to S on C's death. But we need not consider the use now, because we have an easier and safer way of handling our problem. C's tenancy is wealth—wealth in the *form* of land. Why not simply convert C's land wealth to another *form* of wealth, one to which wardship will not attach? Why not, in short, sell the tenancy to some third person—D, let us say—for *cash*? C will be able to hold the cash for as long as he likes and then transfer it to S without difficulty. When S gets the cash, he can, if he wants, buy a tenancy of his own.

Obviously, if D is going to pay a good price for the tenancy, he will insist that the transfer be to D *and his heirs*; but the question for us is whether C shall transfer the tenancy by *substitution* or by *subinfeudation*. Which kind of transfer will produce the larger cash yield? If we transfer by substitution, C will drop off the pyramid, and D will replace him. D will then owe to B the same services that C now owes to B. That will reduce the price D is willing to pay for the tenancy. On the other hand, if the transfer is made by subinfeudation and if C demands from D only a nominal annual service—say, a peppercorn a year—D will undoubtedly pay a higher price. The trouble with that, however, is that C (and later S), by reason of keeping a seignory, will have to go on paying B his regular services. Transfer by substitution or subinfeudation looks like six of one and half a dozen of the other.

But what about the incidents that will attach to *D*'s tenancy? If we transfer by *substitution*, D will be in the same situation C is now in. That is, upon D's death, B will be entitled to the same incidents we are now seeking to avoid. Knowing that, D will take it into account in his bid. If, however, C *subinfeudates* D, the incidents that attach on D's death will run to C (or S) as D's mesne lord. Our choice, therefore, is clear. C subinfeudates to D and his heirs. C can, if he wishes, transfer to D a kind of tenancy to which the incidents will not attach[35]—thereby inducing D to pay a higher price—or C can accept a lower price and retain the right to the incidents as a kind of investment for the future. In either case, the economic benefit of the incidents will run to C (and S).

All right, C now transfers to D and his heirs by *subinfeudation*, exacting from D the service of one peppercorn per year. What happens to B's services and incidents? The services are unimpaired; C (and later S) must go on paying them as before.

---

35. Marriage and wardship attached only to tenure by knight service and to grand serjeanty, a tenure we have not discussed. Holdsworth, 31–32.

But the incidents to which B had been entitled have become worthless. When C dies, B will become entitled to wardship of S, but the *"lands"* of S that B had expected would yield high profits *have been converted into a seignory worth one peppercorn per year.* Voila! Wardship has, for all practical purposes, been avoided. And, obviously, the identical technique can be used to avoid marriage and escheat as well.[36]

SECTION 10.   QUIA EMPTORES

We should note, in looking back on C's tax avoidance gymnastics, that to be successful he obviously had to transfer to D the fullest possible ownership interest—that is, an interest inheritable by lineal and collateral heirs. If C had kept anything more than a bare seignory—say, by transferring to D a life-enjoyment interest only—the price C got from D would hardly have been worth the effort. Moreover, if C had sold D only a life interest, the "seignory" (that is perhaps not the correct term) retained by C might be worth a good deal. Hence B would not be as seriously hurt. The reason that we make this point will become clear in a moment.

It is too late, of course, for B to do anything about C; but it is not too late for him to prevent this kind of thing from happening in the future. B and other B's (barons) like him will repair to the legislature to close this extraordinary loophole. In 1290 they will be crowned with success by the enactment of *Quia Emptores.*[37] How did *Quia Emptores* correct matters? Simply by forbidding further transfer *by subinfeudation* of *generally inheritable* interests. Henceforth, anyone who owns such an interest will, if he wishes to transfer the *whole* interest to someone else, have to do it by substitution. Bare seignories may no longer be retained.

We shall see in our next two chapters that, despite *Quia Emptores,* transferors will ultimately find ways of avoiding their taxes. One way will be the "use," which we have already mentioned. Another will be the transfer of interests that leave the transferor with just a hair's breadth *more* of ownership than a bare seignory. But for our purposes here, it will suffice to

---

36. The example we have been using in this section is taken from Plucknett, 538–39. However, he does not explain the benefit running to C and S in terms of the *incidents* D will owe. But incidents must have played an important part, or else C and S would have obtained no real benefit.

37. The statute *Quia Emptores* . . . , 18 Edw. 1, c. 1 (1290), was so named from its first two words, which mean "since purchasers." The reasons for enacting the statute are set out, with bluntness befitting its purpose, in the preamble, which states that the statute was made "at the prayer of the magnates." See Plucknett, 540–41.

observe not only that alienability of land has become free, but also that the feudal pyramid itself is now destined for collapse.

The reason for its collapse, which will not occur immediately but will take hundreds of years of slow erosion, should be obvious. Putting it in its simplest form, let us assume that a tenant in demesne dies without heirs and without having transferred his full ownership to someone else. What happens? The land escheats to the mesne lord. The mesne lord is, of course, prevented by *Quia Emptores* from subinfeudating it again. Thus the bottom tier of the pyramid is gone forever. Now the mesne lord dies without heirs and without transferring his interest. The land moves up another tier by escheat, and now two tiers are gone. Finally, assuming that these calamities continue, the land arrives back at the king.[38] Must he, too, transfer only by substitution? Not so strangely, *Quia Emptores* did not apply to the king.

SECTION 11. SUMMARY

We set forth in this chapter to explore how the institution of knight service contributed to the development of our modern notions of potentially infinite ownership of land, free alienability of land, and independent ownership. We should see now that the first two notions are intimately related to each other. Land may be owned potentially infinitely because it is *inheritable*; but even where an owner has no prospective heirs to take his tenancy he can, by *alienating it*, give the tenancy a brand new start in life. The death of the transferor without heirs will leave the transferee's potentially infinite interest undisturbed. In a sense, then, the first two notions also feed into the third. That is, the transferee's ownership is *durationally independent* of anyone else's. To be sure, he will still hold *of* someone (his transferor's mesne lord), and he will still have to pay the services his transferor had been paying. Moreover, his tenancy will be burdened by feudal incidents. But as long as he performs his duties, his interest will go on and on, passing to his heirs or his chosen transferee, as he wishes. The slow collapse of the feudal pyramid will ultimately free him from even the feudal duties. In 1660, what vestiges remain of tenure by knight service will be abolished by statute.[39] In 1925, most of the remaining forms of

---

38. Of course, the mesne lord might die without heirs first. His seignory would then escheat to the next higher overlord, carrying with it the tenant in demesne, who would merely have a new overlord. The death without heirs of any tenant (mesne or otherwise) after *Quia Emptores* meant the disappearance of that tier from the feudal pyramid.

39. Tenures Abolition Act, 1660, 12 Car. 2, c. 24 See note 14, supra.

tenure will be swept away in the great reforms.[40]   But we have a long way to go yet to reach 1925.

To link what we have learned to modern American law, we have merely to say that the notions of potentially infinite ownership and free alienability of land were simply absorbed into our jurisprudence from the very beginning as part of the common law.   They are now the *given* of our property law.   Except in one or two states,[41] the idea of tenure—at least in its pure feudal form with full ownership in one person and a bare seignory in another—scarcely got a foothold.   Either *Quia Emptores* was accepted as a common-law rule, or statutes were early passed barring transfer of full owernship by subinfeudation.[42]   In this country, one who has full ownership of land is said to own it allodially—that is, free of feudal services and incidents.   Of course, we do have our property taxes and our inheritance taxes.   If we don't pay them, we can lose our land.   Moreover, if an owner dies without heirs and without having disposed of his land by a valid will, his land escheats to the state—not, of course, by feudal escheat, but by statute.   Is this what lawyers call a distinction without a difference?

---

40.   See notes 1 & 14, supra.   The Crown is still entitled to take as *bona vacantia* lands whose owners die without wills or heirs.   See Cheshire, 28.

41.   The royal charters of Pennsylvania, Maryland, and the Carolinas provided that in certain instances *Quia Emptores* would not be in force, thus allowing new subinfeudation and giving the existence of tenure some meaning.   Today, only two states (Pennsylvania and South Carolina) hold that *Quia Emptores* is not in force. In these states, and in some others, land is still held by tenure; but only in these two does the distinction make any difference.   See 1 American Law of Property § 1.41 (Casner ed. 1952) [hereinafter cited as American Law of Property].

42.   See the state-by-state analysis in Gray, The Rule Against Perpetuities §§ 23–23.2 (4th ed. 1942) [hereinafter cited as The Rule Against Perpetuities].

Chapter 2

A CATALOGUE OF ESTATES

SECTION 1. INTRODUCTION

In our efforts thus far to trace some of the beginnings of our land law, we have found ourselves inevitably speaking of ownership in *durational* terms.   We have seen that "full" ownership by a tenant in knight service during the earliest part of the feudal period meant no more than life enjoyment.   We have also seen how, through bargained-for inheritability, full ownership came to mean potentially infinite enjoyment.   To speak of ownership in terms of time seems as natural as speaking of it in terms of enjoyment.   Indeed, the enjoyment-dimension of ownership— How may I *use* my land?—seems barren without a time-dimension—How *long* may I use it?   In this chapter, and largely throughout the balance of the book, we shall be giving chief attention to the time-dimension of ownership.   To some extent, we shall be able to go forward with our inquiry without reference to history; but from time to time we shall have to return to the feudal period.

Before turning to our task, let us set forth three ground rules under which our inquiry will proceed.   As our first ground rule, we are going to assume that there is such a thing as final and complete legal ownership of a thing.   First-year law students learn early that courts rarely, if ever, make final adjudications of property ownership.   Ownership rights, they learn, are "relative."   Jones may "own" against Smith, in the sense of having a better claim to a thing than he; but Brown may prove next week that his claim is better than Jones's.   We shall not concern ourselves with that point.   When we say in our examples that someone owns an interest in property, we shall assume, for convenience of discussion, that his claim is good against the whole world.

Ground rule two: We will confine our examples to *possessory* interests—that is, interests that are said to entitle their owners, or that may entitle them in the future,[1] to *exclusive*[2] use of prop-

---

1.   In Part I of this book, we shall use the term "present interest" or "present estate" to denote an interest entitling its owner to present possession.   We shall use the term "future interest" or "future estate" to denote an interest entitling its owner to possible future possession.   We shall use the term "possessory interest" to include both present and future interests, and to exclude such interests as easements and profits.   The reader should note that the Restatement of Property uses the term

erty. As the reader may already be aware, or as he will certainly become aware as he pursues his study of property law, there are certain interests in property—easements, profits, running covenants, equitable servitudes, and so on—that are said to entitle their owners to *non-possessory* benefits in property. Although it takes little legal sophistication to recognize that the concepts of possessory and non-possessory interests in property are empty vessels until judges fill them with real-world meaning, it is equally obvious that these concepts have drawn to themselves over time separate sets of official rules and prescriptions that demand separate study and analysis.

Ground rule three: Although all the examples we shall be using in Part I of this book will involve transfers of interests in land, the reader should not draw the inference that there is a wholly different set of rules that apply to transfers of interests in things other than land. To be sure, there are cases in which the form of the wealth transferred will be relevant. To talk, for example, of a future interest in a basket of peaches is probably to talk nonsense. But in the main, the concepts and rules we shall be examining will apply equally to things other than land. Our reason for using land in our examples is simply that the concepts and rules originally grew out of land-transfer cases. Because they are still land-bound in *terminology*, we thought it would probably be easier for the student to grasp their meaning in the context of land transfer.[3]

SECTION 2. THE ESTATE CONCEPT

We have often spoken up to this point of someone's having an "interest" in land. What does it mean to have an interest in land? To take an example with which we are all familiar, Jones, let us assume, is the absolute and complete owner of a parcel of land called Blackacre. He leases it to Smith for two years. Now who owns Blackacre?

The layman is likely to say that Jones is still the owner. The sophisticated lawyer, however, will reply that the question cannot be answered until it is put in a functional context. If, for example, one wishes to know who is the "owner" for the purpose of assessing real estate tax liability, the correct answer might

"possessory" to refer only to interests that entitle the owner to *present* possession. See Restatement, Property §§ 7, 9, 153 (1936).

2. A moment's reflection will show the reader that the term "exclusive" is bothersome even as a conceptual tool. Suppose A owns Blackacre, but he grants to B the right to maintain a pipeline across it. Who owns the *exclusive* right to the portion of Blackacre in which the pipeline is located?

3. Many treatise-writers and Restaters show hesitance to accept the idea of an "estate" in something other than land. See, e.g., Restatement, Property § 9, comment *a* (1936).

be "Jones." But if one wants to know who is the "owner" who can transfer right now full and perpetual possessory rights to the property, the answer is likely to be *both Jones and Smith.* If the transferee is to get possession immediately, he will probably have to get Smith to join in the transfer. It is this second meaning of ownership that will concern us.

How may we distinguish Jones's ownership from Smith's? One distinction we can quickly make is that Smith's ownership includes the right of present possession. Jones's ownership, on the other hand, will entitle him to possession only after Smith's two years are up. Because Smith is entitled to present possession of Blackacre, he is said to have a *present interest* in it. Because Jones is entitled to future possession, he is said to have a *future interest.*[4] (Footnote 4 contains a useful warning.)

But if Jones has only a future interest, how do we conclude that he is an owner *now?* One answer might be that he is now entitled to receive rental payments from Smith. But even if Smith's lease entitled him to possess the property without payment of rent, we would still say that Jones is an owner *now.* What does Jones own *now?* We could say correctly that he owns now the right of future possession, but that is saying no more than we started with.

If we were to reflect on the matter for a while, we would probably conclude that he is an owner *now* because courts will protect his future possession *now.* What he "owns" is present protection of his future possession. Does this present protection derive solely from the terms of his lease with Smith? No. The lease may, of course, entitle Jones to various remedies against Smith; but even without such provisions, Jones would be entitled to present protection of his future possession.

To take an example, suppose some third person were removing valuable topsoil from Blackacre. Would Jones have a present right to prevent further removal of the topsoil? Doubtless he would. Moreover, unless the lease authorized Smith to remove topsoil, Jones would also have a present right to prevent Smith from removing it. To take another example, suppose Jones decided to sell his future right to possession to someone else. Could he sell it *now?* He certainly could. As a matter of fact, if we counted all the *present* rights, privileges, and powers that Jones owns *now* in Blackacre, we would come close to saying that the only right he lacks right now is the right of present possession.

---

4. See Restatement, Property § 154, comment *f* (1936). We will discover later that for some purpose Jones's interest may aptly be described as a "present interest" even while Smith's lease continues. See, e.g., the discussion in Section 6, *infra.*

Why do we call Smith an owner now? The answer is actually the same as the answer for Jones: Smith is an owner now because he is entitled to judicial protection of his *present* possession. The alert reader may be strenuously objecting to this line of thought. We seem to be saying that one is an owner because one is entitled to *present* protection of either present or future possession. Why don't we say that one is entitled to present protection *because* one is an owner?

Actually, we are saying both. When a court gives protection to present or future possession, in theory it first concludes that the person seeking protection has a right to the protection. In our Jones-Smith example, if Smith sought protection of his present possession, the court would presumably wish to satisfy itself that Smith had a valid lease to Blackacre. But if the court does conclude that Smith is entitled to protection, it must also be concluding that the lease is valid. The two questions—whether the lease is valid and whether Smith is entitled to protection of his possession—are precisely the same. In order to avoid difficulty with this point, perhaps we should recast our original statement to say that one is an *owner* in those circumstances in which a court, having recourse to rules of law and policy, will recognize and protect a present or future claim to possession.

Jones and Smith are both present owners in the sense of being entitled to present protection of their claims to possession. *This entitlement to present protection of present or future possession is the central characteristic of what is called an "estate."* An estate, therefore, is an interest in land that entitles its owner, or may entitle him in the future,[5] to possession of land. In our Jones-Smith example, both Jones and Smith own estates in Blackacre. Smith's estate is called a present estate and Jones's estate is called a future estate.

Remember that we started out by describing Jones as "the absolute and complete owner of Blackacre." To put that statement in more lawyerly language, Jones owned a *present estate in fee simple absolute*[6] in Blackacre. We shall discuss this estate in detail below, but for the moment it will suffice to describe a *present* estate in fee simple absolute as one that, by reason of its general inheritability (that is, inheritability by lineal and collateral heirs), entitles its owner to potentially infinite *present* possession of land.

Suppose that Jones, instead of leasing Blackacre to Smith for two years, had delivered to him a deed that stated, "I hereby grant and convey Blackacre to Smith for life." The deed would

5. See Restatement, Property § 9 (1936).

6. See Restatement, Property § 15 (1936) for a definition.

give Smith an "estate for life." [7]   What happened to Jones's estate when he delivered his deed to Smith?   Obviously he gave up his right of *present* possession for the period of Smith's life; but he did not give up his estate in fee simple absolute.   His estate simply became, during Smith's life, a *future* estate in fee simple absolute.   Since Jones's estate was potentially infinite to start with, and since he transferred to Smith an estate that was *not* potentially infinite, he did not give away all that he had. As soon as Smith is dead, Jones will again be entitled to his actual possession for a potentially infinite period.   Since Jones will be entitled to possession again, he is entitled during Smith's life to present court protection of that future possession.   What happens if Jones dies before Smith?   If he leaves no will, his future estate in fee simple absolute will descend to his heirs. If he does leave a will disposing of his estate, the estate will pass to those whom he named as takers.   Let us now examine the estate in fee simple with care.

SECTION 3.   THE ESTATE IN FEE SIMPLE

The estate in fee simple is, as we have said, an estate that is potentially infinite in duration by reason of its transferability and general inheritability.   Whether it is a future estate or a present estate, it may be transferred in whole or in part by a valid deed or will, [8] or left to pass to heirs under the laws of intestate succession.   It is probably apparent to the reader that the estate in fee simple is that "full ownership" we saw developing in Chapter One.   Indeed, the only refinement we have added in this chapter is the notion that ownership may lack the right of present possession and still be durationally "full" if the owner's *protection* is potentially infinite.

The reader may have noticed that we described Jones's estate in our examples in Section 2 as an estate in fee simple *absolute*. We have dropped the "absolute" in our present discussion because there is a kind of estate in fee simple that, though potentially infinite in duration, may nonetheless come to an end *before the line of heirs runs out* by operation of a "special limitation," a "condition subsequent," or an "executory limitation" attached to it at the time of its creation.   Such an estate in fee simple is called an "estate in fee simple *defeasible*." [9]   Since Jones's estate

---

7.   We will discuss the estate for life in Section 5, infra.   See Restatement, Property § 18 (1936) for a definition.

8.   When the owner of an estate transfers it during his lifetime, by deed or otherwise, the transfer is commonly referred to as an "inter vivos" transfer.   A transfer of real property by will is called a "devise,"

and those who take under the will are known as "devisees."

In some rare circumstances, a future estate in fee simple may not be transferable. See Chapter Three, Section 4, infra.

9.   See Restatement, Property § 16 (1936).

in our examples did not have a special limitation, a condition subsequent, or an executory limitation attached to it (or so we assumed), we used the word "absolute" simply to indicate that his estate was not defeasible.   Although it is probably good practice to use the word "absolute" whenever one is referring to an estate in fee simple that is free of special limitation, condition subsequent, or executory limitation, lawyers frequently refer to such an estate as a "fee simple" or even as a "fee." [10]   We may find ourselves slipping into that usage as we go along.   Estates in fee simple defeasible and other defeasible estates will be fully discussed in Section 8 of this chapter.

Lawyers still use the "and-his-heirs" formula to transfer estates in fee simple, whether the estates are absolute or defeasible. [11]   By saying that lawyers still use the formula, we should not be understood to say that they are required to use it.   Statutes in most states now provide that any words that indicate the intent of the transferor to transfer an estate in fee simple will suffice. [12]   Indeed, if there are no words to the contrary, it may be presumed that the transferor intended to transfer an estate in fee simple.   Still, lawyers uniformly use the formula because they believe that it most clearly expresses the intent of the transferor to transfer an estate in fee simple.

Some lawyers, as a matter of fact, not only use the "and-his-heirs" formula but also pile on top of it a whole batch of words to make the transferor's intent more unassailably clear.   Thus, it is not uncommon to read, in deeds transferring an estate in fee simple absolute, such language as "to A and his heirs *and assigns forever in fee simple absolute.*"   The italicized words are wholly unnecessary.   The word "assigns" is intended to indicate that the estate is alienable to third persons, but the estate is alienable without it.   The words "forever" and "in fee simple" are equally redundant, since they merely make explicit the potentially infinite duration that is implicit in the "and-his-heirs" formula.   The word "absolute" is also redundant, since the words "and his heirs," *without words of special limitation, condition subsequent, or executory limitation added,* imply the estate in fee simple absolute.   In this book, we shall uniformly use simply the "and-his-heirs" formula to denote the transfer of an estate in fee simple absolute.   When we wish to denote the transfer

---

10.   Lawyers often use the term "fee" as an adjective.   Thus, a lawyer may refer to a transaction as "fee" transaction, meaning one in which an estate in fee simple absolute was transferred.   In our original Jones-Smith example, lawyers might describe Jones as owner of the "fee" and Smith as owner of the "leasehold" or "term."

11.   The words "and his heirs" are referred to as words of general inheritance. See Restatement, Property § 27 (1936). The use of words of general inheritance has never been required to transfer an estate in fee simple by will.

12.   See 1 American Law of Property § 2.4.

of an estate in fee simple defeasible, we shall add to the formula words of special limitation, condition subsequent, or executory limitation.

Let us give two examples of how we shall be using the "and-his-heirs" formula. Throughout Part I, unless we clearly indicate the contrary, the letter "O" will stand for one who starts out as the owner of a *present estate in fee simple absolute.* O will be our transferor. Example one: O transfers "to A and his heirs." Who owns what? Remembering *Quia Emptores,* we conclude that O has nothing left. A is now the owner of a *present* estate in fee simple absolute. Example two: O transfers "to A for life, then to B and his heirs." Does A have an estate in fee simple absolute? Clearly not. The "and-his-heirs" formula did not apply to A. A owns a present estate for life. What about B? B does own an estate in fee simple absolute. During A's possession, B's estate will be a future one. When A dies, B's estate in fee simple absolute will become a present one. If B dies before A, B's future estate in fee simple absolute will pass either to his heirs or, if there is a will, to those whom he named in it as takers. Does O have anything left? No. Since he used the "and-his-heirs" formula, *Quia Emptores* applies. If, of course, O had not made the transfer to B, or if he had transferred to B only a finite interest, we would say that O kept his estate in fee simple absolute. It would, of course, be a *future* one during the period in which A and B were in possession.

Lest there be concern about the matter, we should mention at this point that *future estates* (more often called "future interests") have special labels that indicate who was the owner of the future estate when it was first created and under what circumstances the estate may become a present one. These labels and their meaning will occupy us fully in later chapters; but the reader may be assured now that they have *no durational content whatsoever.* Therefore, we do not need them for our discussion in this chapter.

It is now time to turn to the two questions we left unanswered at the end of Section 6 of Chapter One. They have been impliedly answered by our discussion in this chapter, but let us make their answers explicit. The first question was this: When the "and-his-heirs" formula was used, did that mean that the transferee's heirs actually got ownership rights *at the moment the transfer was effected?* Let us put the question in the present tense and change its language to reflect our present understanding of the estate concept: Does the use of the "and-his-heirs" give the prospective heirs *present* protection of their possible future possession? Does it give the prospective heirs *estates?* The answer is that for a short time during the earliest development of the inheritability notion, the use of the "and-his-heirs" formula apparently did give at least the transferee's immediate prospective heir protection of his right to inherit.[13]   Whether this was a right of present protection is unclear, but it does appear clear that an heir, upon his ancestor's death, was entitled to possession regardless of the ancestor's prior attempt to transfer full ownership to a third person.   In effect, a transfer to "A and his heirs" during this period gave A only a life estate in the land. He could transfer what he had, but he could not defeat his prospective heir's right to possession by transferring full ownership to another.[14]

It should be easy to see why this notion did not long prevail. Who would buy from A, knowing that the estate he purchased would last only for A's life?   A might die the day after the sale was completed.   If land was to become an object of commerce, it would be necessary to deny the prospective heirs this absolute right to future possession.   And deny it the courts did.   In a very short time, the words "to A and his heirs" came to mean simply that the prospective heirs would be entitled to possession *only if A had not transferred the entire ownership (i.e., the estate in fee simple absolute) to someone else before his death.*   In brief, the entire potentially infinite ownership was thought to reside in A.   He could do with it what he wanted.   If he did nothing with it before his death, then and only then would his immediate heir become entitled to possession.   If the immediate heir did get the possession, the entire ownership was thought to be in him, to do with as he pleased.   And so on and so on.

To sum up, the demand for alienability of land made it necessary to deny prospective heirs the absolute right to future possession.   The consequence of this denial was to change the prospective heirs from owners of estates to owners of "mere expectancies."   Could A defeat his immediate prospective heir's expectancy by leaving the estate to someone else in a will?   Not at law[15] until the enactment of the Statute of Wills in 1540;   but after the statute's enactment it was (and still generally is) possible to defeat by will a prospective heir's expectancy.

---

13. See Plucknett, 526–27. There is no indication that this concept extended beyond the first generation. See id. The reader should be aware that one never has an "heir" until one is dead; one merely has an "heir expectant" (although this concept probably had not been developed in the period we are talking about—see id., 550 n.2). Thus, to say that an heir "owns" anything is conceptually difficult. But, as we shall see in Chapter Three, some unborn heirs may be entitled to the protection of the courts, and thus be said to have estates.

14. It was sometimes possible for A to transfer part of the land, as long as the amount of land he conveyed was not "unreasonable." See 2 Pollock & Maitland at 248.

15. There were ways of making wills in equity prior to 1540; see Chapter Three, Section 8.

The content of the preceding paragraphs may be expressed in technical language as follows: In a transfer "to A and his heirs," the words "and his heirs" are now *words of limitation* (words denoting the duration of the estate), not *words of purchase* (words denoting who is getting the estate). The name "A" is the only word of purchase; A is the only person who is getting an estate. The words "and his heirs" simply mean that A's estate is potentially infinite in duration. Similarly, in a transfer "to A for life," the name "A" is the only word of purchase. The words "for life" are words of limitation indicating that A is getting an estate for life. Suppose the transfer were "to A for life, *then* to the heirs of A." Are the words "then to the heirs of A" words of limitation or words of purchase? We shall have difficulty with this question in later chapters. Let us postpone the agony until then.[16]

Our second unanswered question in Section 6 of Chapter One was this: When the owner of a potentially infinite interest transferred a clearly *finite* interest, such as a life enjoyment interest, what did the transferor keep? Let us recast that question in the present tense and use the language of estates: When the owner of a present estate in fee simple absolute transfers a present finite estate, such as a present estate for life, what does the transferor keep? As we have seen from our discussion in this chapter, he keeps the same estate in fee simple absolute that he started with. It simply becomes a future estate in fee simple absolute while the present finite estate continues. But why isn't the retention by a transferor of a future estate in fee simple absolute forbidden by *Quia Emptores?* The answer is that *Quia Emptores* applied only to transfers of estates in fee simple absolute; it did not forbid a tenant in fee simple to grant estates smaller than the fee simple absolute. It was only through transfers of estates in fee simple absolute that tenants were avoiding the feudal incidents.

Now (and perhaps too early) a delicate question: Did *Quia Emptores* prevent someone who owned a present estate in fee simple absolute from keeping a future estate in fee simple absolute when he transferred a present estate in fee simple *defeasible?* Some scholars have argued that *Quia Emptores* applied to such transfers,[17] but courts have generally recognized that a transferor of such an estate may in fact retain a future estate in fee simple absolute. We shall discuss this matter in Section 8 of this chapter and in Chapter Three.

---

16. The answer involves the Rule in Shelley's Case which we will be examining in Chapter Three.

17. See The Rule Against Perpetuities §§ 31–41.1.

SECTION 4. THE ESTATE IN FEE TAIL

If a transfer by O "to A and his heirs" means that A gets an estate that is not only inheritable by lineal and collateral heirs but also fully transferable by A so as to defeat his prospective heirs' expectancies, is there any formula O may use that will both prevent inheritance by A's collateral heirs and bar A's transferring so as to defeat his lineal heirs? Such a desire on O's part might be wholly natural. A may be O's new son-in-law, and O might not want to see the property go to A's collateral heirs on A's death. Moreover, O might be very attached to the land he is transferring and want it to pass down the generations as a sentimental reminder to his grandchildren and great-grandchildren of their ancestry. Certainly, this was a common ambition of transferors in the early days of English history, when the population was less mobile and land ownership was not computed merely in terms of its cash value.

The formula that transferors used to accomplish these purposes in the late twelfth through mid-thirteenth centuries was "to A *and the heirs of his body*." For a time the formula worked perfectly. Not only did it cut out A's collateral heirs and prevent his defeating his prospective lineal heirs' future possession by transfer, it also gave O, the transferor, the right to get the possession back upon the running out of A's line of lineal descendants. The theory that explained O's getting the possession back was that he had not transferred his entire estate in fee simple absolute. It simply became, therefore, a future estate in fee simple absolute during the period of possession by A and A's lineal heirs.

But there seems to be a puzzle. We observed in the preceding section that, to make land alienable, courts early construed "and his heirs" as giving the prospective heirs no estates. Why should the courts turn around and permit O to make land inalienable simply by using a different verbal formula? Surely, giving effect to O's purposes will make land just as inalienable as it had been when "and his heirs" meant that the heirs had an absolute right to possession.

Actually, there is no puzzle. In a very short time, well before 1285, the courts construed the words "and the heirs of his body" in a way that almost wholly frustrated O's intent. What the courts said, in effect, was this: What O *really intends* by this "and-the-heirs-of-his-body" language is to give A the power to transfer an estate in fee simple absolute provided that a child is born to A.[18] The birth of a child to A, according to the courts'

---

18. Only if the transfer was made *inter vivos*. Transfers of interests in land by will were not generally recognized.

construction, was simply a condition to A's enjoying the power to transfer an estate in fee simple absolute. As soon as a child was born to A (the child did not have to survive), the condition was deemed satisfied, and A was then free to transfer an estate in fee simple absolute—defeating, by such a transfer, not only his prospective lineal heirs' expectancies, but also O's right to get the property back upon the running out of A's line of lineal descendants.

We have said that the courts' construction of the formula "almost wholly" frustrated O's intent. Why did it not wholly frustrate O's intent? Because if no child was born to A, or if, after a child was born, A failed to exercise his power to transfer an estate in fee simple absolute, O's intent was given effect. Thus, if no child was born to A, the right to possession of the property on A's death would return to O rather than pass to A's collateral heirs. The possession would also return to O if, after a child was born to A, A did not exercise his power to transfer and died leaving no lineal heir to take. If A did leave a lineal heir, the estate would pass to the heir, who would hold just as his father had. That is, he too would have the power to transfer an estate in fee simple absolute as soon as a child was born to him. The estate that A got was called an *estate in fee simple conditional.*[19]

To persons like O, the right to get possession back only when A had no children, or when he failed to exercise his power to transfer an estate in fee simple and then died without lineal heirs, did not seem like even half a loaf. As was their wont, they petitioned the Crown for redress. In 1285, they got precisely what they wanted in the form of the statute *De Donis Conditionalibus.*[20] *De Donis* did one simple thing: it took away from A the power to transfer an estate in fee simple absolute after the birth of a child. After *De Donis*, the formula "to A and the heirs of his body" gave to A an estate known as an *estate in fee tail.*[21] Because A had no power to transfer an estate in fee simple absolute, it became theoretically possible for persons like O to tie up the ownership of land in a single family for hundreds of years. We say *theoretically possible* because by 1472 a way would be found for the tenant in tail (as A was called) to transfer an estate in fee simple absolute despite *De Donis*. Let us defer discussion of that point for a moment.

---

19. See Simes & Smith, The Law of Future Interests § 12 (2d ed. 1956) [hereinafter cited as Simes & Smith]. This estate is still said to exist in Iowa, South Carolina, and Oregon. See Simes & Smith § 62 at 48. The reader should be careful not to confuse this estate with estates having similar labels, such as the "estate in fee simple subject to a condition subsequent", to be discussed in Section 8, infra.

20. 13 Edw. 1, c. 1 (1285).

21. See Restatement, Property § 17 (1936) and Cheshire, 238–39.

If we cannot resist the temptation to say that *De Donis* permitted the creation of tailor-made estates, we can at least argue that it is not a pun. Our word "tailor" and the word "tail," as used in "fee tail," come from the same source—the French *tailler*, to cut. The word "tail" in "fee tail" has nothing to do with that which wags the dog. The estate in fee tail was a *cut* estate— either cut in the sense that the collateral heirs were cut out, or cut in the sense that the estate was carved into a series of discrete life-possession periods to be enjoyed successively by A and his lineal heirs. A transferor like O could, moreover, confine the lineal inheritability to a particular class of lineal heirs. He could, if he chose, confine the lineal inheritability to A's male heirs— thereby giving A an *estate in fee tail male*.[22] If he wished to confine the inheritability to female lineal heirs, he could transfer to A an *estate in fee tail female*.[23] He could also confine the inheritability to lineal heirs of A by a particular wife by giving A an *estate in fee tail special*.[24] He could even confine the inheritability to male (or female) lineal heirs by a particular wife by giving A an *estate in fee tail male (or female) special*.[25] Where O used only the words "and the heirs of his body," all lineal heirs of A could succeed to the estate. Such an estate was called an *estate in fee tail general*.[26]

As long as there was a lineal heir to take, the estate in fee tail could go on indefinitely. It would seem, then, that when O conveyed to A an estate in fee tail, he gave away all that he had—an estate potentially infinite in duration. But that is not how the courts viewed the matter. They regarded O as having kept a future estate in fee simple absolute, one that would become a present estate when (if ever) A's lineal succession ended.[27] This is still the rule in those states that recognize the fee tail.

---

22. The appropriate language was: "To A and the heirs male of his body."

23. The appropriate language was: "To A and the heirs female of his body."

24. The appropriate language was: "To A and the heirs of his body by his wife, Mary."

25. The appropriate language was: "To A and the heirs male (or female) of his body by his wife, Mary."

26. One would expect some confusion among these formulas to arise; and it did. See Simes & Smith § 62 at 47 n.7.

27. The reader may occasionally find it helpful to think of estates in terms of length, visualizing the fee simple as the longest and the fee tail, life estate, and estate for years as successively shorter. We will be setting forth the conventional rules respecting the lengths of estates in Section 8 of this chapter. Although this conceptual framework appears to account for the results of transfers—when the owner of a "longer" estate conveys a "shorter" one, he keeps a future estate that will become a present estate as soon as the "shorter" interest runs out—it does not account for the legal theories that produce those results. The "shortness" or "longness" of an estate is likely to be the product of a policy choice either to recognize a later possessory claim or not. When O transfers an estate in fee tail to A, why does the land not escheat to the state upon the expiration of A's lineal succession? Because A's estate was *shorter* than O's, or because we *prefer* O to the state as the next possessor? Is the estate in fee tail still "shorter" than the estate in fee simple? See note 34, infra, and accompanying text.

Looking at the period following *De Donis* and up to 1472—that is, the period during which it was not possible for a tenant in tail to transfer an estate in fee simple absolute—would we be correct in saying that the words "and the heirs of his body" were words of purchase? Did they give the prospective heirs *estates*, with present protection of their future possession? The writers of that period were apparently in disagreement on the point themselves, so we cannot give a clear answer one way or the other.[28] We can say, however, that each successive tenant in tail had no more than life-enjoyment of the land. He could, presumably, transfer his life-enjoyment right to a third person, but he could transfer no more.

What happened in 1472 to restore to the tenant in tail his power to transfer an estate in fee simple absolute? It was decided in Taltarum's Case[29] that a tenant in tail could transfer an estate in fee simple (thereby cutting off his prospective lineal heirs and O's future estate as well) if he replaced the transferred land with a court judgment entitling him to land of equal value from someone else. But how could A's lineal heirs (assuming that A is still our tenant in tail) and O be hurt if A substituted for the transferred land a judgment in A's favor entitling him to equally valuable land? Would not O and A's lineal heirs have the benefit of that judgment? They certainly would. But there was one catch: although the judgment that A substituted for the land was a valid one, *it ran against someone who had no land at all.*

The proceeding through which A accomplished this "disentailing" was called the *common recovery*.[30] Here's how it worked. B, with the connivance of A, would bring a real action against A claiming falsely that he, B, owned the land and demanding recovery of it. A responded by claiming, just as falsely, that he had acquired the land from C and that C had warranted title to the land. When A demanded of C, also an accomplice of A, that he defend the title, C admitted falsely that he had, indeed, warranted the title. C allowed B to take a default judgment against A for the recovery of the land, and allowed A to obtain a default judgment against himself, C, for the recovery of land of equal value. The result of this fancy feudal footwork was to

28. See the discussion in Plucknett, 546–57.

29. Y.B. 12 Edw. 4, 19, pl. 25 (1472).

30. See Simpson, 121–22, and Cheshire, 240–41. Are such fictions tolerated today, by modern courts? They sometimes are. For example, in some states a mortgage-borrower must sign a bond or note creating personal liability for the debt that the mortgage is to secure. A borrower who wishes to avoid such personal liability may, if his lender permits, transfer the property to be mortgaged to a professional "judgment-proof," who signs both bond and mortgage for a modest payment. The judgment-proof then merely reconveys to the borrower "subject to the mortgage." Result? The real borrower is not personally liable for the debt.

leave B with title to the land in fee simple and to leave A with his judgment against C. The judgment against C was viewed by the court as an adequate substitute for the entailed land. But when it came time for O or A's lineal heirs to enforce the judgment, it would transpire that C had been selected by A because he had no land at all! (Why else would C have played along?) Did the courts have any suspicion that A, B, and C were colluding? Of course they did—but how else, in the face of *De Donis*, could they unshackle land from the chains of the fee tail?

Another collusive method of disentailing that would become available to A in the sixteenth century—though one that would cut off only his own prospective lineal heirs, not O—was the *fine*.[31] A would covenant to transfer an estate in fee simple absolute to a collaborator, B. B would then sue A on his covenant. A would capitulate; and A and B, with the leave of the court, would enter into a compromise or "final concord" that would recognize the title in fee simple to be in B. The court's approval of the compromise completed the transfer to B. It might be noted that B's gaining of title in both the common recovery and the fine did not mean he kept it. Dutiful collaborator that he was, he commonly transferred the estate in fee simple right back to A.

The Fines and Recoveries Act[32] of 1833 did away with these collusive law suits and replaced them with a far simpler method of disentailing an estate in fee tail. All the tenant in tail had to do was to transfer an estate in fee simple by deed. The only limitation on this disentailing power was that the tenant had to have present possession. If his estate in fee tail was a future one, he could not disentail without the consent of the tenant in possession. Other changes have since been made in the law in England concerning the estate in fee tail, but to explore them would take us far from our task.[33]

We know of no state in the United States that recognizes the estate in fee tail in its strict 1285–1472 form. Wherever it is recognized, the tenant in tail in possession may disentail it by simple deed. In a number of states, the estate in fee tail has been abolished. Attempts to create a fee tail in such states typically create an estate in fee simple instead. In other states, statutes or decisions of the courts have brought it about that a

31. See Cheshire, 241.

32. 3 & 4 Will. 4, c. 74 (1833). The inventive English property lawyers came up with a device, almost unknown in this country, that retained the effectiveness of the fee tail after the various methods of disentailing such estates had been established. This was called the "strict settlement." An excellent discussion appears in Casner & Leach, Cases and Text on Property 357–58 (2d ed. 1969). See generally Cheshire, 165 and *passim*.

33. See generally Cheshire, 255–62.

transfer to "A and the heirs of his body" gives to A an estate for life, and to his immediate *lineal* heirs a future estate in fee simple absolute. In such states, the words "and the heirs of his body" are treated as words of purchase, entitling the prospective heirs to present protection of their future possession. In still other states, A is said to receive an estate in fee tail without disentailing power, and his immediate *lineal* heirs take, *as heirs*, an estate in fee simple.[34] What is the difference between that and treating the heirs as owners of a future estate in fee simple? It would seem that, unless form is exalted over form, there should be no difference.[35] The reader should, of course, remember that since primogeniture does not generally apply in the United States, all issue of A will share in the inheritance equally.[36]

In states where the estate in fee tail is recognized, though subject to disentailment by deed, may the estate be created as a future interest? Yes. O transfers "to A for life, then to B and the heirs of his body." Who has what? A has a present estate for life. B has a future estate in fee tail. O has a future estate in fee simple absolute. They all have them *now*. May B disentail *now* by transferring a future estate in fee simple absolute by deed? Probably not.[37]

Let us end this section by posing a complicated question. We are in a state that recognizes the estate in fee tail but allows its disentailment by deed only. O transfers "to A for life, then to B and the heirs of his body." While A is still living, O dies intestate, and then B dies leaving a will that says, "I leave all my property, real and personal, to my good friend, C." O is survived only by two daughters and a son. B is also survived only by two daughters and a son. Who owns what?

A, who is still living, still owns his present estate for life. O's future estate in fee simple absolute passes by the laws of intestacy to his children equally.[38] B's will was ineffective to disentail his estate in fee tail, so it passes to his lineal heirs—his three children. Now A dies, leaving a will that says, "I leave all my property, real and personal, to my beloved wife, Mary." B's children get possession. They win out over O's

---

34. The best summary of these various modern treatments of the fee tail in this country is still to be found in the Restatement. See Restatement, Property, Introductory Note 379 (Supp. 1948). See also Simes & Smith §§ 62, 313. The student is cautioned to consult the statutes, decisions, and constitution of his state for its present law.

35. Compare, e.g., Restatement, Property § 91, with id. § 188.

36. They will probably take as "tenants in common." See the discussion in Section 9, infra. It is conceivable that in some states primogeniture may apply to the estate in fee tail.

37. See, e.g., Mass. Gen. Laws Ann. ch. 183 § 45 n.15 (1958).

38. They probably take as tenants in common. See Section 9, infra.

children, since that was the order of possession prescribed by O in the original transfer.   A's will, of course, could pass no interest in this property to his wife, since his estate in it terminated at his death.   Let us now look more closely at the estate for life.

SECTION 5.   THE ESTATE FOR LIFE

The estate for life,[39] the reader will be pleased to know, is just about what its name implies—an estate the duration of which is measured by a human life.   Because it terminates at the end of the measuring life, it is generally thought to be an estate that may not be inherited.   We shall see below that there is an exception to this proposition in the case of the estate *pur autre vie.*

The traditional words of limitation that denote the creation of an estate for life are the words "for life."   O transfers "to A for life."   A has a present estate for life.   Upon A's death, his estate will terminate.   Suppose O transfers "to A for life, then to B for life, then to C for life, then to D for life."   Who owns what?   A, B, C, and D all own estates for life.   Each estate for life is measured by its owner's life.   A's estate for life is *present*, and the rest are all future.   But they all own their estates *now*.   Does O have anything left?   Yes.   O still owns his estate in fee simple absolute.   It is simply a future estate in fee simple absolute during the period in which the life estates continue.   The reason, of course, is that no matter how many estates for life O creates, they will not total an estate in fee simple.   Therefore, when A, B, C, and D are all dead, O (or whoever has succeeded to his interest in the interim) will once again be entitled to present possession for a potentially infinite period of time.

Staying with the transfer to A, B, C, and D, suppose C dies while A, B, and D are still living.   What happens?   C's life estate terminates.   Does that mean C never *had* an estate for life?   No.   It simply means that it never became a present estate.   Once C is dead, D becomes the life-tenant who will be entitled to possession upon B's death.   In other words, although A, B, C, and D all got life estates, the *order* in which they were entitled to *possession* was the order in which their names appeared in the transfer by O.   By carving out the life estates to A, B, C, and D, O placed himself last in line for possession.

Suppose that while A is still in possession (assuming that B, C, and D are still living), A transfers "to E for the life of E."

---

39.   See Restatement, Property § 18 & ch. 6 (1936).

What does E get?   One thing he gets is present possession, since A had that to give him.   But for how long may E keep possession?   The language of the transfer clearly shows that A intended E to have possession for E's full life.   That will be precisely what E gets *if E dies before A*.   But if A dies before E, E's estate will terminate then.[40]   Remember that A had only a life estate to begin with;   if he were allowed to transfer an estate that could last beyond his death, he would be able to delay or even to defeat the possessory right of the next taker in line.[41]

If E dies before A, the right to possession goes back to A, who once again has his present estate for life.[42]   This means that A had a future estate for life while E was alive.   Is our conclusion that A kept a future estate for life an *ex post facto* conclusion— that is, do we say that A kept a future estate for life because we *now know* that E died first?   No—from the moment E got his life estate, we would have said that A had a future estate for life.   From that moment on, the law simply recognized that E might live for a shorter period than A.   In consequence, A was entitled from the moment to court protection of his *possible* future possession.[43]

What A's transfer to E did, in effect, was change O's original transfer to read "to E for the life of E *for so long as A lives*, then to A for life, then to B for life, then to C for life, then to D for life."   B, C, and D cannot complain of A's transfer to E, because it can in no way delay their receiving possession.   O

---

40. E's life estate may be viewed as subject to an implied "special limitation": the prior death of A.   See Section 8, infra, for a discussion of the special limitation.

41. But doesn't the owner of an estate in fee simple absolute defeat the possessory right of the next taker when he transfers to someone else an estate in fee simple absolute and then dies intestate without heirs?   No.   The next taker would be the state by escheat.   By policy preference, the state is not said to have an estate that would be defeated by such a transfer.

42. If A's transfer to E had simply read, "to E for life," would A still have been viewed as having kept a future estate for life?   Not unless the circumstances of the transfer made it clear that A intended E's estate to be measured by E's life.   When the owner of a life estate transfers an estate "for life," and neither the language of the conveyance nor the circumstances surrounding it indicate whose life is to be the measuring life, the law assumes that the transferor has conveyed all that he had—

an estate measured by his own life.   See Restatement, Property § 108, comment *a* (1936), and 1 American Law of Property § 2.15.

43. See, e.g., Restatement, Property § 192 (1936 & Supp. 1948).   We italicized the word "possible" to emphasize what we hope has now become apparent to the reader—namely, that ownership of a future estate does not imply certainty of future possession.   We saw, as a matter of fact, an example earlier in this section of a future estate that never became a present estate.   When we get to future interests, we will see examples of future estates that do not become present estates even when their owners (or, more accurately, *former* owners) are alive at the time the estates might have been expected to become present estates.   The likelihood or unlikelihood of a future estate's becoming a present estate will seriously affect the amount of present protection that its owner will receive from the courts—the less the likelihood, the less the protection.

cannot complain, because his future possession is not delayed either. But may not O complain because E is enjoying possession when O intended A to enjoy it? O has no legal complaint, because he gave to A a life estate, which is a transferable interest in property. B, C, and D can also transfer their interests even while they are future interests.

Suppose the owner of a present estate for life leases the land for five years—that is, transfers an estate for years. Does the transferor keep his estate for life? Yes. It simply becomes a future estate for life during the five-year period.[44] If the transferor dies during the five-year period, both the transferor's future estate for life and the transferee's estate for years terminate. As we have said, the owner of an estate for life cannot transfer more than he has. Suppose the owner of an estate for life transfers an estate for 300 years—does the transferor still keep a future estate for life? In common-law *theory*, he does; but since his chances of being around to enjoy future possession are slim, the courts will not give his interest much present protection.[45]

Going back for a moment to our transfer from A to E, let us assume that A instead transfers "to E *for the life of A.*" Since A has used his own life as the measuring life of E's estate, A has given away all that he had. Because E's estate is measured by the life of someone other than himself, his estate is called an estate *pur autre vie.*[46] A, whose life is the measuring life, is called the *cestui que vie.* If A dies first, E's estate simply comes to an end precisely as it did when A died first after transferring "to E for the life of E." In that case, of course, we thought of E's estate as terminating before its maximum duration had run simply because A could not give E more than A had. In this case, E's estate terminates because its maximum duration—A's life—has in fact run.

But now we have a problem. Suppose that E, in this transfer, dies before A. Where does the right to possession go? Since A is deemed to have given E all that A had, the possession cannot go back to him. A is now just an outsider—simply the measuring life for E's estate. The possession cannot go to B, because B is not entitled to possession until A's death. C, D, and O are even worse claimants than B. Who gets the left-over part of E's estate?

---

44. For reasons that will not become clear until we reach Section 6 of this chapter, an owner of an estate for life who transfers an estate for years may, for some purposes, still be viewed as having a "present interest."

45. See note 43, supra.

46. See Restatement, Property § 18, comment *a* (1936), which calls this an "estate for the life of another." Suppose A had said "to E for the life of F." E's estate would be an estate *pur autre vie*, measured by F's life. Because of the possibility of F's dying before A, A would be viewed as having kept a future estate for life.

Under the common law, whoever got to the property first was entitled to hold it for the left-over period. Such a person, who might even have been a total stranger, was called a *general occupant*. A different result was reached under the common law when the original transfer by A was "to E *and his heirs* for the life of A." In that case, when E died before A, E's heirs were permitted to hold the property for the left-over period as *special occupants*. Technically speaking, the heirs did not get the property by inheritance, since E's estate *pur autre vie* was not regarded as an inheritable estate. Today, in the United States, statutes typically provide that an owner of an estate pur autre vie may devise it to whomever he wishes.[47] If he dies intestate, the left-over portion will pass in some states as real property to his heirs and in other states as personal property to his personal representative for distribution to his next of kin.

As we have earlier indicated, we have not thought it central to this book's purposes to explore the niceties of the widow's or widower's claim to the deceased spouse's property. Suffice it to say that under the common law, a widow was entitled to an estate for life in one-third of the lands of which her husband had been seised of a *legal*[48] inheritable estate during the marriage. This *dower interest* of the wife could not be defeated either by *inter vivos* transfer by the husband (unless, of course, the wife joined in the transfer, which would *release her dower*) or by will. A husband was entitled, provided issue was born to the marriage (the issue did not have to survive), to an estate for life in *all* (not merely one third) his wife's *legal and equitable*[49] inheritable estates in land of which she was seised during the marriage. The husband's interest, called *curtesy*, was effective during the marriage, and continued if the husband survived the wife. The wife could not defeat his interest by *inter vivos* transfer (unless he joined in it) or by will. Neither the husband nor the wife was considered an "heir" of the deceased spouse.

In many states today, common-law dower and curtesy have been wholly replaced by statutes that make the surviving spouse an "heir" of the deceased spouse and fix a *minimum* percentage of the decedent's estate (real and personal) to which the survivor will be entitled regardless of efforts of the deceased spouse to prevent it *by will*. This statutory minimum—called the *statutory forced share*—is typically an estate in fee simple, not merely a life estate. A serious disadvantage to the surviving spouse under many of these statutes, however, is that the minimum

---

47. See Restatement, Property § 151 (1936 & Supp.1948).

48. We shall see in later chapters that "equitable" estates may also exist. It

would not serve our present purposes to explore the differences between "legal" and "equitable" estates at this point.

49. See note 48, supra.

percentage applies only to property owned by the decedent *at death.* Both husbands and wives can, under such statutes, defeat their spouses' forced shares by *inter vivos* transfer.[50]

Some states still recognize dower and curtesy in substantially their common-law forms.[51] *In those states, it is essential that both husband and wife join in transfers of inheritable estates if the transferee is to take free of dower and curtesy.* (Note that dower and curtesy, and statutory replacements for them, are relevant only where the husband or wife owned an inheritable estate in his or her own name. In this country, a husband and wife will typically take title to land in *both names.* We shall speak briefly of the characteristics of that ownership in Section 9 of this chapter.)

SECTION 6.   THE ESTATE FOR YEARS, WITH A PRELIMINARY ANALYSIS OF THE CONCEPT OF SEISIN

An estate for years,[52] also commonly called a term of years or a lease for years, is an estate the duration of which is absolutely computable (in years, months, weeks, and days) from the moment of its creation, or at least from the moment when it becomes a present estate. O transfers "to A for five years." Because we know at the moment of the estate's creation that A will enjoy possession for five years, our definitional requirement is met. A has a present estate for years. Another example: O transfers "to A for life, then to B for five years." Does B have an estate *now*? Yes. It is a future estate. Do we know its duration now? Obviously not, since we do not know when A will die. But will we not know, as soon as A is dead, the *remaining duration* of B's estate? Yes. It will then be a present estate for five years. So again we have met the definitional requirement. A final example: O transfers "to A for so long as B remains a teetotaler." Since we cannot tell how long B will remain a teetotaler, we cannot tell precisely how long A's estate will last. A does not have an estate for years.[53]

Is an estate for years transferable by *inter vivos* transfer? The answer is yes, unless the lease provides to the contrary.

---

50. For a discussion of this point, see Haskell, The Power of Disinheritance: Proposal for Reform, 52 Geo. L.J. 499, 503–06 (1964).

51. See 1 American Law of Property §§ 5.5 and 5.60.

52. See Restatement, Property § 19 (1936).

53. Views may differ on what A does have. It will depend on whether words of inheritance are needed after "to A" in order to create a fee simple estate. If no such words are needed, A may have a fee simple determinable that will become a fee simple absolute if B remains a teetotaler for his entire life. If words of inheritance are needed, the grant will create a determinable estate for life in A, to be measured by either A's or B's life. See Section 8, infra, for a discussion of determinable estates.

What happens when the owner of an estate for years dies before the term is up? The answer to this question is slightly more complicated. Under the common law, the estate for years was not treated as "real property"; it was thought of as "personal property."[54] When the owner of an estate for years died intestate before the term of his estate had run out, the unexpired portion did not descend to his "heirs." One *inherited* only real property, such as estates in fee simple in land. The estate for years passed instead to the decedent's administrator. The estate for years and any other personal property the decedent had owned at his death were used before any of the real property to satisfy his debts. Whatever was left of the personal property would then be distributed by the administrator to the decedent's spouse and the decedent's "next of kin." A decedent's "heirs" and his "next of kin" were not always the same persons,[55] so personal property might go to some people and real property to others.

Although the estate for years continues to be conceptualized as personal property today, some of the common-law consequences of that conceptualization have been changed by statute. For example, real property and personal property generally pass to the same persons under modern laws of intestate succession. Some states tax estates for years as real property, and a few have enacted statutes that convert certain kinds of long-term leases into real property for specified purposes. Even so, the general rule that an estate for years is personal property can have unexpected (and sometimes unwanted) consequences. A, believing wrongly that his estate for years is real property, executes a will in which he leaves "all my real property to B and all my personal property to C." Who gets the estate for years on A's death?

For the purposes of this book, a lengthy examination of the estate for years would be an inexcusable frolic and detour. The relations between landlord and tenant in the modern lease are a curious and complicated blend of the law of property and the law

---

54. The Restatement characterizes it as an "interest in land," but not as "real property." See, in this order, Restatement, Property §§ 19, 9, and 8 (1936). So far as we have been able to detect, the Restatement, Second, Property (Landlord and Tenant) (1977), does not take a stand on the matter. Its focus is not upon how the tenant's interest is to be conceptualized as property, but rather upon what the substantive relationships (i.e., rights and duties) of landlords and tenants will be once a "landlord-tenant relationship" has been found to exist. As noted infra in the text of this section, the estate for years is still generally regarded as personal property.

A few states, by statute, have converted some kinds of long-term leases into real property (freehold estates) for specified purposes.

55. For example, a decedent's father might be counted as his next of kin but not as his heir. This state of affairs, which seems to us anomalous, occurred because different courts had jurisdiction over the two types of property (feudal courts over real property, and ecclesiastical courts over personal property), and entirely different rules were used in each. See Plucknett, 727–29.

of contract.   Those relations deserve detailed study in the classroom.   Indeed, we would not even have mentioned the estate
for years were it not for the historic role it played in the development of our law of future interests.   In this chapter, we
can give only the barest hint of what that role was.

In its earliest development, the estate for years was commonly
used as a device to secure the payment of debts.   Thus, O,
wishing to borrow from A, would transfer an estate for years to
A in exchange for the borrowed sum.   A would simply collect
his debt out of the profits that the land yielded during his *occupancy*.   We italicize "occupancy" for a very important reason.
In feudal theory, A's use of the land was not thought of as *possession* of the land—at least, not that glorified feudal possession
called *seisin*.[56]   Although A enjoyed the actual physical use and
profits of the land for the fixed period of his estate for years,
the seisin was thought still to reside in O.   In the eyes of a
common lawyer of the feudal period, O, despite A's occupancy,
had a *present* estate in fee simple that was merely subject to
(burdened or encumbered by) the estate for years in A.   Although it is perfectly proper today to say that O, having transferred an estate for years, has a future interest,[57] we will be
finding it useful, particularly when we get to Chapters 3 and 4,
to remind ourselves that a transfer by O in the feudal period of
an estate for years, without more, left the seisin in O.   We will
express that idea, when appropriate, by saying that O has a
"present" estate in fee simple, subject to the estate for years.
The quotation marks around "present" will be intended to indicate that O, though seised, is not in physical possession of the
property.[58]

But why would a feudal lawyer view O as still seised after
he had transferred an estate for years?   To answer that question,
we shall have to improve upon that loose definition of seisin we
gave in Chapter One.   There, the reader will recall, we defined
seisin as meaning, roughly, possession.   Actually, it meant something more than physical occupancy of land.   It meant primarily
that dominion over land one had when one owned what was called
a present *freehold estate* in the land.   The only freehold estates
were the estate in fee simple, the estate in fee tail (or, earlier,
the estate in fee simple conditional), and the estate for life.   A
common characteristic of these estates was that they were all
created by *feoffment with livery of seisin*.   The estate for years

---

56.   1 American Law of Property § 3.1
at 176–177.

57.   Called a reversion.   We will be
looking at reversions in Chapter Three.

58.   We use the quotation marks as our
own mnemonic device.   They are not part
of the traditional language of future-interest law.

was not created by feoffment with livery of seisin.   It was created by simple agreement between the parties *plus physical en-
try by the tenant for years* (or *termor*, as he is sometimes called).[59] > termor
The estate for years was not a freehold estate, and the termor
was not "seised."   He had physical occupancy of the land, but
the dignified possession called seisin was thought to reside in the
owner of the "present" freehold estate.

This is all well and good—but did the concept of seisin play
any functional role?   It did.   It expressed the right-duty relationship between feoffer and feoffee.   Turning back to our pre-
Quia-Emptores days, let us assume that O, by feoffment with
livery of seisin, transferred to "A and his heirs" by subinfeudation.   This meant that A held his estate in fee simple absolute
of O, owing to O such services as had been agreed on.   The
ceremonial transfer of seisin from O to A was the operative act
that established the right of O to look to A for performance of
the services and the duty of A to perform them.   To be seised,
therefore, did not mean merely to own a freehold estate; *it also
meant to be bound to perform the feudal duties.*   If one was not
seised, one was not bound.

From the notion that one must be seised of an estate in freehold to be bound to perform the feudal duties grew an extraor-
dinarily important rule of feudal land law: *There must never be
a moment when the seisin cannot be located in someone owning
an estate in freehold.*   To put this rule in its more common form,
there could be no "gap" in the seisin.   The reason for the rule
should be obvious.   If there were ever a time when nobody was
seised, who would perform the feudal duties?   Since the feudal
duties must always be performed, someone must always have the
seisin.

We cannot, without leaping into the heart of future interests,
say much more about seisin at this point than we have.   We can,
however, point in the direction of our later inquiry by giving a
few examples of the relevance of the concept to the estate for
years during the feudal period.   We will be using our "present-
estate" locution.   Example one: O transfers "to A for five years."
O is still seised of a "present" estate in fee simple absolute,
subject to a term of five years in A.   O is still bound to perform
the feudal duties.   Example two: O, effectively transferring his
entire estate in fee simple absolute, transfers "to A for five years,
then to B and his heirs."   O makes livery of seisin to A *for the
benefit of B*, who is seised of a "present" estate in fee simple
absolute subject to the term of five years in A.   If the transfer

---

59. Before the termor took possession,
he had an *interesse termini*.   See Cheshire, 388.   The requirement that the termor had to enter upon the land for his estate for years to begin will become relevant
in our later discussion of conveyancing.

is made by subinfeudation (before *Quia Emptores*), B holds of
O. If the transfer is made by substitution, B holds of O's mesne
lord. In either event, B must perform the feudal duties.

Let us try a slightly more complicated example. Prior to
1536,[60] O attempts to transfer "to A for five years, then to the
heirs of B in fee simple." B is living at the time of the transfer.
Where is the seisin? It cannot be in A, since A has only an
estate for years. It cannot be in the "heirs of B," because B
does not yet have any heirs. Since the seisin must be some-
where, it must still be in O. Result? O still has his "present"
estate in fee simple absolute, subject to a term of five years in
A. B's "heirs" get absolutely nothing—not even a future interest. Since the seisin could not pass to them when the transfer
was made (they were not identifiable at that time), it will never
get to them unless O enfeoffs them after B's death.[61] We will
have much more to say about this example when we get to future
interests.

Our last example: O, by feoffment with livery of seisin, transfers "to A for life, then to B and his heirs." Since an estate for
life is a freehold estate, A has the seisin. If A transfers "to C
for five years," A remains seised of a "present" estate for life,
subject to a term for years in C. When A dies, the seisin will
pass automatically to B (or to whoever has succeeded to B's future
estate in fee simple absolute). B's estate is also a freehold estate
capable of bearing the seisin. The message to the reader from
these examples? Begin to alert yourself to look for the seisin
when we speak of transfers during the feudal period.

We have one final point to make. Although the "present-
estate" locution is particularly useful to us as a reminder of the
importance of seisin in the feudal scheme of things, we should
not conclude that it is inappropriate to use it in connection with
modern-day transfers. When O transfers today "to A for five
years," we can say *either* that O has a future interest [62] *or* that
he has a "present" estate subject to a term for years in A. Similarly, when O, transfers today his entire estate in fee simple
absolute by a conveyance "to A for five years, then to B and his
heirs," we can say *either* that B has a future interest [63] *or* that
he has a "present" estate subject to a term for years in A. Unhappily, the fact that we have two locutions available to us can
be a source of confusion, as we shall be seeing in later chapters.

---

60. This is the year in which the Statute of Uses, 27 Hen. 8, c. 10 (1535), became
effective. We will discuss the significance of this statute in Chapter Four.

61. Until 1536 (see note 60, supra) seisin
could not automatically "spring out" of a
grantor at some future date: he had to
deliver it. We will clarify this point later.

62. See notes 4 and 57, supra.

63. Called a remainder. We will be
looking at remainders in Chapter Three.

SECTION 7.   SEISIN: A FROLIC AND DETOUR

The material in this section appeared in the first edition of this book, and produced mixed reactions.   Some students judged it to be an undigestible and useless lump of stuff;   others found it to be a skeleton key to an elusive concept.   About the most we will say of it is that reading it will cause little permanent damage.   It *is*, however, something of a frolic and detour, and we give you our permission to skip it.   If you have not already studied adverse possession, you had better skip it.

Our aim here is to find the feudal meaning of "seisin" by analyzing use of the term in a statute of limitations for actions to recover possession of real property.   The state of XYZ, let us assume, has a statute reading as follows:

> No action for the recovery of possession of real property shall be brought or maintained unless the person bringing or maintaining the same shall have been *seised of an interest* in the property at some time within the twenty years next preceding the commencement of such action.

Assuming, as we probably safely can, that the framers of this statute had in mind the usual purposes of an "adverse possession" statute (it is, in fact, a rather common form of such a statute), its *intent* is to say that if land has been adversely possessed continuously for 20 years, anyone who had a present possessory claim to the land immediately before the adverse possession started may no longer recover possession (unless he was under some legal disability such as insanity or infancy when the adverse possession started).   He has lost his "title."   Let us try to define the words "seised of an interest" so as to give effect to what we properly assume is the statute's purpose.

Might we define one who was "seised of an interest" as one who had "good title" [64] to the land?   Our statute would then say, in effect, that no one could bring an action to recover possession of land unless he had "good title" to it at some time during the 20 years prior to his bringing his action.   Does that make sense? A moment's reflection should tell us that it does not.   Assuming O had "good title" just before A entered into adverse possession 20 years ago, when does O *lose* it?   He loses it right now.   But if he loses it *now*, he must have had it yesterday.   If he had it yesterday, he has, under our proposed reading of the statute, 20 years from yesterday to bring his suit.   Thus, A would have to stay in adverse possession for almost another 20 years to defeat O.   As a matter of fact, if we say that O can bring a suit to

---

64.   We *are* using "good title" here in a relative sense, despite our ground rule to the contrary.

recover possession only when he has "good title" (what other theory would explain it?), it is obvious that A can *never* defeat O's right to possession. We must, therefore, abandon "good title" as an adequate substitute for "seised of an interest."

How about using "possession?" Will the statute make sense if we read it to say that one may not bring an action to recover possession of real property unless he had "possession" of the property at some time during the 20 years preceding commencement of the action? If we take possession to mean at least some kind of physical presence on the land, we may be in trouble. Suppose O, with his "good title," has not been physically present on the land for 21 years. A entered into adverse possession of the land *only two years ago.* May O recover possession from A? We would certainly assume that the actual statute we started out with would permit O to recover possession; but as we have now worded it, O cannot recover possession. Why? Because O has not been physically present on the land for 20 years!

Let us make one last try. Suppose we recast the statute to read as follows:

> No action for the recovery of possession of real property shall be brought or maintained unless the person bringing or maintaining the same shall, at any time during the twenty years next preceding the commencement of such action, either (a) *have been in actual adverse possession thereof,* or (b) *have been in actual possession thereof as owner of an estate in freehold therein,* or (c) *have owned an estate in freehold therein while the land was not adversely possessed by another person.*

As impossibly cumbersome as the italicized language is, it comes about as close to the idea of being "seised of an interest" as we can get—at least without turning the statute into a book. The remarkable thing is that the statute we have proposed not only serves the purposes we imagined the original statute had, but also expresses almost precisely the feudal notion of seisin. Note that in our proposed statute, a person may be seised of an interest (a) when he physically possesses as an adverse possessor, or (b) when he physically possesses as owner of an estate in freehold (not a term of years), or (c) when, though not in physical possession, he owns an estate in freehold at a time when no one else is adversely possessing the land. That was just about what seisin meant during the feudal period.

But how can we say that an adverse possessor may be seised of an interest? Was not seisin given to persons only by feoffment? Let us go back to the feudal period for a moment. O enfeoffs "A and his heirs." Now B arrives on the scene and ousts A from the land. Where is the seisin? To say that A still has the seisin might make theoretical sense, but it would not make practical sense.　The person who is seised must perform the duties, and how can A perform the duties if he doesn't have the land?　With a lively alertness to the needs of the lords, the feudal courts decided that the seisin was in B.　B was held to have *disseised* A.　For as long as he remained in possession, B, the *disseisor*, was thought to be seised of an estate in fee simple absolute.　A, the *disseisee*, would be permitted to recover possession by writ of right if he commenced his action within the then-prescribed period for the limitation of such actions;[65]　but while A was gathering his writs, B was bound to perform the feudal duties.

SECTION 8. DEFEASIBLE ESTATES

The reader may be pleased to know that we have described all the estates we are going to.　The label "defeasible" does not introduce a new kind of estate—it merely describes a characteristic that may appear in the estates we have already studied. There *are* some other kinds of estates—estates at will, estates at sufferance, estates from year to year[66]—but an understanding of them is not essential for our purposes.　They may more profitably be studied as part of the law of landlord and tenant.　From here on, we shall be talking only about *present* or *future* estates in fee simple, in fee tail, for life, and for years.

Although we have not made much of the matter up to this point, it now becomes important for us to note that the durational labels we have discussed indicate the *maximum* durations of estates.　Thus, when we speak of an estate in fee simple, we mean an estate whose *maximum* duration is until its owner dies intestate and without lineal or collateral heirs surviving.　The *maximum* duration of an estate in fee tail is until the last lineal heir of the original tenant in tail dies.　The *maximum* duration of an estate for life is until the death of the person whose life is the measuring life.　The *maximum* duration of an estate for years is until the fixed number of years is over.

---

65. Because of the importance to feudal landholders of seisin and of real property in general, the writ of right has been called "the most solemn of all actions." Plucknett, 112.　Nevertheless, it was believed that the time within which such a complainant would be allowed to prove an ancestor to have been seised of the estate in question must be limited.　At first this was done by selecting an arbitrary date in the past, before which "legal memory" would not run.　The date initially was Dec. 1, 1135 (the death of Henry I); in 1236 it was changed by statute to Dec. 19, 1154 (the coronation of Henry II);　and in 1275 it became Sept. 3, 1189 (the coronation of Richard I).　Finally, in 1540, an arbitrary period of sixty years was set as the period of "legal memory."　See id., 719.　The latter change was probably made because it was felt that a 350-year statute of limitations was somewhat awkward.

66. See generally Restatement, Property §§ 20–22 (1936).

defeasible

In this section, we shall concern ourselves with estates that are *defeasible*—that is, estates that may come to an end before their maximum duration has run.   Before we turn to that subject, let us make explicit some notions that have lain implicit in our discussion of estates in previous sections of this chapter.   In a number of places in our earlier discussion, we saw examples of a person's transferring an estate and "keeping" a *future* estate with the same label as the present estate he had to start with. For example, A, the owner of an estate for life, transfers to B a life estate measured by B's life.   We have said that B gets a present estate for life and A keeps a future estate for life.   Yet there is no way to be certain that A will outlive B.   In fact, if A is an octogenarian at the time the transfer is made and B is a man in his prime, the odds are that B will live longer.   Why, then, do we say that A has kept a future estate for life?

When we say that A has kept a future estate, we are saying that we *prefer* A as the next possessor if B *in fact* dies before A.   By saying that we "prefer" A as the next taker after B, we do not mean, of course, that we have really explored the social consequences of choosing A as the next possessor.   We mean simply that the choice of A is, rightly or wrongly, imbedded in the way we think about ownership of land.   It is part of our "law."   Since we have done nothing to change it, we seem to think it is all right.

What we hope is emerging from our discussion is the idea that the "future estate" labels we have been using are simply a way of saying that we prefer this person to that person (or to the state) as the next person to enjoy possession of property after the present estate has ended.   As long as the person we prefer is around,[67] we will not only give him possession when his chance comes, we will also protect his *future* possession while the present estate lasts.   Suppose O transfers "to A for life, then to B for life."   A has a present estate for life; B has a future estate for life.   When both life estates have expired, we wish possession to return to O (or his successor in interest) rather than escheat to the state; so we say that O has a future estate in fee simple. Of course, when we say that *we* prefer A, B, and O in that order, we simply mean that we prefer to defer to O's judgment as to the order of possession.   How is *our* preference expressed?   In our continuing commitment to private control of resources—i.e., "private property."[68]

---

67. Of course, if the estate is inheritable—one in fee simple or in fee tail—the original owner of the future estate need not be around.

68. Interesting questions may be raised as to whether the right to create future interests in property is itself "property" protected by the fourteenth amendment.

Let us summarize the rules that determine when a transferor keeps a future estate. (a) If the owner of an estate in fee simple transfers any number of estates in fee tail, for life, or for years, or any combination of such estates, the transferor is deemed to have "kept" a *future* estate in fee simple. (b) If the owner of an estate in fee tail transfers any number of estates for life or for years, or any combination thereof, the transferor is deemed to have kept a *future* estate in fee tail.[69] (c) If the owner of an estate for life transfers any number of estates for life *measured by the lives of persons other than the transferor*, or any number of estates for years (no matter how long), or any combination of such estates, the transferor is deemed to have kept a *future* estate for life. (d) If the owner of an estate for years transfers any number of estates for years of shorter aggregate fixed duration than the one he had, the transferor is deemed to have kept a *future* estate for years. In sum, whenever the owner of an estate transfers a *lesser* estate—that is, an estate whose conceptual maximum duration is shorter than that of the estate he had to start with—he is deemed to have kept a future estate.

It would seem fair to assume that when a transferor transfers an estate or estates that *equal*, in conceptual maximum duration, the estate he had to start with, he keeps nothing. That is precisely what happens in many cases. A, owning an estate for life measured by his own life, transfers "to B *for the life of A*." Since the transferred estate for life is measured by the life of the *transferor*, it does not fit within rule (c). Hence A is deemed to have kept no future estate. Another example: O transfers "to A and his heirs." Since the transfer does not fit within rule (a), O has not kept a future estate. Has he kept a seignory? No—*Quia Emptores* forbids that. A final example: O transfers "to A for life, then to B and his heirs." The transfer to A meets the requirements of rule (a), but O has also transferred his estate in fee simple to B. Since A's and B's estates together equal the maximum conceptual duration of O's original estate, O has kept nothing.

But we would be in error if we concluded from our rules (a) through (d) that it is never possible to retain a future estate when one transfers an estate or estates that equal, in conceptual

---

69. Note that when an owner of an estate in fee tail transfers an estate for life measured by the transferee's life, the transferred estate will end either upon the transferee's death or upon the transferor's death, whichever first occurs. Similarly, if he transfers an estate for years, the transferred estate may end either at the expiration of the fixed period or at the transferor's death, whichever first occurs. No matter when the transferred estate for life or transferred estate for years ends, possession returns to the owner of the estate in fee tail. If, of course, the termination of the transferred estate occurs by reason of the death of the transferor, possession goes to his immediate lineal heirs.

maximum duration, the estate one had to start with. If the transferor attaches a "special limitation" [70] or a "condition subsequent" [71] at the time of the transfer, the transferor will be deemed to have kept or created in himself a future estate having precisely the same durational characteristics as the estate he had to start with. Here is an example: O transfers "to A and his heirs *for so long as the premises are not used for the sale of alcoholic beverages.*" O has attached a special limitation to the transfer. O has, therefore, retained a future estate in fee simple absolute. Here is another example: O transfers "to A and his heirs; *but if the premises are ever used for the sale of alcoholic beverages, O, or whoever has succeeded to his interest, may enter and terminate the estate granted.*" O has attached a condition subsequent to the transfer. O has, therefore, created in himself a future estate in fee simple absolute. Let us look at each of these transfers separately.

Since the "and-his-heirs" formula was used in the first transfer, it is obvious that the estate transferred is an estate in fee simple. Thus, the transfer does not fit rule (a). The *maximum* duration of A's estate is conceptually identical with the *maximum* duration of O's original estate in fee simple absolute. But it is quite obvious that if the italicized words used by O in his transfer are given effect, the transferred estate may very well come to an end before any owner of the estate dies intestate and without lineal or collateral heirs surviving. Those words will be given effect. They are called *words of special limitation*—"special," because they prescribe special circumstances under which A's estate may expire *before* the maximum duration implied by the words "and his heirs." What O in effect said in his transfer was this: "I am transferring to A an estate the duration of which is to be the *shorter* of these two durations: (a) until any owner of the granted estate dies intestate without lineal or collateral heirs surviving, *or* (b) until alcoholic beverages are sold on the property. If the estate ends by reason of the sale of alcoholic beverages, I am to be restored to my original present estate in fee simple absolute."

That is precisely the way the courts treat the matter. If any owner of the transferred estate dies intestate and without lineal collateral heirs surviving, the estate will simply escheat to the state. If, however, before that occurs, alcoholic beverages are sold on the property, the estate will *automatically expire*, and O (or whoever has succeeded to his interest) [72] will be entitled

---

70. See Restatement, Property § 23 (1936).

71. See Restatement, Property § 24 (1936).

72. The reader is probably tired of reading this parenthetical material, so we will discontinue the use of it.

to present possession with an estate in fee simple absolute.   (Please read the footnote to the preceding sentence.)   A's estate is one kind of a class of similar estates called, generically, *defeasible estates*.[73]   Defeasible estates are estates that may come to an end before their maximum duration has run by reason of the operation of a special limitation, a condition subsequent, or an executory limitation.[74]   When an estate is defeasible by operation of a special limitation, it is called a *determinable* estate.   Hence, A's estate in our first example is called an *estate in fee simple determinable*.[75]

O used the "and-his-heirs" formula in the second transfer as well; so it is clear that the transferred estate is an estate in fee simple.   Thus, O does not keep a future estate by operation of our rule (a).   His future estate is created by the remaining words of the transfer—the *condition subsequent*.   Note that the words creating the condition subsequent do not state that A's estate will automatically expire upon the sale of alcoholic beverages. They simply say that if alcoholic beverages are sold on the property, O *may* enter and terminate the granted estate.   He doesn't have to.   If O chooses not to do so, A's estate will continue merrily on its way.   If he does choose to enter and terminate,[76] then (and only then) will A's estate end and O become entitled to possession with his original estate in fee simple absolute. Therein lies the major difference between the estate transferred to A in the first example and the estate transferred to A in the second example.   Upon the sale of alcoholic beverages in the first example, A's estate *automatically expires*[77] because its duration was so limited by the special limitation.   In the second example, A's estate ends only if O chooses to *cut it short*[78] by exercising his power to terminate it.   A's estate in the second example, also a defeasible estate, is called an *estate in fee simple subject to a condition subsequent*.[79]

---

73. See Restatement, Property §§ 44–58 (1936).

74. See Restatement, Property § 25 (1936).   Estates subject to an executory limitation will be discussed at the end of this section, and again in Chapter Four.

75. It is also called an estate in fee simple subject to a special limitation.   See Restatement, Property, Introductory Note, 117–18 (1936).

76. He probably will not actually enter.   He is more likely to telephone A and ask him to leave.   Failing in this, he will sue to recover possession.   The process by which this occurs is often described as O's "declaring a forfeiture" of A's estate.

77. The *concept* of automatic expiration is one thing, but it will certainly be the rare case in which A will voluntarily relinquish possession.   For all practical purposes, O may have to do precisely what he would have to do if he were exercising a power of termination.

78. We shall see that the concept of the "cutting short" of estates was at one time important, although it in no way reflects real-world facts.

79. It is also called an estate in fee simple subject to a power of termination.   See Restatement, Property, Introductory Note, 118 (1936).

What told us that O's transfer in the first example created an estate in fee simple determinable, and what told us that O's transfer in the second example created a fee simple subject to a condition subsequent? As a matter of legal theory, we simply looked to the intent of the parties.[80] Any language of a transferor expressive of the intent to transfer subject to a special limitation will be given effect as such. Any language expressive of an intent to transfer subject to a condition subsequent will also be given effect. There are no *required* formulas. In our two examples, O's intent was fairly clear. The "for-so-long-as" language in the first transfer certainly gives the impression that A's estate was not intended to go on after alcoholic beverages were sold. In the second transfer, O specifically reserved the power to terminate A's estate, thereby giving clear evidence that he did not intend A's estate to terminate automatically.[81]

But what does a judge do when the intent is not so clear? Are there any rules to guide him? Over the years, certain words used by transferors have come to be invested by courts with presumed meaning. Thus, if a deed or will uses such words as "for so long as," "while," "during," or "until" to introduce the circumstances under which an estate may end prior to its running its maximum course, it is generally assumed that a special limitation was intended. If, however, the deed or will uses such words as "but if," "on condition that," "provided, however," or "if, however," it will generally be assumed that a condition subsequent was intended.[82]

The two transfers we have used to demonstrate the special limitation and the condition subsequent involved transfers of estates in fee simple. But special limitations and conditions subsequent may be used in transfers of any estates. Here is an example: A, owner of an estate for life, transfers "to B for the life of A *while B remains unmarried.*" Since the *maximum* duration of B's estate is measured by the transferor's life, A cannot claim to have kept a future estate for life by operation of our rule (c). But A does keep a future estate for life by reason of having attached a special limitation to the transfer. (Note the word "while" that introduced the circumstances under which B's estate might terminate before B's death.) B's estate is therefore a *determinable estate pur autre vie*. If A had said, instead, "to B for the life of A; *provided however*, that if B shall not remain single, A may enter and terminate the estate," B

---

80. See 1 American Law of Property § 2.8 at 102–03.

81. Specific reservation of the power is said not to be required, but good drafting certainly commends use of this language. See, e.g., Post v. Weil, 115 N.Y. 361, 22 N.E. 145 (1889).

82. See 1 American Law of Property § 2.6 at 96–97.

would have an *estate pur autre vie subject to a condition subsequent.*   In the first example, B's marriage would automatically bring his estate to an end.   In the second, B's marriage would give A the power to terminate B's estate.

May one transfer an estate, keeping a future estate *both* because the transferred estate is shorter in duration *and* because one used a special limitation or condition subsequent?   Yes.   O transfers "to A for life for so long as A remains single."   O has a future estate in fee simple absolute not only because he transferred to A a lesser estate than the one he had to start with, but also because of the special limitation used in the transfer. A's estate is a *determinable estate for life.*   O could have made A's marrying a condition subsequent, in which event A would have *an estate for life subject to a condition subsequent.*[83]

May a special limitation operate so as to transfer possession to someone other than the transferor?   Yes.   O transfers "to A and his heirs *until* A marries, then to B and his heirs."   What is the name of A's estate?   The name that the *Restatement of Property* assigns to it is so long that we barely have room for it.   It is an *estate in fee simple with an executory limitation creating an interest that takes effect at the expiration of a prior interest.*[84]   We shall see in the next chapter why that title is assigned to A's estate.   For the time being, the reader is asked simply to accept the fact that it is another form of defeasible estate.   When the stated event occurs, B becomes automatically entitled to possession with an estate in fee simple absolute.   While A's estate is a present one, B has a future interest in fee simple absolute.   Oddly enough, if O had transferred "to A *for life* for so long as he is not married, then to B and his heirs," A's estate would simply be called a *determinable life estate.*   Again, we must ask the reader to wait until the next chapter for an explanation.[85]

---

83. When we get to the next chapter, we shall see that the future estate a transferor keeps by reason of having transferred a lesser estate bears a future-interest label different from that applied to the future estate he keeps by reason of having used a special limitation or condition subsequent; but the introduction of those labels now would not be helpful.

84. Restatement, Property § 47 (1936). The words *"until* A marries" constitute the special limitation.   It makes A's estate determinable.   The words "then to B and his heirs" constitute an executory limitation.   We will be looking more carefully at executory limitations later, especially in Chapter Four.   For now, it will suffice to say that executory limitations always create future interests in persons other than the grantor.   It's a bit more complicated than that.   See Restatement, Property § 25 (1936).

85. See Restatement, Property § 112 and illustration 4 (1936).   Note that the transfer in the text accompanying note 84, supra, was to "A and his heirs," whereas this transfer is to "A for life."   The explanation of the difference in resulting labels involves the rule that one may not limit a "remainder" after an estate in fee simple.

Suppose O transferred "to A and his heirs, *but if* A during his lifetime becomes a user of alcoholic beverages, then to C and his heirs." The "and-his-heirs" formula again informs us that A is getting an estate in fee simple. The "but-if" formula indicates that A's estate in fee simple is subject to a condition subsequent. Hence, we might reasonably assume that A's estate will not automatically end when he becomes a user of alcoholic beverages. We would, however, be wrong in so assuming. Despite the "but-if" formula, and despite the fact that the "but-if" formula is still said to create a condition subsequent,[86] A's estate is *automatically cut off*[87] as soon as he becomes a user of alcoholic beverages. The rule is simply that *when a condition subsequent is created in favor of someone other than the transferor, no power of termination need (or can) be exercised.*[88] A's estate is nonetheless thought to be *cut off*. It is not thought to *expire naturally* as it is thought to do when a special limitation is used. When a condition subsequent is created in favor of someone other than the transferor, the *Restatement of Property* calls the condition subsequent an *executory limitation*.[89] It calls A's estate an *estate in fee simple subject to an executory limitation*.[90]

As we have indicated, some of the points we have made about these defeasible estates (particularly those described in the last two paragraphs) will not become clear until we get to future interests. But we ought to be able to make some useful general comments about defeasible estates here. The one characteristic that all defeasible estates share is the chance that they may come to an end before they have run their *maximum* course. Except for that single characteristic, defeasible estates are practically identical with their non-defeasible counterparts. If a non-defeasible estate is transferable by *inter vivos* transfer or by will, its defeasible opposite number is also. Defeasible estates, like non-defeasible estates, may be present estates or future estates. Thus, O transfers "to A for life, then to B and his heirs for so long as the premises are not used for the sale of alcoholic beverages." B owns *now* a future estate in fee simple determinable. Whether a defeasible estate is present or future, its owner may transfer lesser estates to others. An example: A, owner of a present estate in fee simple subject to a condition subsequent, transfers "to B for life, then to C for life." B now owns a present estate for life, and C now owns a future estate for life. A, of

---

86. The Restatement of Property confines use of the term "condition subsequent" to language in a transfer that creates a future interest called a power of termination in the transferor. See Restatement, Property § 24 (1936). We do not so confine it in this book.

87. See note 78, supra.

88. See Restatement, Property § 24, comment *d* (1936).

89. See Restatement, Property § 25 (1936).

90. See Restatement, Property § 46 (1936).

course, has kept a future estate in fee simple subject to a condition subsequent. What happens if the specified event that made A's original estate defeasible occurs while B is in possession? If O (who, we assume, was A's transferor) chooses to exercise his power to terminate, B's present estate, C's future estate, and A's future estate will *all be cut off*. If, of course, A's estate had been an estate in fee simple determinable, the occurrence of the specified event would have resulted in the *automatic expiration* of B's, C's, and A's estates.

To summarize the preceding paragraph in a sentence: except for their defeasibility, defeasible estates have all the characteristics of non-defeasible estates that we have heretofore studied. How may the owner of a present defeasible estate actually use the land? Putting the question another way, what protection does O have against A when O transfers "to A and his heirs for so long as the premises are not used for the sale of alcoholic beverages?" Since O has a future estate in fee simple absolute by reason of the special limitation in the transfer to A, O is entitled to present protection of his possible future possession. Thus O may be able to prevent A from treating the land in such a fashion as will injure O's possible future possession. As we have indicated before, the *amount* of protection that the owner of a future estate will have against the owner of a present estate or against third persons will be a *function* of the likelihood of the future estate's becoming a present one.[91] Efforts to quantify such protection in terms of absolute legal prescriptions are futile.[92] Suffice it to say that, in the example we have given, O's protection will be pretty thin.

SECTION 9. CONCURRENT ESTATES

Since the reader will undoubtedly study concurrent estates as part of his regular course in property, we shall limit our discussion of these estates to matters relevant to our purposes.

A concurrent estate is simply an estate—whether present or future, defeasible or non-defeasible, in fee simple, in tail, for life, or for years—that is owned by *two or more persons at the same time.* O transfers "to A and B and their heirs." A and B own a present concurrent estate in fee simple absolute. There are three kinds of concurrent estates: the tenancy in common, the joint tenancy, and the tenancy by the entirety. Let us examine each of these separately.

---

91. See Restatement, Property §§ 187–99 (1936 & Supp. 1948).

92. And possibly dangerous. The likelihood of a future estate's becoming a present one certainly cannot be expressed in terms of the labels that the future estates bear. So-called "contingent" interests may be far more likely to become present estates than so-called "vested" interests.

Generally speaking, a transfer to A and B will *today* be deemed to create a tenancy in common unless the transferor specifies otherwise. Thus, if O transfers Blackacre "to A and B and their heirs," it will probably be assumed in most states that A and B own Blackacre in fee simple absolute as tenants in common. The same would be true if they received the estate by will or by intestate succession. As tenants in common, A and B *each* owns in his own name, and of his own right, half of Blackacre. Does that mean a physically identifiable half? No. It means that each owns separately half of the total ownership. A and B can, if they want, physically divide the land between them by *voluntary partition;* and each can force such division on the other by *judicial partition*. If they do partition the land, each will then own an estate in fee simple absolute in his own separate parcel of land.

If they do not partition the land between them, they will each continue to own an un-partitioned (or, more technically, *undivided*) half of the whole. Each is entitled to share with the other the possession of the whole parcel of land. Each may transfer his undivided half-interest as he wishes, so long as the transfer does not impair the possessory rights of the other tenant in common. Each may transfer his undivided half-interest by will. If either dies intestate, his undivided half-interest will pass to his own heirs. Thus, assuming that A died intestate leaving C and D as his sole heirs, C and D would own as tenants in common a half-interest in Blackacre in fee simple absolute. They would be tenants in common between themselves as to their half-interest, and they would, together, be tenants in common with B as to the entire parcel. In effect, C and D would each own, in his own name and of his own right, a quarter-interest in Blackacre in fee simple. The central characteristic of a tenancy in common is simply that each tenant is deemed to own by himself, with most of the attributes of independent ownership, a physically undivided part of the entire parcel.

In states that permit it (most states do), a transfer by O "to A and B and their heirs as joint tenants, with right of survivorship," will create a *joint tenancy* in fee simple in A and B. In the case of the joint tenancy, A and B are not thought to be separate and independent owners. They are viewed, in a sense, as a single owner. What does this mean? In the only relevant sense, it means simply that if either joint tenant dies without having transferred his ownership by *inter vivos* transfer, the surviving tenant becomes the sole owner of the entire estate. No interest in Blackacre passes to the deceased tenant's heirs or to any person to whom he might have tried to devise his interest in Blackacre. In *theory*, the tenant's death does not pass an interest to the survivor. The deceased tenant's ownership is simply thought to cease upon his death, while the survivor's ownership swells to absorb the whole of the estate. Not so surprisingly, the Internal Revenue Service views the matter somewhat differently.[93]

May A or B transfer his ownership by *inter vivos* transfer? Yes. If A transfers by *inter vivos* transfer "to C and his heirs," he thereby converts the joint tenancy into a *tenancy in common* in B and C. Thus, it is said that a joint tenancy may be "destroyed" by an *inter vivos* conveyance by either joint tenant. Joint tenants may, if they wish, convert their joint tenancy into a *tenancy in common*. They may also, voluntarily or by judicial proceeding, physically divide the parcel between them—in which event, of course, there is left neither a joint tenancy nor a tenancy in common. Each then owns his parcel of land separately. The rules for creation of a joint tenancy are these: The joint tenants must get their interests at the same time. They must become entitled to possession at the same time. The interests must be physically undivided interests, and each undivided interest must be an equal fraction of the whole—e.g., a one-third undivided interest to each of three joint tenants. The joint tenants must get their interests by the same instrument—e.g., the same deed or will. The joint tenants must get the same kinds of estates—e.g., in fee simple, for life, and so on.

The third form of concurrent estate is the *tenancy by the entirety*. This estate is not recognized in a number of states. Where it is recognized, it may exist only between a husband and a wife. It resembles, in most respects, the joint tenancy. The only major difference is that a tenant by the entirety may not destroy the other spouse's right of survivorship by transferring his or her interest to another. Whether a tenant by the entirety may transfer *any* interest to a third party—for example, the right of present possession or the contingent right of survivorship—is a matter on which the states differ. Most take the view that no interest may be transferred. The husband and wife may, of course, together convey their estate to a third person. If they *both* wish to convert their tenancy into a tenancy in common or a joint tenancy, they may do so. Upon the death of a tenant by the entirety, no interest passes, in theory, to the surviving spouse. As was true of the joint tenancy, the survivor's ownership is thought simply to expand to absorb the relinquished ownership of the decedent.

---

93. See Int. Rev. Code of 1954, § 2040, as amended.

Chapter 3

REVERSIONARY INTERESTS, POWERS OF TERMINATION, REMAINDERS, AND EQUITABLE USES

SECTION 1. INTRODUCTION

If the reader has studied the preceding chapters with care, he already knows a formidable amount about future interests. We shall be spending much of our time in this chapter merely applying future-interest labels to the future estates we have already met. Whatever label we apply to a future estate, we may be confident that the future estate is in fee simple, in fee tail, for life, or for years. Its *duration* will be determined by the *estate label* that it carries; its *characteristics as a future estate* will be indicated by the *future-interest label* that it carries. The ground rules under which our discussion of future interests will go forward will be the same as those we set forth in the beginning of Chapter Two.

A future interest, simply defined, is an interest that is not now a present interest but that may become a present interest. To own a future interest *now* means not only to be entitled now to judicial protection of one's possible future possession, but also (in most cases) to be able to make transfers now of that right of possible future possession. As we saw in Chapter Two, the fact that one owns a future interest does not necessarily mean that one will enjoy possession at some future date. If a person who owns a future estate for life dies before his time for possession arrives, he will never get possession. That does not mean he never *had* an estate; it simply means his estate never became a present one. We shall be seeing some slightly more complex examples in this chapter of future estates that do not become present estates.

SECTION 2. THE REVERSION

When the owner of an estate transfers a lesser estate,[1] the future estate that the owner keeps is called a *reversion*.[2] Sup-

---

1. We have defined a "lesser" estate as an estate that is conceptually shorter in duration than the estate the transferor had to start with; see our rules (a)–(d) in Chapter Two, Section 8. See also Restatement, Property § 154, comment *d* (1936).

2. Compare Restatement, Property § 154(1) (1936).

56

pose that O, our hypothetical owner of an estate in fee simple absolute, transfers "to A for life." We said in Chapter Two that as soon as A is dead, O will once again be entitled to present possession for a potentially infinite period: in the language of future interests, O has kept a *reversion in fee simple absolute.* O may transfer any number of lesser estates and still keep a reversion. For example, suppose that O transfers "to A for life, then to B and the heirs of his body, then to C for life." Although O has given away two life estates and an estate in fee tail, he has *not* given away an estate in fee simple; so O has kept a reversion in fee simple. As soon as all the estates he has transferred come to an end, O will be entitled to possession again. What if C dies before B's estate in fee tail has expired—does O get possession immediately? No. C's death merely brings C's future estate for life to an end; O will not be entitled to possession until B's estate in fee tail ends as well.

Here is a slightly more complex example: O transfers "to A for life"; A then transfers "to B for the life of A," and B transfers "to C for the life of C." Since the only estate O has transferred is an estate for the life of A, O has kept a reversion in fee simple absolute. As soon as A is dead, O will automatically be entitled to possession again. Did A keep a reversion? No. He transferred to B all that he had—an estate measured by his own life. B's estate *pur autre vie* will not end until A dies, so the right to possession will not return to A. Since the estate that B transferred to C is measured by C's life rather than by A's, B kept a reversion. If C dies before B *and* A, B will again be entitled to possession until A dies. What happens if B then dies before A? The estate cannot return to A, who has kept no reversion; and it cannot yet return to O, who is not entitled to possession until A dies. When B dies, the possession goes either to those to whom he left it by will or to his intestate successors.[3]

The owner of a reversion may transfer the reversion. Suppose O transfers an estate "to A for life," keeping a reversion in fee simple absolute. O then transfers his reversion "to B and his heirs." B now owns the reversion in fee simple absolute. Note that the future interest is still called a reversion even after O has transferred it to B. The characteristic that makes it a reversion is the fact that it was, *at the time it was created,* an interest *retained* by O, the transferor of the life estate. A person who owns a reversion is called a *reversioner.*

If the reversion is in fee simple, it may be devised as any present estate in fee simple may be devised.[4] If O transfers "to

---

3. In some states, it may pass on intestacy as a chattel real to B's personal representative for distribution to his next of kin. In others, it may pass as real property to his heirs.

4. Obviously, an estate that does not survive its owner's death may not be devised. An estate in fee tail may not be devised either. See Restatement, Property § 81 (1936).

A for life," and, while A is still living, O dies leaving a will in which he devises all his real property to X, X now owns the reversion in fee simple absolute.   If, instead of devising his property, O dies intestate, his reversion will simply pass to his heirs with any other inheritable real property he owns at his death.   Whether O leaves a will or dies intestate, his death will not make the reversion a present estate.   It will remain a reversion until A's death.

SECTION 3.   THE POSSIBILITY OF REVERTER

Suppose O transfers "to A and his heirs for so long as the premises are used solely for the purposes of a public tavern." A's estate in fee simple determinable is potentially infinite in duration—it will not end unless the premises cease to be used solely as a tavern—so A's estate is not a "lesser estate" as we have defined the term.   O, therefore, cannot have kept a reversion.   But if the premises *are* used for some other purpose, A's estate will automatically expire, and O will be entitled to possession with an estate in fee simple absolute.   We call O's right to regain possession in these circumstances a *possibility of reverter*.   A possibility of reverter is the future interest a transferor keeps when he transfers an estate whose maximum potential duration equals that of the estate he had to start with and attaches a special limitation that operates in his own favor.[5]

Suppose that A, the owner of the estate in fee simple determinable in our preceding example, transfers "to B for life, for so long as B remains unmarried."   O still has his possibility of

---

5.   If the reader were to ask where we got this definition for the possibility of reverter, we should be forced to admit that we simply made it up.   Most treatise-writers define the possibility of reverter as the interest a transferor keeps when he transfers a fee simple determinable or a fee simple conditional.   See, e.g., 1 American Law of Property § 4.12; Simes & Smith § 281.   Although this definition is all right as far as it goes, it fails to provide for interests less than the fee simple that are granted on special limitation.   Suppose A, the owner of an estate measured by his own life, transfers "to B for the life of A for so long as B remains unmarried." The determinable life estate that A has transferred has a potential maximum duration equal to that of the estate he had to start with, so A cannot have kept a reversion.   If we are to give a name to A's interest—and it seems that we should—we must call it a possibility of reverter even though A has not transferred a fee simple determinable or fee simple conditional.

The Restatement does not restrict the possibility of reverter to the transferor of a fee simple interest; instead, it defines a possibility of reverter as "any reversionary interest which is subject to a condition precedent."   Restatement, Property § 154(3) (1936).   (The Restatement regards the special limitation as a kind of condition precedent.)   Yet if the transferor transfers a *lesser* estate than he had to start with and attaches a special limitation, the Restatement views him as having kept only a reversion even though his interest would seem to fall within the Restatement's definition of a possibility of reverter.   See Restatement, Property § 23, Illustrations 3, 5, 6, & 7 (1936).   The paragraph of text following this footnote gives an example of this sort of transfer.

Although we call the possibility of reverter an "estate," the courts of an earlier era would probably have called it a "possibility of becoming an estate."   See Casner & Leach, Cases and Text on Property 322 (1969).

reverter: if the premises cease to be used as a tavern while B is in possession, both B's present interest and A's future interest will expire naturally, and O will be entitled to possession. B has a determinable estate for life. What about A? He has not transferred an estate whose maximum potential duration is equal to that of the fee simple determinable he started with, so he cannot have kept a possibility of reverter. But since A started with an estate potentially infinite in duration, and he transferred to B only a life estate, he must have kept a reversion. A will automatically be entitled to possession of the property if B marries, because the special limitation on B's estate operates in A's favor; A will also be entitled to possession of the property when B dies, because A has kept a reversion. In theory, A owns only one future estate; it just happens that there are two ways in which it might become a present estate.

Possibilities of reverter are transferable *inter vivos*.[6] If the owner of a devisable and inheritable estate grants that estate on special limitation, the possibility of reverter that the grantor keeps may pass by will to his devisees or by the laws of intestacy to his heirs. Like the reversion, the possibility of reverter is an interest that is retained by the transferor *at the time it is created*. A possibility of reverter that is transferred *after* its creation generally continues to be called a possibility of reverter no matter how or to whom it passes.

SECTION 4. THE POWER OF TERMINATION

A *power of termination* is the future interest that a *transferor creates in himself*[7] when he transfers an estate and attaches a condition subsequent that operates in his own favor. Another way of putting it is to say that when a transferor transfers an estate subject to a condition subsequent, reserving to himself the power to terminate the transferred estate upon the occurrence of a specified event, he has a power of termination.[8] Suppose O transfers "to A and his heirs; *but if* the premises cease to be used for the purposes of a public tavern, the grantor herein, or anyone who has succeeded to his interest, may enter and ter-

---

6. In most states. See 1 American Law of Property § 4.70.

7. The Restatement regards a power of termination that operates in the transferor's favor as a new interest that the transferor creates in himself at the time of the transfer rather than as a portion of his original estate that he keeps. Since the power of termination is not an interest *retained* by the transferor, it is not regarded as a *reversionary* interest like the rever-sion and the possibility of reverter. See Restatement, Property § 154(1) and comment *a* (1936).

8. See Restatement, Property § 155 (1936). This future interest is still probably more commonly called a "right of entry"; but the Restatement's choice of the term "power of termination" seems to us a good one. See Restatement, Property § 24, Special Note to comment *b* (1936).

minate the granted estate." O has kept a power of termination. Since O's original estate was in fee simple, his power of termination is in fee simple. If A ceases to use the premises for a public tavern, his estate will not expire *automatically*, as it would if O had attached a special limitation; instead, A's estate will continue until O exercises his power to cut it short.

Here is another example: A, owner of an estate for life, transfers "to B for three years, *provided, however*, that if B fails to make timely payment of any installment of rent, A shall have the power to enter and terminate the term granted herein." A has kept a power of termination for life. Note that A has also kept a reversion for life, since he transferred to B only an estate for years.[9] When B's term of years expires, A's reversion will automatically entitle him to possession. But if B fails to make timely payment of an installment of rent during his term of years, his estate will continue until A takes the affirmative step of terminating it.

It is quite clear that a person who owns *both* a reversion *and* a power of termination may transfer both interests together. Whenever a landlord transfers his reversion, the transfer carries with it such powers of termination as are set forth in his leases. But in a substantial number of states, one who owns only a power of termination may *not* transfer it—at least, not by *inter vivos* transfer![10] As a matter of fact, the general common-law rule is that a power of termination may not be transferred unless it is incident to a reversion. One theory offered to explain this curious rule is that free alienability of powers of termination

9. As we pointed out in Section 6 of Chapter Two, feudal courts viewed the owner of a freehold estate who granted a term of years as owning a *present* estate *subject to the term* in the grantee. The seisin remained with the grantor, who was still obligated to perform the feudal duties; the grantee was a mere occupant of the land. This construction prevails today in some circumstances: a tax assessor, for example, would usually regard the landlord rather than the tenant as the "owner" of the rental property. When we get to Section 8 of this chapter and Section 2 of Chapter Four, we will be finding it useful to characterize the estate retained by an owner of a freehold estate who transfers an estate for years as a "present" estate subject to the estate for years. For the time being, though, use of the reversion locution is perfectly acceptable.

We observed in footnote 5 in the preceding section that one who transfers, on special limitation, a lesser estate than the estate he had to start with is *not* viewed as having kept both a possibility of reverter and a reversion; instead, he is regarded as having kept only a reversion. The reader may have found it surprising, then, that a transferor who transfers a lesser estate and attaches a condition subsequent that operates in his own favor *is* regarded as having kept both a reversion and a power of termination. We can only observe that the reader who has reached this point in our book and still expects to find logic in the law of future interests has not read very attentively.

10. See Restatement, Property §§ 160, 161 (1936 and Supp. 1948); 1 American Law of Property § 4.68; Simes & Smith § 1862.

would permit "maintenance" [11]—that is, interfering in or financing another's cause of action. Whatever the original theory, it is quite difficult to see why the rule, if it is to apply today at all, does not apply equally to possibilities of reverter.[12] Suffice it to say, a good number of states have enacted statutes that make powers of termination as transferable as possibilities of reverter.[13] In such states, there appears to be no serious objection to transferring a power of termination separately from a reversion to which it may be incident. In states that permit *inter vivos* transfer of a power of termination, the interest, if it is in fee, is inheritable, and it is also transferable by will. This is probably the rule even in states that forbid its *inter vivos* transfer.

We have seen in the preceding paragraph one example of how it may make a crucial difference to an owner whether a court finds his future interest to be a possibility of reverter or a power of termination: one may be transferable and the other not. Are there other circumstances in which this determination will be important? There are. Let us give an example: O transfers "to A and his heirs *on the assumption that* the premises will be used solely for the purposes of a public tavern." We find nothing in our catalogue of traditional formulas that resembles this "on-the-assumption-that" language. Since we do not know whether the language creates a special limitation or a condition subsequent, we cannot tell whether the transferor has kept a possibility

---

11. See Restatement, Property § 160, comment *a* (1936); Simes & Smith § 35. The thesis that the prohibition of the transfer of powers of termination was intended as a restraint on maintenance may have originated with Lord Coke. In his Commentary on Littleton, first published in 1628, Coke wrote: "Here Littleton reciteth one of the maxims of the common law; and the reason hereof is, for avoyding of maintenance, suppression of right, and stirring up of suits; and therefore nothing in action, entrie or re-entrie can be granted over . . . ." Cook on Littleton 214a (Butler 18th ed. 1823). Harvard Law School's Professor Thorne has raised one small objection to Coke's thesis: namely, that it is not true. Thorne, Sir Edward Coke 15–17 (Selden Society Lecture, 1952). Thorne regards the prohibition as a rule of seisin. See infra Section 8, note 89.

12. The Restatement's justification for the rule is that it "emphasizes the personal character" of the power of termination. See Restatement, Property § 160, comment *a* (1936). But why emphasize it? And why not emphasize the equally "personal" choice the owner of a possibility of reverter must make when he asserts his right to possession?

In several states, courts have held that an attempt to transfer a power of termination not incident to a reversion results in destruction of the power of termination. See Simes & Smith § 1863. Michigan has abolished this rule by statute—Mich. Comp. Laws § 554.111 (1948)—and other states that formerly embraced the doctrine may now be willing to let it die a natural death. See Restatement, Property § 160, comment *c* (Supp.1948); Simes & Smith § 1863.

13. The Restatement lists some states that have statutes making powers of termination transferable. See Restatement, Property § 160, Special Note to comment *d* (Supp.1948). See also Simes & Smith § 1862 nn. 88–89.

of reverter or a power of termination. Now let us assume that A, with O's knowledge, converts his tavern into a bowling alley; and let us also suppose that the state in which the property is located has a ten-year statute of limitations for the recovery of real property. O waits eleven years to sue A for possession. Does O prevail?

If the court finds that O kept a possibility of reverter, O may be out of luck. Since O was automatically entitled to possession as soon as A violated the special limitation, the court might conclude that A's continued possession was wrongful and that O's cause of action accrued immediately.[14] Under this view, O's time for bringing an action to recover the property from A has run. If, however, the court finds that O kept a power of termination, it might conclude that O had no cause of action against A until he exercised the power and A refused to leave. On this theory, O might prevail.[15] Is there any policy that justifies the different real-world consequences that may flow from a "finding" that an interest is a possibility of reverter rather than a power of termination? We leave that question to the classroom.

SECTION 5. THE REMAINDER

A remainder is a future interest *created in someone other than the transferor* that, *according to the terms of its creation,* will become a present estate (if ever) *immediately upon, and no sooner than, the expiration* of all prior *particular* estates[16] *created simultaneously with it.*[17] That is quite a mouthful, so let us give

14. On the other hand, the court might find that A's continued possession was permissive. Under this view, the statute would not begin to run until A resisted O's demand for possession or otherwise openly denied O's title.

It is also possible that the court would view the "on-the-assumption" language as creating neither a special limitation nor a condition subsequent. For example, the language could be viewed as creating merely a covenant on the part of A (and perhaps of his successors) to use the premises solely as a public tavern. Under that interpretation, O would be viewed not as having a future interest, but rather as having only a right to sue for damages in case of breach (or, possibly, for an injunction against further breach).

15. Or he might not. If O waited too long to exercise the power (and "too long" may mean a period far shorter than the period allowed to bring an action to recover real property), the court might con-

clude that he "waived" the right to exercise it. See 1 American Law of Property § 4.9.

16. A "particular" estate is one of limited duration—that is, a fee tail, a life estate, or an estate for years.

17. See Restatement, Property § 156 (1936). Some authorities have said that the prior estates and the remainder must be created by the same instrument. See, e.g., Cheshire, 294–95. Others have held that the prior estates and the remainder may be created by two separate instruments, as long as the instruments are part of the same transaction. See 1 American Law of Property § 4.29. In any event, it is clear that if O transfers "to A for life," and later transfers his future estate "to B and his heirs," B does not have a remainder. The first transfer leaves a reversion in O; the second transfer gives the reversion to B, but B's interest is still *called* a reversion.

an example. Suppose O transfers "to A for life, then to B and his heirs." Is B's interest a remainder? Since B is someone other than the transferor, our first requirement is met. B's interest may become a present estate immediately upon, but not before, the expiration of A's estate for life. (Note that when B's estate becomes a present estate, it will not *cut short* A's estate for life; nor is there any gap between A's death and the time when B's estate will become present.) Therefore, our second requirement is met as well. A's estate is prior in order of possession to B's, and was created simultaneously with B's. Finally, owing to the fact that A's estate is shorter than an estate in fee simple—e.g., is merely *part* of an estate in fee simple, it is a particular estate. Since all our definitional requirements are met, B must have a remainder. (The owner of a remainder is called a *remainderman*.) The language of the transfer gives the remainder "to B *and his heirs*," so B has a *remainder in fee simple absolute*.

The reader has probably noticed that B's future interest looks very much like the future interest O would have kept if O had merely transferred "to A for life." Had O done that, we would have said that O had kept a *reversion* in fee simple absolute. We call B's interest a *remainder* because the right to possession *remains* with B at the time when, had O kept a reversion, the right to possession would have returned to O. The remainder given to B in our example is, for all practical purposes, a "reversion" created in a third person.

In our first example, B got the whole of what would have been O's reversion. In some cases, the creation of remainders may simply *delay* a reversion's becoming a present estate. Thus, if O transfers "to A for life, then to B and the heirs of his body, then to C for life," B and C both have remainders, and O has a reversion in fee simple. Let us check B's and C's remainders against our original definition. Both B and C are persons other than the transferor. B's future interest will become a present interest, if it ever does, only when A's life estate expires naturally at A's death. Since A's estate for life was created simultaneously with B's future interest, B's interest must be a remainder; and since the terms of the transfer granted an estate to B *and the heirs of his body*, B's remainder is a remainder in fee tail. C's future interest will become a present estate for life, if it ever does, only when A's estate for life and B's estate in fee tail have expired naturally. Since C's future interest was created simultaneously with A's and B's estates, it must be a remainder; and since the terms of the transfer gave C an estate for life, his remainder must be a remainder for life. Of course, if C dies before B's lineal descendants give out, C's remainder will never become a present estate; but this does not mean that C never *had* a remainder.

What about O? The two life estates and the estate in fee tail that he transferred do not amount to an estate in fee simple, so he has kept a reversion in fee simple. If the remainders in this example become present estates, they will simply delay the reversion's becoming a present estate.

Here is another example: A, the owner of a present estate for life, transfers "to B for the life of B, then to C for the life of C." B, obviously, gets a present estate for life. What about C? He gets a future estate for life that will become a present estate, if it ever does, only upon the natural expiration of B's estate—in other words, he gets a remainder for life. If A dies while B and C are still living, both B's present estate for life and C's future estate for life will come to an end. But suppose B and C die while A is still living—will A be entitled to regain possession? Yes: A kept a reversion for life. How is it that A, who owned only an estate for life, could transfer estates for life to B and C and still keep a reversion? Remember our rule from Chapter Two: If the owner of an estate for life transfers *any number* of estates for life measured by the lives of persons *other than himself*, then the transferor is deemed to have kept a future estate for life. Here, each estate for life transferred by A is to be measured by the *transferee's* life.

One more example: O, effectively transferring his entire estate in fee simple absolute, transfers "to A for five years, then to B and his heirs." When we imagined this transfer's being made in the feudal period (Section 6 of Chapter Two), we observed that livery of seisin would be made to A for the benefit of B, and that B would be viewed as having a "present" estate in fee simple subject to the term in A. Similarly, when we imagined O's merely transferring "to A for five years" during the feudal period, we said that a feudal lawyer would likely view O as having a "present" estate in fee simple, subject to the term in A. A lawyer today would not be the least bit uncomfortable saying that a transfer from O "to A for five years, then to B and his heirs" gives to B a remainder in fee simple absolute.[18] Nor would he feel uncomfortable saying that a transfer from O "to A for five years" leaves O with a reversion in fee simple absolute. These modern locutions reflect the fact that seisin is not as significant a concept in today's law as it was in the feudal legal system. But we must warn the reader once more that we will be finding the "present estate" locution useful later on in this chapter and in Chapter Four. For the time being, however, we may say that a transfer today from O "to A for five years, then

18. See Restatement, Property § 156 and illustration 9 (1936).

to B and his heirs" is commonly viewed as giving A a present estate for years and B a remainder in fee simple absolute.

Let us go back to our first example: O transfers "to A for life, then to B and his heirs." We have said that B has a remainder in fee simple. His remainder has all the characteristics of a reversion in fee simple: it may be transferred in whole or in part by *inter vivos* transfer; it may be devised, and it may be inherited by his general heirs under the laws of intestate succession. It is, in sum, full durational ownership, lacking only present possession. To make this point quite clear, let us assume that B dies intestate while A is still living. B's remainder does not expire with him; it simply passes to his heirs. When A dies, either B's heirs or persons to whom the heirs have transferred the remainder in the interim will be entitled to possession with an estate in fee simple.

When we looked at determinable estates in the last chapter, we noted that an estate that comes to an end automatically by operation of a special limitation is thought to *expire naturally*. Since remainders may follow estates that expire naturally, may we assume that if the special limitation were created to operate in favor of a third person, that person would have a remainder? There are many instances in which this assumption would be correct. For example, suppose O transfers "to A (a widow) for life until she remarries, then to B and his heirs." B has a remainder, one that will become a present estate either when A dies or when she remarries.

But suppose O transfers "to A *and her heirs* for so long as A does not remarry, then to B and his heirs." A's estate is a fee simple determinable—that is, one that will expire naturally should she remarry. If she dies without remarrying, then the limitation will no longer have any effect; her estate will blossom into an estate in fee simple absolute. Does B have a remainder? No. When we defined "remainder," we said that the interest becomes a present estate upon the expiration of all prior *particular* estates—that is, estates of limited duration. *A remainder may never follow any estate in fee simple.* The reasons for this rule are entirely historical. They stem from the notion that if the owner of an estate in fee simple transfers another estate in fee simple, there is nothing left out of which to make a remainder. Apparently, the idea of creating in a third person an interest equivalent to a possibility of reverter either never occurred to the feudal lawyers or was rejected by the feudal courts.[19] More-

---

19. Gray argues at some length that the possibility of reverter itself could not be created after 1290 because it violated the statute *Quia Emptores*. See The Rule Against Perpetuities §§ 20–42. A number of scholars have disagreed with this view. See 1 American Law of Property § 2.6 and authorities there cited.

over, since the remainder was, until 1536,[20] the only kind of interest recognized by the law courts that could be created in a third person,[21] B would have received no legal interest whatever if the transfer had been attempted before 1536.

But if O attempted the transfer today, would B still get no interest? The answer is that he *would* get an interest, but it would not be a remainder. The interest that B would get is called an *executory interest.*[22] B's interest looks and acts like a remainder; but since a remainder cannot follow an estate in fee simple, we cannot *call* B's estate a remainder. What about A's estate? We said in the preceding paragraph that it is a fee simple determinable, and so it is; but to distinguish it from the fee simple determinable that leaves a possibility of reverter in O, the *Restatement of Property* gives it this handy little label: an *estate in fee simple with an executory limitation creating an interest that takes effect at the expiration of a prior interest.* We ran into that estate in Chapter Two,[23] and sadly enough we will run into it one more time in Chapter Four. We shall be talking more seriously of executory interests in Section 7 of this chapter and in Chapter Four, so the reader need not remember anything more at this point than that a remainder may not follow any estate in fee simple. (We will learn in the next chapter, by the way, that many executory interests do *not* look like remainders.)

At the beginning of this section, we defined a remainder as a future interest created in someone other than the grantor that will become a present estate upon the natural expiration of prior particular estates created simultaneously with it. It is now our painful duty to inform the reader that there are two kinds of remainder: the *vested* remainder and the *contingent* remainder. A contingent remainder cannot become a present estate until some condition *in addition to* the natural expiration of prior estates is met. We shall have to postpone careful examination of the contingent remainder until we have wrestled with the concept of "vestedness."

SECTION 6. THE CONCEPT OF VESTEDNESS

A future interest is *vested* if it meets two requirements: first, that there be no *condition precedent* to the interest's becoming

---

20. The date when the Statute of Uses, 27 Hen. 8, c. 10 (1535), became effective.

21. See Section 8 of this chapter for a discussion of the interests recognized in equity that could be created in a third person prior to 1536.

22. See Restatement, Property § 158 (1936).

23. See Chapter Two, Section 8, note 84 and accompanying text. Compare Restatement, Property § 47 (1936) (in which the adjective "determinable" is *not* used to describe A's estate) with id. § 25, illustration 7 (in which the adjective "determinable" *is* used to describe A's estate).

a present estate other than the *natural expiration* of those estates that are prior to it in possession; and second, that it be *theoretically* possible to identify who would get the right to possession if the interest should become a present estate *at any time.* In our example in which O transferred "to A for life, then to B and his heirs," B's remainder is vested. No condition precedent other than the natural expiration of A's estate stands in the way of the remainder's becoming a present interest, and it is possible to identify the person who will get the right to possession whenever A's estate ends. That person will be B (for so long as he is alive and has not transferred the remainder) *or* B's heirs (if B has died before A without transferring the remainder *inter vivos* or by will) *or* the persons to whom B has transferred the remainder *inter vivos* or by will. No matter when A dies, we will always be able to point to a specific living person or to a specific group of living people and say, "The possession goes there." [24]

Suppose O transfers "to A for life, then to B for life, then to C for life, then to D and his heirs." A has a present estate for life. B and C have remainders for life. D has a remainder in fee simple. B's, C's, and D's remainders are all vested. Why? First, because each one, in order to become a present estate, has merely to wait for the *natural expiration* of the estates in front of it. Second, because it is always possible to tell who will get possession when the present estate ends. If, for example, C dies before A, C's remainder for life will expire; so the sequence of possession will run from B to D and his heirs.

What is the importance of our saying that a future interest is vested? The reader must possess his soul in patience, for it will be some time before we can answer this question fully. We can, however, tell him this much: the importance of "vestedness" owes to the fact that an interest that is not vested (a "contingent" interest) is subject to various legal disabilities that do not affect the vested interest. In a few states, a contingent interest will be destroyed if it has not vested by the time the prior interests have expired. In a substantially larger number of states, a contingent interest will violate the Rule Against Perpetuities (and so become a nullity) if it is not certain to vest within a certain period after its creation. We shall be discussing these matters in some detail later in this book. [25]

---

24. We are assuming, as the courts do, that we will know of all transfers B has made and that we will know who B's heirs are when he is dead. When a remainder is described as "vested," it is irrelevant that there may in fact be difficulty in determining what transfers have been made or in locating B's heirs.

25. We discuss the destructibility of contingent remainders in Section 7; see infra notes 44–46 and accompanying text. The Rule Against Perpetuities occupies a prominent place in Part II of this book; See, e.g., Part II, Chapter Eight.

Let us examine the future interests we have already defined to see whether we may describe them as being "vested." We have defined a reversion as the interest a transferor keeps when he transfers a lesser estate. If O transfers "to A for life," O keeps a reversion. Is O's reversion a vested interest? Clearly, nothing stands in the way of the reversion's becoming a present estate except the natural expiration of A's life estate. Moreover, the person or persons who will get possession when the reversion becomes a present estate are identifiable at all times from the moment the reversion is created. If O is still alive when A dies, and if he has not transferred the reversion, he will be entitled to possession. If he has transferred it, the transferee will be entitled to possession. If O has predeceased A without having transferred the reversion *inter vivos*, either his heirs or devisee will be entitled to possession. Because the reversion has the two characteristics we associate with vestedness—the absence of a condition precedent to its becoming a present estate, and the presence of an identifiable taker at any time it should become a present estate—it is a vested interest.

Suppose O transfers "to A and his heirs for so long as the premises are used solely for the purposes of a public tavern." Is O's possibility of reverter a vested interest? It, too, becomes a present estate automatically upon the expiration of a transferred estate, and we can always point to the person or persons who will be entitled to possession if the transferred estate expires by reason of the special limitation. Nevertheless, some have said that the possibility of reverter is not vested because the occurrence of the specified event is a *condition* to its becoming a present estate.[26] One writer has almost suggested that it cannot be vested because its *name* implies the contrary.[27] This is a question of considerable interest to some scholars, but not to us. Our own view is that this is one case in which it makes no difference whether the interest is vested or not.[28]

We said in the preceding section that a remainder can follow a determinable particular estate (remember that a remainder *cannot* follow a *fee simple* determinable). In our example, we said that if O transfers "to A (a widow) for life until she remarries, then to B and his heirs," B has a remainder. Is B's remainder vested? From the moment the remainder is created, we can identify the person who will be entitled to possession when the

---

26. See Restatement, Property § 154 comment *e* (1936).

27. "[It] is difficult to see how an interest described as a 'possibility' could be vested." Simes, Handbook of the Law of Future Interests 29 (1966).

28. The Rule Against Perpetuities, which is the bane of many contingent interests, does not apply to the possibility of reverter. See Part II, Chapter Eight, Section 7 for a discussion of which future interests are subject to the Rule, and why.

remainder becomes a present estate. What is more, the only thing that stands in the way of the remainder's becoming a present estate is the natural expiration of A's estate, either by reason of A's death or by reason of her remarriage. B's remainder meets our two requirements for vestedness.

Let us return for a moment to our example in which O transfers "to A for life, then to B for life, then to C for life, then to D and his heirs." We said that B, C, and D all have vested remainders. But the reader, if he has not nodded off by now,[29] may be raising an objection. It is clear that B will never get possession unless he survives A, and that C must outlive both A and B to enjoy possession. Are not both remainders subject to a condition precedent in addition to the natural expiration of the prior estates—the condition that the remaindermen *survive* the owners of the prior estates? Even D's remainder in fee simple will never become a present estate if D dies intestate without lineal or collateral heirs and without having transferred his remainder *inter vivos*. But if we were to say that D's remainder is subject to a condition precedent that D or some heir or transferee or devisee of D's survive to take possession, there could be no such thing as a vested remainder.[30]

The law of future interests solves the puzzle by providing that whenever a remainderman must survive to enjoy possession *solely because the durational character of the estate he is getting implies it*, the survivorship is not a condition precedent to the vesting of his estate. B, C, and D each owns, right now, a fixed right of future possession: each remainder is *vested in interest.* If B or C lives long enough for his remainder to become a present estate, it will *vest in possession.* D's estate will *vest in possession* when all the prior estates come to an end.

The fact that an interest is vested does not imply that its owner is certain eventually to get possession. We have seen in the preceding paragraphs that B's and C's interests may expire before they become present estates. B's and C's remainders meet the tests of vestedness while B and C are alive; but if either remainderman dies before his interest vests in possession, the remainder simply expires. Even D's remainder in fee simple may expire before it vests in possession if D dies intestate without

---

29. If the reader *has* nodded off, he can expect a rude awakening when he takes his final exam; but the nap may be worth it.

30. The reader may, by this point in our discussion, have concluded that the world would be a happier place if there *were* no such thing as a vested remainder.

As we pointed out in the text accompanying note 25, however, a remainder that is *not* vested is subject to various legal disabilities that make its existence a perilous one. From the point of view of the remainderman, at least, a vested remainder is a thing of beauty and a joy forever.

lineal or collateral heirs surviving. Let us examine some other circumstances in which a vested interest may be reduced or destroyed before it becomes a present estate.

Suppose O makes this transfer: "To A for life, then to the children of B and their heirs." B, let us assume, is a living person who has two living children at the time the transfer is made. The interest that the children get meets all our definitional requirements for a vested remainder. If A dies while both children are living, the children will take a present estate in fee simple absolute. If one child dies before A, that child's heirs or transferees will be entitled to the deceased child's share of the estate when A dies; and if both children die before A, the estate will pass to the heirs and transferees of both on A's death.[31] But what happens if, *before A dies,* another child is born to B? The answer is that the shares of the first two children will be reduced (or *partially divested*), so that the three children will each get a third of the estate. We can put this example in rule form by saying that where a remainder is created in a "class"— such as "the children of B"—members of that class who are living at the time the remainder is *created* have (assuming there are no conditions precedent to their enjoying possession other than the natural expiration of prior estates) *vested remainders subject to partial divestment.* Such remainders are also described as being *vested subject to open*.[32] In the example we have given, the class "closes" at A's death, when the remaindermen are entitled to possession. Any child of B born after A is dead will get nothing unless O expresses an intent that afterborn children share in the estate.

Although B's two children in the preceding example may have to share the estate in fee simple with children who were not around when the remainder was created, it is at least certain that they (or their successors in interest) will enjoy possession. But not all vested remainders in fee simple are certain to vest in possession. Suppose O transfers "to A for life, then to B and his heirs; *but if* the premises are ever used for the sale of al-

---

31. Unless, that is, a court decides that the children's interests are subject to an *implied condition of survivorship*. If O intended that only the children who survived A should take, then the children's remainders would not vest until A's death. The heirs or transferees of a child who predeceased A would take nothing; instead, the entire estate would pass to the child who survived A. If none of B's children survived A, the remainder interest would fail.

There is a strong preference for "early vesting" as a rule of construction: in the absence of compelling evidence that O intended to subject the remainder to a condition of survivorship, a court would probably find that the interest in B's children vested as soon as it was created. Conditions of survivorship will be discussed in Part II, Chapter Five.

32. See Restatement, Property § 157 (b)(1936).

coholic beverages, then the grantor herein, or anyone who has succeeded to his interest, may enter and terminate the estates granted." The transfer is clearly subject to a condition subsequent. It seems obvious that for as long as alcoholic beverages *have not* been sold on the property, B's interest meets the two tests of a vested remainder. All that it waits for is the natural expiration of A's estate for life; and the person or persons who will get possession are identifiable. If, however, A sells alcoholic beverages on the property and O exercises his power to terminate the estates, both A's estate for life and B's remainder in fee simple will be cut off. B will never get possession. B's remainder in our example is described as *vested subject to complete divestment*, or as *vested subject to total defeasance*.[33]

Here is another example: O transfers "to A for life, then to B and his heirs; *but if* B does not survive A, to C and his heirs." We have stepped into quicksand. It is clear that B will never get possession unless he survives A. Certainly it does not seem inaccurate to describe B's surviving A as a condition precedent to his remainder's becoming a present estate. It seems obvious, therefore, that B's remainder cannot be vested. But if B's remainder in this paragraph is not vested, how did we describe B's remainder in the preceding paragraph as vested? Was there not in that case as well a condition to B's getting the possession—the condition that A *not* sell alcoholic beverages?

Believe it or not, B's remainders are vested in both cases. Both remainders are vested subject to complete divestment—the first by O's exercise of his power of termination, the second by B's failing to survive A. But why are B's remainders vested at all if, in addition to the natural expiration of A's life estate, there are conditions that stand in the way of the remainders' becoming present estates? The answer is that although there *are* conditions in both transfers, they are conditions *subsequent*—not conditions *precedent*. What are the conditions "subsequent" to? They are subsequent to the vesting of the remainders. A condition subsequent operates to divest a vested interest.

This will all become reasonably clear in a moment, but let us first add a bit more chaos to our confusion. Suppose O transfers "to A for life, then to B and his heirs; but if B does not survive A, to C and his heirs." We have just had this transfer, and we have labeled B's remainder a vested remainder subject to complete divestment. Now let us try this one: O transfers "to A

---

33. See Restatement, Property § 157 (c)(1936).

for life, then if B survives A, to B and his heirs; otherwise to C and his heirs." Did O intend the same consequences in each transfer? It certainly looks as though he did. But B's remainder in the second example is traditionally regarded as non-vested. Why? Because in the second example B's surviving A is thought of as a *condition precedent.* "Precedent" to what? Precedent to the vesting of the remainder.

By this point the reader will not be surprised to discover that it is simply *the way in which O expressed himself* that determines whether B's surviving A is a condition subsequent or a condition precedent. Here are the mechanical rules that determine which is which: *When conditional language in a transfer (e.g., "but if," "provided that," "on condition that") follows language that, taken alone, would be said to create a vested remainder, the condition so created is a condition subsequent. If, however, the conditional language appears before the language creating the remainder, or the conditional language seems to be a part of the description of the remainderman, the condition created thereby is a condition precedent.* The rules we have given, we hasten to add, are not fixed rules of law. The intent of the parties to the transfer will, in theory, determine whether a condition is subsequent or precedent to the vesting of the remainder. But absent evidence of intent to the contrary, courts will use these mechanical rules to determine what the intent was. The rules are pretty much a fixture of our law of future interests.

The transfer "to A for life, then to B and his heirs; but if B does not survive A, to C and his heirs" and the transfer "to A for life, then if B survives A, to B and his heirs; otherwise to C and his heirs" illustrate the operation of the rules in two classic cases. In the first transfer, note that the "but-if" language *follows* what looks like a plain vested remainder. It is as though O had added the conditional language as an afterthought. The condition is subsequent. In the second transfer, the conditional language—"if B survives A"—*precedes* the language giving B his remainder. It does not look like an afterthought. The condition is precedent. Let us look at one more example: O transfers "to A for life, then to B and his heirs if B reaches the age of 21." Here, although the conditional language follows language appearing to give B a plain vested remainder, one has the feeling that the conditional language is not an afterthought of O's. There is not even a comma separating the word "heirs" from the word "if." The "if" language seems to *describe* the remainderman as one who must reach 21 to qualify as owner of a vested interest. The condition, therefore, is probably precedent. May real world consequences turn on such gossamer stuff as this? Sadly enough, they sometimes do.

If a remainder is not vested when a condition precedent stands in the way of its becoming a present estate, what is it? It is *contingent.*

SECTION 7. THE CONTINGENT REMAINDER

Unlike a vested remainder, a contingent remainder is *either* subject to a condition precedent (in addition to the natural expiration of prior estates), *or owned by unascertainable persons, or both.* But the contingent remainder, like the vested remainder, "waits patiently" for possession. It is so created that it can become a present estate (if ever it does) immediately upon, and no sooner than, the natural expiration of particular estates that stand in front of it and were created simultaneously with it.[34]

Now for an example. Suppose O transfers "to A for life, then if B survives A, to B and his heirs; otherwise to C and his heirs." We said in the last section that B's remainder is contingent because it is subject to the *condition precedent* of B's surviving A. (Note that the conditional language, "if B survives A," precedes the language creating the remainder in B.) What about C's interest? It may become a present estate only upon the natural expiration of A's estate for life, which was created simultaneously with it; so it fits within the definitional requirements of the remainder. Because C's remainder is subject to the condition precedent of B's *not surviving* A, C's remainder is also contingent. In this situation, B and C are traditionally said to have *alternative contingent remainders.*[35]

Here is another example: O transfers "to A for life, then to the heirs of B." B, let us assume, is a living person when the transfer is made. We will not know who B's heirs are until he is dead; in fact, some of the persons who will become B's heirs may not be born yet. And unless B dies before A, there will be no "heirs" of B to take when A's life estate expires. Do we

---

34. Since a contingent remainder *is* a remainder, it must meet the definitional requirements set forth in the first sentence of Section 5 of this chapter. But when the contingent remainder is a freehold estate, the particular estate that immediately precedes it must, itself, be a freehold estate. Another way in which this rule is often expressed is this: a contingent remainder that is a freehold estate cannot follow an estate for years. The reason for this curious rule will be explained in Section 8 of this chapter and in Chapter Four. It has to do with the concept of seisin.

35. Since it looks certain that either B will get the possession on A's death or that C (or successors to his interest) will, it is tempting to argue that B's and C's interests, taken together, amount to a vested interest. But who would be entitled to the possession if, while B was still living, A's estate came to an end *before A's death?* Could that happen? We will be seeing later that it could. See notes 62–67, infra, and accompanying text.

have to conclude, therefore, that O's transfer created no re-mainder? No. As difficult as it may be to conceive of unas-certained or even unborn persons "owning" a future estate *now*, the transfer is said to create a remainder. The remainder is contingent until the takers are identified.[36]

We have said that in a transfer "to A for life, then if B survives A, to B and his heirs," B's remainder is contingent because it is subject to the condition precedent that B survive A. Suppose O transfers "to A for life, then if B survives A, to B *for life*": is B's remainder contingent in this transfer as well? Many com-mentators describe B's remainder in the second transfer as vested. Their theory is that the "if-B-survives-A" language sim-ply makes explicit the implicit condition that a remainderman for life (unlike a remainderman in fee simple) must always survive to get possession. But one may argue the other way.[37]

Here is a semi-tricky example: O transfers "to A for life, then to B's eldest son and his heirs." At the time the transfer is made, B has one son. Before A dies, B has a second son. Then, while A is still living, B's first son dies. Now A dies. Who gets possession? A court may conclude that possession should go to the *first* son's heirs (which may, of course, include the second son) or to anyone to whom the *first* son has transferred his remainder by will or *inter vivos* transfer. The court could reach this result by reasoning that B's first son is, by definition, B's eldest son; and since O did not say that B's eldest son *had to survive* A to take, he had a vested remainder from the very beginning. If this reasoning is not clear, try substituting the name of B's eldest son in the transfer. Assume it was, to pick a name at random, Bosavern Penlez. Now the transfer reads "to A for life, then to Bosavern Penlez and his heirs." Clearly, Bosavern has a vested remainder. He need not personally sur-vive A, since his vested remainder is in fee simple. The court will not necessarily conclude, however, that O's transfer created

---

36. In some states, if B is still alive at A's death, the courts may conclude that O intended the possession to go to those who would be B's heirs if B were in fact dead at that time. See Simes & Smith §§ 153–65. In other states, the possession may return to O until B dies. See Restate-ment, Property §§ 239–40 (1936). In the few states that still follow the rule of des-tructibility of contingent remainders, A's death while B is still living may destroy the remainder. See notes 43 and 44, in-fra, and accompanying text. See also Section 8 of this chapter.

37. It seems equally plausible to say that B's interest is contingent. If O had meant to give B a vested remainder, he could have done so by transferring "to A for life, then to B for life." One could argue, then, that O would not have added the "if-B-survives-A" language if he had not meant to make B's interest a contin-gent interest. Whether we describe B's interest as "contingent" or "vested," of course, B will not get possession unless he survives A; but if B's interest is a *con-tingent* interest, it may be destroyed in a few states by operation of the doctrine of merger in combination with the rule of des-tructibility of contingent remainders. See notes 63–67, infra, and accompanying text.

a vested remainder in Bosavern. It might decide that "eldest son" means "eldest son surviving at the time of A's death." This interpretation would require that possession go to B's *second* son on A's death.[38]

Let us consider another example: O transfers "to A for life; then, if B marries C before A's death, to B for life; then to D and his heirs." B's remainder for life is clearly contingent, since it is subject to the condition precedent of his marrying C. What about D's remainder? All it waits for is the natural expiration of the estates prior to it in possession; and there is no difficulty in identifying who will be entitled to possession when it becomes a present estate. D's remainder is vested. The point here is simply that a vested remainder may be created to follow a contingent remainder.

By this point in our discussion, it must be obvious to the reader that a contingent remainder is simply a remainder that cannot become a present estate until the takers are identified or until conditions precedent prescribed by the creator of the interest have been satisfied. In other words, a contingent remainder can never become a present estate unless it first becomes vested. In some cases, it may happen that the condition precedent becomes impossible to satisfy. Thus, if O transfers "to A for life; then, if B survives A, to B and his heirs," B's dying before A will make it impossible for the remainder ever to become a present estate. The remainder becomes a nullity. Similarly, if O transfers "to A for life; then, if B has reached the age of 21 by A's death, to B and his heirs," A's dying before B reaches 21 (even though B may later reach that age) makes the remainder a nullity.

In that last example, where will the possession go if A dies before B reaches 21? Since A's death makes B's remainder a nullity, and since O has named no alternative remainderman, the possession must go back to O. This means that O, when he made the transfer, must have kept a reversion in fee simple. But *Quia Emptores* declared that O could not transfer an estate in fee simple and still keep a seignory; does it not violate the statute to say that O transferred a contingent remainder in fee simple and still kept a reversion in fee simple? It does not, for this reason: only vested interests count as part of the fee simple. Until B's remainder vests, it will not be considered a full-fledged future estate in fee simple. O, whose reversion is vested, is, in legal theory, the only owner of the future estate in fee simple.

---

38. An argument in favor of that interpretation might be that O would have used the first son's name had he intended to give him a vested remainder. O's transfer is an excellent example of bad drafting.

In terms of factual probabilities, of course, there is no reason to assume that the owner of the vested reversion is more likely to get possession than the owner of the contingent remainder. It is clear that O's reversion will never become a present estate unless B fails to reach 21 before A's estate ends.[39]   As long as we know what we are saying, there is no objection *today* to saying that O's reversion is just as "contingent" as B's remainder.[40]   In the earliest common-law days, however, courts were unable to view matters that way.   They thought it essential that the future ownership of property not be in a doubtful state at any time. Thus, until B reached 21 before A's death, O was the person who owned the future estate in fee simple, although O's reversion in fee simple was subject to complete divestment by the vesting of B's remainder in fee simple.   B's reaching 21 before A's death was regarded, therefore, as a *condition precedent* to the vesting of B's remainder and as a *condition subsequent* divesting O's reversion.   It is still so regarded.

Assume that B does reach 21 before A's estate ends.   Does the behavior of B's remainder conform to our definition of a remainder?   Is not a remainder supposed to wait patiently for the *expiration* of estates that are prior to it?   Here, we have a remainder, by vesting, cutting short or divesting an estate in fee simple, O's reversion.   Is that not conduct unbecoming a remainder?   Our definition of a remainder requires a remainder to await the expiration of all prior *particular* estates created simultaneously with it.   A contingent remainder *can*, by vesting, divest a reversion;   but it cannot, without losing its common-law characteristics, divest any other interest.[41]

Suppose O transfers "to A for life;   then, if B marries A, to B for life;   then to C for life."   Now A dies.   Where will the possession go if B did not marry A?   If C is still living, he will

---

39. If, when O makes the transfer, A is 35 and B is 20, and both are in good health, the probability of O's reversion's becoming a present estate will be far lower than the probability of B's contingent remainder's vesting (thereby divesting the reversion).

40. *If*, that is, we are thinking of "contingency" solely in terms of the factual probability of future possession.   The difference between a "contingent" and a "vested" interest is today only relevant for the purpose of determining whether the interest runs afoul of the Rule Against Perpetuities, discussed in Chapter Four of Part I and more thoroughly in Part II, or (in those few states that still recognize it) of the rule of destructibility of contingent

remainders, discussed in this section and Section 8 of this chapter.

41. Most states now protect remainders from the rule of destructibility of contingent remainders (which we are about to reach in the text).   In those states, a remainder that has not vested by the time of expiration of the particular estate or estates created simultaneously with it, may, if it vests later, divest a *present* estate in O.   That means either that our definition of a remainder must be modified, or that a remainder saved from the destructibility rule is no longer a remainder—but rather an executory interest.   We assure the reader that this will all become clear in due course.

get possession. If C is not living, the possession will go back to O, the reversioner. The rule to remember, then, is that the possession always moves to the next vested interest. In this example, C's remainder for life was vested from the beginning. Since O had fixed the order of possession as running from A to B to C to O, giving the possession to C when A dies means simply carrying out O's intent.

Thus far, the only meaning we have assigned to the word "contingent" is the notion that a remainder will not become a present estate if a condition precedent specified by the creator of the interest has not been satisfied or if the persons he wished to have possession are not identifiable. These requirements mean no more than that transferors' wishes will be carried out. Surely that elemental idea cannot justify the gymnastics we went through a few pages back to distinguish between "remainders vested subject to total defeasance" and "contingent remainders." What does justify it?

Let us give two simple examples of contingent remainders. First, O transfers "to A for life; then, if B reaches 21 *by A's death*, to B and his heirs." Second, O transfers "to A for life; then, if B *ever* reaches 21, to B and his heirs. Is there any difference between the transfers? Certainly. In the first transfer, O insisted that B reach 21 *by A's death* in order to get the property. In the second transfer, O apparently wanted B to get the property even if B reached 21 *after* A's death. In both transfers, of course, B's remainder will become a nullity if he dies before reaching 21. The possession, on A's death, will simply return to the reversioner, who will again have a present estate in fee simple. Also, in the case of each transfer, B's remainder will immediately vest if he reaches 21 before A's estate ends. In the process of vesting, the remainder will divest the reversion in O. Once B's remainder has vested, it makes no difference whether B survives A or not. If he dies before A, his vested remainder will pass to his heirs or devisees.[42]

Our only problem arises in the situation in which B is living but has not reached 21 by A's death. Under the terms of the first transfer, B's remainder simply becomes a nullity. That result is precisely what O intended, and it is precisely what actually happens today. In our second transfer, however, if O's intent is to be carried out, B still has a chance of getting the property. But *will* he get it? If we try to carry out O's intent, we are left with the question of where the possession is to go during the period between A's death and B's reaching 21.

---

42. Unless, that is, a court finds that B's interest is subject to an implied condition that he survive A. See note 31, supra.

The answer seems simple enough: since O has not yet actually transferred more than an estate for life, the possession must go back to O. Since B might never reach 21, and since O in that case will be permitted to keep the property forever, we had better call O's estate a present estate in fee simple. But wait: if we say that O has a present estate in fee simple, how can we give effect to B's remainder? After all, it is quite clear that remainders may not follow estates in fee simple. Moreover, if we give effect to B's remainder, it can become a present estate only by *cutting short* a present estate in fee simple. That, as the reader knows, is something a remainder is not supposed to do. It is quite obvious that if we are to preserve our carefully crafted definition of a remainder, we must inform B that he can never have the property. If B is a good citizen, he will take comfort from the fact that although he will not get the property, at least the definition of a remainder will have been preserved.

But what about O's intent? He *wanted* B to have the property if B *ever* reached the age of 21. If O were still alive at A's death, he could, of course, convey the property to B when B reached 21. But, sadly enough, O is dead. As a matter of fact, he made the original transfer as a final disposition of his property. Therefore, his heirs or devisees, who succeeded to his reversion, are now owners of the estate in fee simple absolute. May they not transfer it to B when he reaches 21? Certainly they may. *Will* they? Not likely. It is evident that O's intent *has been frustrated by the definition of a remainder!*

It is almost impossible to believe that courts could ever have been so shackled by definition as to frustrate O's intent in this fashion. But this is precisely the result the early common-law courts reached. The rule they applied in order to reach this bizarre result was this: *Unless a remainder shall be vested at or before the termination of all estates prior to it in possession, it shall be destroyed.*[43] The rule was referred to as *the rule of destructibility of contingent remainders.*[44]

Now, at last, we have a meaningful distinction between a contingent remainder and a vested remainder subject to total defeasance. In the case of a contingent remainder, the intent of the transferor and the hope of the remainderman could be frustrated by application of the destructibility rule. In the case

---

43. In our example in the text, we have the rule applying when the life estate expires naturally by A's death. But we will see in Section 8 of this chapter that it also applied when the prior particular estate ended "prematurely." See notes 62–67, infra, and accompanying text.

44. We will analyze this rule more carefully in Section 8. See generally 1 American Law of Property §§ 4.59–4.62. As the reader will soon discover, the destructibility rule had its origins in the concept of seisin.

of a vested remainder subject to total defeasance, the destructibility rule would not apply.

Could not a transferor always avoid the destructibility rule by using a vested remainder subject to total defeasance instead of a contingent remainder?   No, because he could not accomplish precisely the same purposes.   Let us try using a vested remainder subject to total defeasance in our standard example. The challenge is to give B his possession even if he reaches 21 after A's death.   O transfers "to A for life, then to B and his heirs; but if B does not reach 21, the grantor herein, or anyone who has succeeded to his interest, may enter and terminate the granted estate."   B's remainder is indestructible.   Has O accomplished his original purposes?   Let us assume B is four years old when A dies.   Where does the possession go?   To B.   Since his remainder is vested, and since he has not yet failed to reach 21, he is clearly entitled to possession.[45]   That is certainly not the result O had in mind when he used a contingent remainder.

We should not leave this section without informing the reader that the destructibility rule has been abolished in all but a few states either by specific statute or by judicial decision.[46]   Today, in most states, B's contingent interest will be preserved for him until he reaches 21 after A's death.   If he does reach 21, he will be entitled to his estate.   In the interim between A's death and B's reaching 21, the reversioner will be entitled to possession with an estate in fee simple subject to divestment by the vesting of B's interest.   Are courts today likely to *call* B's interest during that interim a *remainder?*   If they care to preserve the traditional definition of a remainder, they will have to find another label for it.   They might, for example, call it an executory interest that used to be a remainder.[47]   But why bother to preserve the traditional definition in states that no longer have the destructibility rule?   We will be asking that question again.

---

45. Even if B had died before reaching 21, his heirs would be entitled to possession until the transferor exercised his power of termination.

46. The destructibility rule still exists in its old common-law form in Florida. Various authors have suggested that it also exists unchanged in Arkansas, North Carolina, Oregon, Pennsylvania, South Carolina, and Tennessee; but there are no statutes or recent decisions to clarify the rule's status in these states.   For a brief survey of the scholarship on the subject, see Dukeminier & Krier, Property 457 n.42 (1981).

Five jurisdictions have enacted statutes preserving the contingent remainder only when the prior estates are *prematurely* determined—as, for example, by merger. See notes 62–67, infra, and accompanying text.   In these jurisdictions, a contingent remainder that has not vested when all prior estates terminate *naturally* will still be destroyed.   See D. C. Code § 45–214 (1981);   Maine Rev. Stat. Title 33 § 157 (1964);   Miss. Code Ann. § 89–1–17 (1972);   R.I. Gen. Laws § 34–4–4 (1970); Tex. Rev. Civ. Stat. Ann. 1290 (1980).

47. See the discussion in Restatement, Property § 240, comment *e* (1936).

What is an executory interest? Here is a pretty good definition: *An executory interest is any future interest created in a person other than the transferor that is not a remainder.*[48] Here are five classic examples of executory interests: (1) O transfers "to A for life; then, one day after A's death, to the heirs of A." The transfer creates a springing executory interest in those who will be A's heirs. (2) O transfers "to A for 200 years if he shall so long live, then to the heirs of A." This transfer also creates a springing executory interest in A's prospective heirs. (3) O transfers "to A and his heirs five years from the date of this deed." A owns a springing executory interest. (4) O, when B is fifteen, transfers "to A for life; then, no sooner than one day after A's death, to B and his heirs if B ever reaches 21." B owns a springing executory interest. (5) O transfers "to A and his heirs; but if A marries X, to B and his heirs." B owns a shifting executory interest.

We have now done for the executory interest just about what we did for the reversion, the possibility of reverter, the power of termination, the vested remainder, and the contingent remainder. We have defined it, and we have given some examples of its use. Is that enough? Unless we are badly mistaken, it is not. The examples leave too many questions unanswered. Why are not some of these interests remainders? Why should anyone want a future interest to become a present estate one day after the death of the life tenant? Why would anyone transfer "to A for 200 years if he shall so long live"? Why do we describe four of these executory interests as "springing" and the fifth as "shifting"? Why, in the first two examples, does O create future interests in favor of "the heirs of A"? Sadly, enough, it will take us a long time to answer these questions. To get the answers, we shall have to retreat once again into the feudal period.

SECTION 8. PROBLEMS OF THE PRE–1536 CONVEYANCER: THE RISE OF THE USE

The year, let us say, is 1500. Feudalism is not quite the vigorous institution it used to be; but the feudal pyramid, though beginning to crumble, is still standing. Mesne lords continue to demand annual services, and tenants in demesne continue to feel the weight of the feudal incidents, which have been given new life by *Quia Emptores*. It is still the goal of every right-thinking tenant to avoid the incidents upon his death, and it is still the firm intent of every mesne lord to protect his ancient privileges. The only obvious difference between this period and

---

48. Compare Restatement, Property § 158 (1936).

the earlier feudal period is that transferors are tending more and more to use future interests to maintain control of the future use of their property. One reason for this change is that the estate in fee tail may now be disentailed by fine or common recovery.[49] By using future interests, a transferor may make those whom he wants to have the property in the future "purchasers" instead of heirs. As purchasers, they will have protection of their future ownership rights. Moreover, the transferor may be able to avoid the incidents by having his successors take the property as purchasers.

If we look closely, we will note another important difference between this period and the earlier feudal period. No longer are the feudal law courts the sole courts to which one may go for protection. The King's Chancellor is affording remedies that the *law* courts simply cannot offer.[50] Armed only with the principle that law should accord with divine moral command, the Chancellor is requiring people to perform their *moral* duties even in cases in which the law courts would recognize no *legal* duties. How is he "requiring" them to do their moral duties? By commanding them to perform the duties, and by fining them or putting them in jail if they disobey. In short, the *court of equity* has arrived on the scene, and its weapon is the *injunction*.

In the law courts, seisin is still king. Around the concept of seisin has grown a whole cluster of technically refined and highly conceptual legal rules that have one purpose: *to preserve continuity of the seisin*. In this section, we shall present five examples of the ways in which the donative purposes of tenants in demesne were frustrated by application of these rules. In each example, we shall show how, by recourse to the equity powers of the Court of Chancery, a tenant in demesne could accomplish the very ends that the law courts denied him. Most of the transfers we shall be examining will be "testamentary" in character: they will represent final dispositions of property by persons who wish to control the property's use from the grave. The reader is urged to examine the problems with care. If he understands them, he will understand our modern law of future interests.

Problem 1: No transfers of land by will

The law courts of 1500 simply did not recognize testamentary transfer of interests in real property.[51] Although the origins of

---

49. For a discussion of these disentailing methods, see Chapter Two, notes 30 and 31 and accompanying text.

50. See generally Plucknett, 180–81, 187–89, 685–86. During the formative period in which the Chancellor first began to "do equity" in earnest, the holders of that office were usually ecclesiastics. See id. at 685.

51. Except according to certain local customs. See Plucknett, 564, 582, 735–36.

this notion are difficult to trace, it seems reasonable to suppose that it was related to the character of feudal land ownership. Allowing testamentary transfers of land would have greatly reduced the mesne lord's chances of profiting from a wardship or an escheat, and would also have created an exception to the rule that an interest in land must pass by livery of seisin.[52]   Free *inter vivos* alienability seems to have been accepted (though perhaps reluctantly) as a practical response to the increasing demand for land;[53]   but there was probably no equivalent pressure for the acceptance of testamentary transfer.   If one could transfer freely while alive, and if one's heirs could transfer freely after one's death, why would testamentary transfers be necessary?

Although many testamentary purposes could be accomplished by the *inter vivos* creation of legal estates and future interests, the creation of these estates was not always an adequate substitute for testamentary transfer.   Thus if O, a widower with a brother A and a son B, wished to leave his brother an estate for life and his son a remainder in fee simple, he had merely to transfer his entire estate in fee simple to a trusted third person, T, who would reconvey "to O for life, then to A for life, then to B and his heirs."   Not only would the vested remainders in A and B be given effect, but also A and B would have become purchasers who would not be burdened by the feudal incidents. Nevertheless, it is not difficult to see why O might hesitate to use the simple device we have described.   If O was forty when he made the transfer, how could he be sure that his purposes would not change before his death?   A and B might predecease him.   He might have a new wife and another child to provide for.   He might find himself in financial distress that required him to sell the entire property to someone else.   If wills were permitted, O could make a will and simply modify or revoke it as circumstances changed.   But wills are not permitted—at least at law.

They are, however, permitted in equity!   Here is how it works. O transfers his entire estate in fee simple, by feoffment with livery of seisin, "to T and his heirs *to the use of O and his heirs.*" By using the magical words "to the use of O and his heirs," O created between himself and T a relationship of trust that was deemed by the Court of Chancery to be morally binding on T. The words "to the use of O and his heirs" mean, roughly, "for the *purposes* of O and his heirs."[54]   Thus, T holds a *legal* estate

---

52. See Cheshire, 43; Holdsworth, 103–04.

53. See Painter, 194.

54. The word "use" here is said to be derived from an Old French corruption of the Latin "opus," meaning benefit or work, rather than from the Latin "uti, usus," meaning to use.   Plucknett, 576.

in fee simple in the property *subject entirely to the control of O!*
If T fails to carry out any instruction of O's concerning the property, O has merely to ask the Court of Chancery to order T to
comply.   If T disobeys the order, he may be fined or jailed for
contempt.

But how does O make his will?   He simply instructs T in
writing to transfer the legal estate, upon O's death, "to A for
life, then to B and his heirs."   If O wishes, he may revoke the
instructions or modify them to suit his later purposes.   Assuming
O does not change the instructions, A and B will have no difficulty
in forcing T to make livery of seisin upon O's death to create the
two estates.   They have merely to ask the Court of Chancery
to command him to do so.

But there are two problems.   First, suppose T, in violation
of his moral duty, sells the property to a third person who knows
nothing of O's *equitable* interest in it.   May such a person keep
the property?   Yes.   A *bona fide* purchaser who pays value for
the property is as deserving of protection as O.[55]   A technique
will have to be devised to reduce the risk that T will make a
dishonest disposition of the property.   Second, T may die before
he has discharged his duties.   T's heir will be under the same
moral obligation as T was to follow O's instructions;   but the
burden of the incidents will fall upon the inheritance, since T has
replaced O on the feudal pyramid.

The solution to both problems is for O to enfeoff three or four
persons as *joint tenants with rights of survivorship*.   It is certainly less likely that *all* the feoffees will be dishonest.   Moreover, when one feoffee dies, nothing will pass to his heirs.   The
legal ownership of the other feoffees will simply swell to absorb
the relinquished ownership of the deceased feoffee.   When the
group of feoffees looks as though it is getting dangerously close
to the point at which a single feoffee might be left with the
property, it will not be difficult to restore the group to its original
number by making a new series of enfeoffments.[56]

What do the *law* courts make of this business?   They may
not be particularly happy about the competition they are getting
from the Court of Chancery, but there is nothing they can do
about it.   *Their* rules are being followed to the letter.   There
is no problem with the seisin: it was transferred to T by livery
as required.   The mesne lord, under whom T now holds the

---

55.   This is still a basic rule of property
law.   The common statement of the rule
is that a sale to a *bona fide* purchaser for
value by one having "legal" title cuts off
"equitable" interests.

56.   In future examples, we shall be us-

ing only one feoffee, T.   It is simply too
cumbersome to do otherwise.   The reader
is asked to assume that "T" stands for a
group of feoffees owning as joint tenants.   (We have chosen the letter "T" to
imply "trustee.")

property, is entitled to his services as before. He cannot complain of O's transfer to T, since *Quia Emptores* specifically permits substitution. In a *law* court, O is probably viewed simply as T's *tenant at will*—that is, as a tenant whose estate may be *legally* terminated at any time by T.[57] In equity, however, O (who is called the *cestui que use*) is regarded as the beneficial or *equitable* owner of the estate in fee simple. In both the law courts and the Court of Chancery, T—the so-called *feoffee to uses*—is recognized as the owner of the legal estate in fee simple. The moral of it all? Where there's a will, there's a will.

Problem 2: No transfers without livery of seisin

If the Court of Chancery could find a way to permit the making of a will, surely it could also find a way to permit transfer of present freehold estates without that elaborate and *public* ceremony, livery of seisin. Suppose O wishes to sell his present estate in fee simple to A. Neither O nor A is particularly anxious to make the transfer a matter of public knowledge. How may O get the seisin to A without livery?

Actually, O could accomplish his purpose without recourse to the Court of Chancery. First, O and A would enter into an agreement of lease under whose provisions A would be entitled to a term of years when he entered the property. Upon A's entry, O would simply *release* his interest[58] to A by a written instrument. Once A owned both the term and the freehold interest, the two interests would *merge* to form one estate in fee simple. This procedure (which was called a *lease and release*) was fully acceptable to the courts of law, presumably on the theory that livery of seisin to one already occupying the land was unnecessary.[59] But the procedure had one serious disadvantage: it required A actually to enter possession of the property.

By using the Court of Chancery, A could avoid having to make an actual entry upon the land. Here is the procedure: O and A entered into a written agreement—called a *bargain and sale*— for the sale of the land. If the agreement recited that A had given valuable consideration for the purchase, the Court of Chancery regarded A for most practical purposes as the owner. The agreement was said to have *raised a use* in A. This meant that O had become morally bound (and therefore subject to equitable command) to perform his side of the bargain by treating the property as A's. O's position was, in effect, the same as that

---

57. For a discussion of this estate, see generally 1 American Law of Property §§ 3.28–3.31.

58. As we have been pointing out here and there, a feudal court would probably

have regarded O's interest as a present estate in fee simple subject to the term rather than as a reversion in fee simple. See 2 Pollock & Maitland, 35–37.

59. See 2 Pollock & Maitland, 92–94.

of a feoffee to the use of A and his heirs. The courts of law had no complaint—from their point of view, O had never transferred his interest.[60] The result of the bargain and sale was to leave the *legal* estate in fee simple in O and to create an *equitable estate in fee simple in A*.

Problem 3: Destructibility of contingent remainders

In our earlier discussion of destructibility,[61] the example we used to demonstrate the rule was this: O transferred "to A for life; then, if B ever reaches 21, to B and his heirs." Despite O's intent (and B's expectations) to the contrary, B's contingent remainder was destroyed if A died when B was 19, even though B might later reach 21. One might infer from this example that if B *did* manage to reach 21 by A's death, his remainder would necessarily be good. This was not always the case. The destructibility rule applied not only when A's estate for life *expired naturally* at A's death, but also when it *terminated prematurely*. One circumstance in which A's life estate might terminate prematurely was that in which A committed a serious enough breach of his feudal duty of loyalty to justify *forfeiture* of his estate.[62] If the estate was forfeited, and if *at that time* B had not reached 21, B's contingent remainder was destroyed.

Another way in which A's life estate could terminate prematurely was by operation of the doctrine of *merger*.[63] The doctrine of merger, in its simplest application, worked this way. O transfers "to A for life." After the transfer, A has a present estate for life and O has a reversion in fee simple. Now O *releases*[64] his reversion to A. It seems silly to say that A now has both a life estate and a reversion in fee simple. After all, the entire ownership is now in A. He must, therefore, have a

---

60. The same effect as a bargain and sale resulted when a person covenanted to "stand seised" for a close relative. Equity regarded the close relative as the owner of the estate to be transferred, but the legal estate remained with the covenantor.

The notion in our modern law that the execution of a contract for the sale of real property passes "equitable title" to the purchaser—thus permitting him to use the equitable remedy of specific performance—seems directly traceable to the early notion of bargain and sale. Deeds commonly used in many states are still called "deeds of bargain and sale."

61. See supra Section 7, text accompanying notes 43–45.

62. A breach of this nature—originally called a "felony"—included such activities as the attempted transfer by a life tenant of an estate in fee simple. This "tortious feoffment" actually conveyed a fee estate to the transferee until the reversioner took action to recover possession. See 1 American Law of Property § 2.17.

A life tenant's estate might also be forfeited by breach of any condition subsequent.

63. See Simes & Smith § 197 at 223 for a discussion of the operation of the doctrine of merger.

64. A *release* was a form of grant; like the grant, it was an instrument under seal. All owners of future interests could release them to the owner of the present estate.

present estate in fee simple.   His estate for life has terminated by reason of having *merged* into the estate in fee simple.   Had A *surrendered*[65] his estate for life to O, the transfer would have had a similar result.   O would be the owner of a present estate in fee simple absolute, and the life estate would have terminated by merger.

But suppose O, instead of making the original transfer simply "to A for life," transfers "to A for life; then, if B survives A, to B and his heirs."   In the eyes of the feudal court, B has no real ownership.[66]   He has, at most, a bare possibility of *getting* ownership.   Hence, if A surrenders his estate for life to O, or if O releases his reversion to A, merger will occur just as though no contingent remainder had been created.   B's contingent remainder will be destroyed in the process.[67]

Why would O *want* to give B a contingent remainder and then destroy it by releasing the reversion to A?   It might be that B behaved badly, but chances are that O wanted nothing of the kind.   O fully intended that B get a present estate in fee simple if he survived A; but someone who succeeded to O's reversion on O's death might not have felt the same solicitude for B.   As a matter of fact, the termination of A's estate by forfeiture or merger was often a matter arranged by the life tenant and the reversioner *for the sole purpose of squeezing out the contingent remainderman.*[68]   When B's contingent remainder was destroyed in this fashion, the result was usually to frustrate O's original intent.

But we have yet to discover how this strange destructibility rule ever came into existence.   Was there any reason for this flagrant disregard of O's intent?   The feudal courts believed that there was: they regarded the destructibility rule as a *fundamental rule of seisin.*   At the heart of the rule was the idea that voluntary livery of seisin was necessary for the creation of any *freehold* estate.   Since livery of seisin implied the delivery

---

65. A *surrender* of a present estate to the owner of a future interest required no writing until enactment of the Statute of Frauds, 29 Car. 2, c. 3 (1677).

66. Courts were slow to recognize the contingent remainder; in fact, contingent remainders probably did not exist as we have described them before the fourteenth century. See Plucknett, 562–64. After they came to be generally recognized, beginning with the sixteenth century, destructibility was always one of their major characteristics. See id., 590–92.

67. Under no circumstances could a *vested* remainder be destroyed by the merger of other estates or by the forfeiture of any estate prior to it.

68. One can get a sense of what the motivation might have been by imagining, in our example in the text, that B is a healthy 25 and that A is 85 and failing rapidly. An estate in fee simple in the land would be worth two million pounds. How much might the reversioner be willing to pay A for his life estate? Alternatively, how much might the reversioner be willing to pay Gyp the Blood to see to it that B does not survive A?

of *present* possession, it was impossible for a transferor to make livery of seisin *so as to take effect in the future*. A transferor could do nothing to make the seisin spring out to him at a future date. Thus, if O attempted to transfer "to A and his heirs five years from the date hereof," the attempted transfer was a nullity from the very beginning. Similarly, if O tried to transfer "to A and his heirs when A marries B," the attempt failed. No seisin had passed. In both cases, O would continue as owner of a present estate in fee simple.

The notion that O could do nothing to make the seisin spring out of him in the future found expression in the rule that one could not create a legal freehold estate *in futuro*. Although the rule sounds as though it forbade the creation of all future freehold estates, that was not its purpose or effect. The rule simply limited the *way* in which a future freehold estate could be created. According to the rule, a transferor who wished to create a *future* freehold estate in a third party had to create simultaneously a *present* freehold estate to carry the seisin to the future free-holder. The present freehold estate could not be in fee simple; it had to be either an estate in fee tail or an estate for life. (To keep things simple, we will be using the estate for life in our examples.) Thus, if O wished to give A a future estate in fee simple that would become a present estate upon O's death, he could not do it by transferring "to A and his heirs upon O's death." But he could accomplish his purpose by transferring his entire estate to a trusted third person who would retransfer "to O for life, then to A and his heirs."[69] This would work because O's life estate could carry the seisin to A.

An obvious corollary of the rule that one must create a present estate capable of carrying the seisin to the future freeholder was the rule that the future freehold estate must be created in such a way as to make it possible, though not necessarily certain, that the future freeholder will be able to take the seisin *immediately* upon the expiration of the present estate. If, for example, O transferred "to A for life, then *one month later* to B and his heirs," the attempted transfer to B would fail. Since B could not under any circumstances take the seisin immediately upon the expiration of A's present estate, he got no estate at all.

We should now be able to understand how the rule of des-tructibility of contingent remainders came into existence. Con-fining ourselves, for this discussion, to freehold remainders, we can see that the contingent freehold remainder does, at the time of its creation, satisfy the rules of seisin. For example, if O

---

69. If O transferred his entire estate to A and A retransferred "to O for life," the practical result would be the same; but A would have a reversion instead of a remainder.

transfers "to A for life; then, if B ever marries C, to B and his heirs," B's future interest is *capable* of becoming a present estate immediately upon the expiration of A's estate.[70] B *may* marry C before A's estate ends. What is more, A's life estate is a present freehold estate created simultaneously with B's future interest that is capable of carrying the seisin to B. Because B's future interest is capable of complying with the rules of seisin, there is no reason to declare it a nullity at the time of its creation. But if it turns out that B has not married C by the time A's life estate ends, his future interest becomes a nullity then.[71]

But if B, on the termination of A's estate, was still capable of marrying C, why could not the feudal court allow the seisin to go back to O temporarily and then let it spring to B if B later married C? The court could not do that, for that would mean that O's original transfer had given B a legal freehold estate *in futuro*. That was forbidden. If O still wants B to have a present estate in fee simple upon his marrying C, he must make livery of seisin to him. O cannot make the seisin spring out of himself *automatically* at a future date.[72]

A careful examination of the rules of seisin we have been considering reveals the important fact that the only *legal* future *freehold* estate that a pre-1536 transferor, O, could create in someone other than himself was the remainder. To the feudal lawyer that meant a future *freehold* estate that was so created as to be capable of becoming a present estate immediately upon, and no sooner than, the expiration of a present particular *freehold* estate (or estates) created simultaneously with it. Except for the fact that our definition of a remainder in the first sentence of Section 5 of this chapter contemplates, in accordance with modern usage, a vested freehold remainder's following a term for years as well as a particular freehold estate, our definition is very close to the feudal lawyer's definition.[73] We will be seeing below that a *contingent freehold remainder* cannot follow a term of years.

But our task here is to show how the pre-1536 conveyancer might have avoided the destructibility rule by using enfeoffments to uses. O, let us assume, wants to give A a present life estate. Upon A's death O wants B, who is now 12, to have a present

---

70. The word "capable" here implies no certainty that the interest will be ready to take the seisin. It simply means that the terms of creation contemplate the possibility of the estate's becoming present at that time.

71. Note that the feudal court would probably not say that B's contingent remainder had been *destroyed*. It would

probably say that the remainder never became an estate at all.

72. The obverse of this statement is that a remainder could not become a present estate by cutting short a reversion that had become a present estate.

73. See note 16, supra.

estate in fee simple if B has reached 21 by that time. If B is alive but less than 21 when A dies, O wants B to get a present estate in fee simple if he later reaches 21. As we have seen, if O attempts to accomplish his purposes *at law*, the contingent remainder he must use will be destroyed if B has not reached 21 by A's death. Indeed, it may be destroyed earlier than A's death by premature termination of A's life estate. Can O avoid the destructibility rule in equity? He can. He enfeoffs "T and his heirs *to the use of A for life;* then, if B *ever* reaches the age of 21, *to the use of B and his heirs.*" As far as the law courts are concerned, T owns a perfectly good legal estate in fee simple. He is seised, and he must perform the feudal duties.[74] A owns nothing at law; but in equity he owns an *equitable estate for life.*[75] B, too, owns nothing at law; but in equity he owns *an equitable contingent remainder in fee simple.*

Now the critical question. What happens if A dies when B is 19? Since the seisin remains in T, there is no problem with the destructibility rule. Since O intended B to get the property whether he reached 21 before or after A's death, *equity will see to it that his intent is carried out.* But who actually enjoys the property during the interim between A's death and B's reaching 21? To answer this question, the court of equity went through these steps of reasoning: (1) O made no special provision in his enfeoffment to T for the disposition of the property between A's death and B's reaching 21. (2) Certainly O could not have intended the possession to reside in T for that period; T's job was merely to hold the seisin for the benefit of others. (3) It seems obvious, therefore, that O intended the possession to go to whoever would have been entitled to it *had O granted legal estates to A and B.* That person would be the *legal* reversioner—either O himself, if he is still alive, or the person who has succeeded to his legal reversion.[76] (4) Therefore, we must award possession to that person.

In awarding possession to O, the court of equity simply concluded that O's enfeoffment of T had impliedly created an *equitable reversion* in O. Since O made no alternative disposition

---

74. One imagines that T would not have accepted the fee simple without assurance that the land would yield the wherewithal to discharge the duties. No doubt the beneficial owners actually performed the duties.

75. Whether A's estate actually bore this label in the court of Chancery we cannot say. In this section we shall be applying labels to the interests that could be created by feoffments to use; we adopt these labels not for the sake of historical accuracy, but rather to prepare the reader to cope with the technical labels that become part of the vocabulary of future interest law as a result of the enactment of the Statute of Uses, 27 Hen. 8, c. 10 (1535).

76. Although O may well have shuffled off his mortal coil before A's death, we shall continue to use the letter "O" to designate the person who would have succeeded to his legal reversion.

of the property between A's death and B's reaching 21, he was said to be entitled to possession by *resulting use*. Now, what shall O's interest be called during the period in which he will be in possession? We can no longer properly call it an equitable reversion, because it is a present equitable estate. Since it is an estate that may go on forever (B may not reach 21), we can label it tentatively a present *equitable estate in fee simple (by resulting use)*.

If B reaches 21, equity will award possession to him precisely as O intended.[77] But what shall we call B's equitable future interest while O is back in possession? Calling it an equitable contingent remainder *now* seems a bit awkward. After all, the word "remainder," when used *at law*, denotes an interest that cannot follow, much less cut short, a present estate in fee simple. In this situation, B will get possession, if he does, only by cutting short O's present equitable estate in fee simple. In a sense, the possession will *spring* from O to B without any act on O's part. To capture this idea of possession springing from O to B, let us call B's interest a *springing use*. B now owns a *springing use in fee simple*. Now we can give O's present equitable estate a label that reflects the fact that it may be cut short by B's reaching 21. It is a present *equitable estate in fee simple (by resulting use) subject to a springing use in B in fee simple*.

Let us now briefly review the labels we have applied to all the interests that O's enfeoffment of T created:

(1) T gets a *legal estate in fee simple*. The seisin remains with him until it is finally determined that O or B, one or the other, is entitled to a present estate in fee simple absolute.

(2) A gets an *equitable estate for life*.

(3) Until A dies, B can be said to have an *equitable contingent remainder in fee simple*.

(4) Until A dies, O can be said to have an *equitable reversion in fee simple (by resulting use)*.

(5) If A dies while B is alive but under 21, O owns a present *equitable estate in fee simple (by resulting use) subject to a springing use in B in fee simple*.

(6) If A dies while B is alive but under 21, B owns an equitable future interest called a *springing use in fee simple*.

These labels may seem confusing to the reader. Labels (2) through (4) are simply the equitable labels for the legal interests that the parties would have had if O had attempted his transfer at law. The last two labels designate interests that could not

---

77. B will be able to require T to enfeoff him with the legal fee simple.

be created at law before 1536. At law, if A died while B was 19, O would have a present estate in fee simple, and B, owing to the destructibility rule, would have nothing. In equity, however, O's interest may be cut short by B's reaching 21. Consequently, we describe O's interest as an equitable estate in fee simple (by resulting use) *subject to a springing use in B.* We call B's interest a *springing use* to indicate that it no longer acts like a legal remainder. A remainder *at law* could not become a present estate by cutting short a present estate in fee simple. A remainder could not even follow an estate in fee simple.

While we are discussing springing uses, we might as well show how they could have been used to accomplish some other purposes that could not have been accomplished at law before 1536. Let us imagine that O, sometime before 1536, wants to give A a future estate in fee simple that will become a present estate upon A's marrying B. Can O make a *present* transfer *at law* that will take effect when A marries B? It is difficult to see how he could. An attempt to transfer "to A and his heirs when A marries B" would not be effective. Since seisin would not pass to A at the time of the transfer, A's interest would fail as an unlawful estate *in futuro.* Moreover, there seems to be no way in which O could transfer his entire estate to a trusted third person and get a retransfer that would work. O would surely want an estate in fee simple, for A may never marry B; but if he gets back an estate in fee simple, A will not have a contingent remainder. Remainders cannot follow estates in fee simple.[78]

The solution is for O to enfeoff "T and his heirs to the use of A and his heirs when A marries B." T, of course, gets a legal estate in fee simple. What about O and A? First we must look to see what interests would have been created at law by a transfer "to A and his heirs when A marries B." As we saw above, A would get nothing. O, therefore, would have his original present estate in fee simple. By analogy, then, to what O would have had at law, we say that O has a present *equitable estate in fee simple (by resulting use).* (We will come back to O.) The court of equity will award the possession to A upon his marrying B. Here again, because we can think of the possession as springing to him from O, we can call A's interest a *springing use in fee*

---

78. How about this for a try: O transfers his entire estate to X, who re-transfers "to O and his heirs; but if A marries B, to A and his heirs"? When we get to Problem 5, infra, we will see that it was impossible prior to 1536 to make a condition subsequent operate at law in favor of anyone other than a transferor. Because the attempt here is to make a condition subsequent operate in favor of a third person, A, it will fail. Remember that the only future freehold estate that could be created in a third person at law before 1536 was the freehold remainder! When, after 1536, we find O successfully making a condition subsequent operate in favor of a third party, the third party will not have a remainder; he will have a kind of executory interest.

simple. Since O's present equitable estate is liable to be cut short by A's marrying B, its full label should be a present *equitable estate in fee simple (by resulting use) subject to a springing use in A in fee simple.* The seisin will remain with T until he enfeoffs whoever of the two, O or A, is finally determined to be entitled to a present legal estate in fee simple absolute. The law courts cannot complain, for their rules have been obeyed to the letter.

We have now accomplished our chief purpose in this discussion: to show that O, before 1536, could use *equitable* estates *in futuro* (springing uses) to avoid the destructibility rule and to accomplish other conveyancing goals that could not be achieved by the use of *legal* estates. O had merely to deposit the seisin with a trustworthy T with appropriate instructions, and the Chancellor did the rest.

Before moving on to Problem 4, we must remind the reader of a point that we made originally back in Section 6 of Chapter Two. That point was that in the feudal period an estate for years was incapable of "supporting" a freehold remainder. O *could* make an effective transfer "to A for five years, then to B and his heirs," but feudal lawyers would not judge B to have a remainder. Why? Because O, to accomplish his transfer, made livery of seisin to A *for the benefit of B.* In the feudal lawyers' view of things, B was seised of a present estate in fee simple, subject to the estate for years in A. Similarly, if O merely transferred "to A for five years," feudal lawyers would not judge O to have a reversion. Owing to the fact that O remained seised, he too would be viewed as having a present estate in fee simple, subject to the estate for years.[79] Lawyers today would not object to calling B's interest a remainder or O's a reversion, but they would find the "present-estate" locution at least as acceptable."[80]

When we get into discussion of Problem 4, and particularly when we reach post-1536 conveyancing in Chapter Four, we will be adopting the "present estate" locution, using quotation marks around "present" to remind us that the owner of the estate being described is not in occupancy himself. But the "present-estate" locution has a pertinence to us right here. Consider this pre-1536 transfer that we looked at in Chapter Two: it is from O

---

79. We are not suggesting that feudal lawyers actually used the words "present estate" or "subject to." We mean to say only that they would *not* have said B had a remainder or O a reversion.

80. In some circumstances more acceptable. If O today, owning property that is leased to A, conveys the property to B, he will rarely state in his deed that he is conveying a "reversion." He will simply convey the fee simple "subject to the lease."

"to A for five years, then to the heirs of B in fee simple." B is alive when O attempts the transfer. Who has what?

A's estate for years looks all right, but what do B's heirs have? Answer: absolutely nothing. The explanation is quite simple. Since O cannot create a legal freehold estate *in futuro* (one that will become a present estate by reason of the seisin's springing out of O), B's heirs' future interest stands or falls on whether or not the seisin has already left O. Unhappily for those who will be B's heirs, the seisin has remained with O. B's heirs cannot have gotten the seisin either directly from O or through A's taking it for their benefit.[81] Why? Because B *has* no heirs yet! A cannot have gotten the seisin on his own account, because an estate for years does not carry the seisin. The seisin is still in O. He is seised of a "present" estate in fee simple, subject to the estate for years in A. The seisin will not spring from him to B's heirs even when we know who they are.

We have a number of points to make about this failure of O. The first is that he could have succeeded by an enfeoffment to T with appropriate instructions. The second is that his failure did not owe to operation of the rule of destructibility of contingent remainders. The destructibility rule is, to be sure, grounded in the same rule we see operating here—the rule that barred the creation of legal freehold estates *in futuro;* but the destructibility rule destroyed interests that were valid interests when created. In this case, no interest whatever was created in the heirs of B. Our last point is that the rule that we see operating in our example here is commonly *phrased* this way: *a legal contingent freehold remainder can never follow an estate for years.* A feudal lawyer, as we have noted *ad taedium,* would have denied that even a vested freehold remainder could follow an estate for years; but the phrasing ought to be acceptable to us so long as we know that what is really operating here is the rule that barred the creation of legal freehold estates *in futuro.* We will see in Chapter Four that the Statute of Uses, enacted in 1535, abolished that rule; thereby permitting O to give to the unknown future heirs of B a perfectly valid legal future interest. But that future interest will not be a remainder; it will be a springing executory interest. Now, on to Problem 4.

Problem 4: The Rule in Shelley's Case

In Chapter One, we examined at some length the historic development of the concept of alienability. The development

---

81. A termor could accept the seisin for the freeholder (e.g., for B in our example where O transferred "to A for five years, then to B and his heirs") only when the freeholder's estate was vested. Here, the heirs of B cannot have a vested estate because they have yet to be identified.

reached its culmination when the words "and his heirs" in a transfer were thought to give full durational ownership to the immediate transferee and no ownership whatever to his heirs.   This notion was expressed in the statement that the words "and his heirs" are words of limitation and not words of purchase.   They indicate the durational character of an estate, not its taker.

We also noted in Chapter One that the incidents of wardship, marriage, and escheat attached only upon the *inheritance* of property.   The question now is whether the introduction of future interests as devices to control the use of property in the future could also help to avoid feudal incidents.   O, let us say, is about to transfer a tract of land to his ne'er-do-well brother, A.   O has two things in mind.   In the first place, he does not want his brother to be able to disinherit his heir expectant by selling the estate in fee simple to a stranger.   In the second place, O would like to save A's heir from the feudal incidents that will attach on A's death.   How can O accomplish these ends?   It appears that the solution would be to transfer an estate for life to A and give a remainder in fee simple to A's heir.   In that way, A would be unable to disinherit his heir expectant by transfer.   As a remainderman, A's heir would take by purchase rather than by inheritance, so he would also avoid the feudal incidents.

Since O does not know who will turn out to be A's heir, he will have to use a generic term to describe the remainderman. O decides to make his transfer "to A for life, *then to the heirs of A.*"[82]   Now A dies, leaving one son surviving.   Does the son take the property as a remainderman—that is, as a purchaser— and avoid the incidents, as O had hoped he would?   No—*the son takes by inheritance.*   What rule of law has thwarted O's intent? It is, of course, the famous (or infamous) Rule in Shelley's Case.[83] The rule did not bear that name in 1500: Shelley's Case was not decided until 1581.   But the rule was in existence as early as the middle of the fourteenth century, and perhaps even earlier.[84]

Let us look at Coke's classic formulation of the rule as he presented it in his argument for the defendant in Shelley's Case.[85] As we set it forth, we shall insert parenthetical comments show-

82. The words "heirs of A," if used today, would mean those persons living at A's death and entitled to share his inheritable estates under the laws of intestate succession.   In England, during the period we are discussing, "heirs of A" meant the potentially infinite succession of heirs from generation to generation.   Under primogeniture, eldest sons were the preferred inheritors from generation to generation.   Daughters took only when there was no son to take.

83. 1 Rep. 88(*b*) (1581).

84. Provost of Beverley's Case, Y.B. 40 Edw. 3, Hil. No. 18 (1366); Abel's Case, Y.B. 18 Edw. 2, 577 (1324).   See Plucknett, 564–66.

85. Coke was also, curiously enough, the court reporter for the case.

ing how the rule applies in O's transfer "to A for life, then to the heirs of A":

> It is a rule of law, when the ancestor *(A in our example)* by any gift or conveyance *(the transfer from O)* takes an estate in freehold *(the life estate)*, and in the same gift or conveyance an estate *(the remainder in fee simple in our example)* is limited mediately or immediately *(in our example,* immediately, *since no estate intervenes between the remainder and the life estate)* to his heirs in fee or in tail *(ours is in fee);* that always in such cases "the heirs" are words of limitation of the estate *(meaning the estate received by A)* and not words of purchase.

One is tempted, on reading Coke's statement of the rule, to conclude that its operation simply converts A's estate into an estate in fee simple. More modern statements of the rule make clear, however, that it operates only to give the remainder to A. It is the doctrine of merger that then converts the life estate and the remainder into a single estate in fee simple.[86] To demonstrate what this means, let us suppose that O transfers "to A for life, then to B for life, then to the heirs of A." Does the Rule in Shelley's Case operate? Yes. It simply gives the second remainder to A. Thus the transfer reads, in effect, "to A for life, then to B for life, then to A and his heirs." Does merger occur? No. The presence of the vested life estate between A's life estate and his remainder in fee prevents merger.

Would merger occur if the intervening life estate were a contingent remainder? Probably not, at least while the two estates remained in A's ownership. Generally speaking, merger does not apply to destroy a contingent remainder where the life estate and vested remainder in fee are created in the same person simultaneously. It is simply assumed that the transferor would not have created the intervening contingent remainder if he had expected it to be destroyed. Merger may occur, however, if A transfers both his estates to a third person.

Now let us examine closely the elements necessary for the Rule in Shelley's Case to apply (1) A must get a freehold estate: this could be either an estate in fee tail or an estate for life. (2) The estate that O attempts to give to the heirs must be a remainder. (3) The same instrument must create both the estate in the ancestor and the remainder. (4) The estate in the ancestor and the remainder must both be legal or both be equitable estates.

Now that we know the rule, let us try to avoid it *at law.* Why do we not violate condition (1) by giving A a determinable

---

86. In order to give a full fee, the doctrine of merger must operate along with the rule in Shelley's Case. See, e.g., 1 American Law of Property § 4.41 at 481.

estate for years instead of a freehold estate? The transfer might read, "to A for 200 years if he shall so long live, then to the heirs of A." The transfer has one fatal flaw: since the "heirs of A" are unknown, the interest that O is trying to create in them is a contingent interest. As we have just learned in our discussion of Problem 3, a legal contingent freehold remainder can never follow an estate for years—seisin does not pass to either the termor or the remainderman. Is there any way we can violate condition (2) by giving the "heirs of A" a future interest that is not a remainder? Not at law in 1500—the remainder is the only future interest that can be created in someone other than the transferor. Condition (3) may give us a chance. If we can give the estate for life to A by one instrument, then transfer O's reversion to the "heirs of A" by another, we will be in business. But to whom would we transfer the reversion? A does not *have* any heirs yet. O would have to wait for A's death to transfer the reversion to A's heirs. O could not, of course, make a present transfer to take effect in the future: the creation of legal freehold estates *in futuro* is not permitted. Rule (4) contemplates the creation of an equitable estate, so we cannot count it as a technique available at law. *Law* has failed us badly.

Let us try the Court of Chancery. First, let us see if we can violate condition (4) by giving A an equitable estate for life and the "heirs of A" a legal remainder in fee simple. O's feoffment runs as follows: "To T and his heirs *for the life of A to the use of A for life*, then to the heirs of A." T's legal estate *pur autre vie* runs only for A's life. At A's death, T's legal estate *pur autre vie* will terminate, and A's heir will take the legal estate in fee simple absolute. Since A's estate for life is equitable and the remainder to the "heirs of A" is legal, we have avoided the Rule in Shelley's Case.[87]

How about this technique: O enfeoffs "T and his heirs to the use of A for life, then to the use of the heirs of A"? Since the life estate and remainder are both equitable, the Rule in Shelley's Case applies. A, owning the entire equitable estate in fee simple, will be able to demand from T the legal estate in fee simple and transfer it as he wishes. If he does not demand the legal estate, however, O's incident-avoidance purposes may still be accomplished despite application of the Rule in Shelley's Case. Incidents attach only on the inheritance of *legal* estates. In this case, A's heirs will "inherit" only in equity.

---

87. We have found no clear evidence that feoffments to use were in fact used to avoid the Rule in Shelley's Case at this time. It seems probable that they were. See Simpson, 171 n. 1. The techniques that we demonstrate here serve the primary purpose of preparing the reader to understand avoidance techniques *after* the Statute of Uses.

A less doubtful technique might be this: <u>O enfeoffs "T and his heirs to the use of A for 200 years if he shall so long live, then to the use of the heirs of A."</u> In this case, A's equitable determinable estate for years is clearly not the equivalent of a legal freehold; so the <u>Rule in Shelley's Case cannot apply.</u> Moreover, since A's estate is not an equitable freehold, we cannot call the interest in A's "heirs" an equitable contingent remainder. Why? Because at law, from which we draw our analogy, the attempted creation of a contingent remainder following an estate for years would be ineffective from the beginning. A's "heirs," therefore, must have a springing use. From whom does it theoretically spring? From O. Since at law O would be regarded as having a present estate in fee simple subject to the determinable estate for years in A, by analogy we say that O has an equivalent "present" equitable estate in fee simple (by resulting use), subject both to an equitable determinable estate for years in A and to a springing use in fee simple in the "heirs" of A.

One final technique: O enfeoffs "T and his heirs to the use of A for life; then, <u>one day after A's death</u>, to the use of the heirs of A." A has an equitable estate for life. Do the "heirs" of A have an equitable contingent remainder? No. We cannot call it that, since it would not be a contingent remainder at law. Why not? Because according to the terms of its creation, it cannot become a present estate upon A's death. Since it is not a remainder, we have violated condition (2) and thus avoided the Rule in Shelley's Case. Does O have any equitable estate? If the transfer had been made at law, O would have a reversion in fee simple; so in equity we can label O's interest while A is living an equitable reversion in fee simple (by resulting use). What do we call O's estate for the one-day period after A is dead? By analogy to what he would have at law, we must call it a present equitable estate in fee simple, since the interest in the heirs of A would not be given effect at law. Will the interest of the heirs of A be given effect in equity? Yes. Since it will cut short O's equitable estate in fee simple, we must call the interest of the heirs of A a springing use in fee simple. Thus O's one-day present estate is an equitable estate in fee simple (by resulting use) subject to a springing use in the heirs of A in fee simple.

We shall return to the Rule in Shelley's Case in our next chapter; but lest the reader be wailing and gnashing his teeth for fear that the rule is part of the modern lawyer's daily life, we are happy to say that it has been <u>abolished by statute in a substantial majority</u> of states. Other states have rejected it by judicial decision. In the few states in which the rule still exists, it is sometimes justified on the ground that it makes land alienable at an earlier date. The notion, basically, is that if A gets the remainder, he is free to sell the property; but if the heirs get it (as they now do in most states), the property may not be sold until A is dead. Even assuming (though one should not uncritically do so) that early alienability is a desirable social policy,[88] it seems absurd to try to effectuate such a policy with a rule that may be avoided by the simplest of drafting techniques. Because the rule merely penalizes bad drafting, it is just a trap for the unwary.

Problem 5: No conditions in third persons

In Section 6 of this chapter we used the following transfer to illustrate a vested remainder subject to total defeasance: O transfers "to A for life, then to B and his heirs; *but if* B does not survive A, to C and his heirs." B's remainder was the interest that we described as vested subject to total defeasance. The reader may have noted that we were strangely silent about C's future interest. Is it a remainder? Technically, it is not. It is an executory interest. Why? Because a remainder may not divest any estate other than a reversion. Since B's future interest is a *vested* remainder potentially infinite in duration, C's interest cannot become a present estate without divesting B's estate. Remainders cannot do that.

Let us examine this notion briefly in the context of the rules of seisin existing in 1500. O wishes to transfer "to A for life; *but if* A marries B, to C for life." Are there problems with the proposed transfer? Yes. Since livery of seisin was made to A when he got his estate for life, the seisin will, as we have noted before, stay with him until his estate expires or until he *voluntarily* makes livery to another. Livery is an act of volition, the deliberate transfer of possession. To be sure, if O were to reserve a power of termination, he could, upon breach of the condition subsequent by A, declare A's estate forfeited; but this special power is reserved only to transferors. The reason for this is probably that the earliest conditions subsequent were merely expressions of the highly personal duty of loyalty each tenant owed to his transferor-lord.[89] In a sense, all feudal transfers

---

88. A critical evaluation of this policy would entail, among other things, a careful examination of the economist's notion of "efficient use" of resources. If O *willingly* gives the heirs of A the contingent remainder, does that necessarily mean that the transfer was an efficient one? Does abolition of the Rule in Shelley's Case reflect a social preference that overrides considerations of efficiency?

89. Professor Thorne uses the concept of seisin to explain the relationship be-

tween the feudal structure and the rule against giving powers of termination to third persons:

> Let us look now at a right of re-entry for default reserved on a lease for life. . . . [I]n the fourteenth century only the grantor could recover on default the seisin to which he had a claim. He had once had seisin, had given it to the life tenant, and could recover it. Writs were framed for the recovery of seisins, and if a man had once had seisin, whether by purchase or by descent, it was proper

were subject to the "condition subsequent" that the transferee not breach his pledge of fealty.   Thus, an early transfer by subinfeudation "to A and his heirs" could properly be translated to read "to A and his heirs; *but if* the tenant shall violate his pledge of loyalty, the grantor, or anyone who has succeeded to his seignory, may enter and terminate the estate granted."

From the notion that the power to declare forfeiture was a product of the personal relations of lord and vassal grew two corollary notions.   One was that the power could not be transferred by the grantor to anyone else.   As we have seen, this notion still exists in some of our states.[90]   The other was that the power could not be created in a stranger.   It is this second notion that causes O his difficulty with the proposed transfer. What O seems to want to do is to give to C the same right to enter and terminate that, according to the rules of law, he could only reserve to himself.   In short, O wants to make the condition subsequent operate in favor of a stranger.   This he cannot do.

There is, however, a simple solution for O.   He has merely to transfer "to A for life *for so long as* A is not married to B, then to C for life."   One minor difficulty with this solution is that C will definitely get an estate for life if he merely survives A.   The reason, of course, is that since A's estate for life is subject to a special limitation—that is, A's estate is one that will expire naturally *either* on A's death *or* on A's marrying B—C's estate for life becomes a vested remainder.   It does not *cut short* A's estate; it becomes a present estate whenever A's estate *expires naturally*.   Thus, if A dies next week, C will be entitled to possession even though O may not have wanted him to have it unless A in fact married B.   Another difficulty with the proposed solution, though one that O may regard as insignificant, is that A's marrying B will *automatically* bring about the expiration of A's estate.   It is possible that O hoped C might have the *choice* either to allow A's estate to continue or to cut it short. Of course, C does have that choice anyway, since he has merely to reconvey to A if he prefers that A continue in possession. Generally speaking, the use of the determinable estate for life in A seems like an adequate solution to O's problem.

But there were other problems in 1500 that did not yield to such easy solutions *at law*.   Let us take the transfer with which we started this section.   Why should O in 1500 have *wanted* to

---

that he should regain it.   But if he had never gotten it, as the assignee of a right of entry or re-entry never had, the system did not protect him.   . . .   [H]e had no former seisin on which to base his case.

Thorne, Sir Edward Coke 15 (Selden Society Lecture, 1952).

90.   See supra Section 4, notes 10–12 and accompanying text.

transfer "to A for life, then to B and his heirs; but if B does not survive A, to C and his heirs"? The answer is that O wanted to avoid the destructibility rule. He could have said "to A for life, then, if B survives A, to B and his heirs; otherwise to C and his heirs." But that would have made B's and C's remainders both contingent,[91] so that they would both have been subject to destruction by the premature termination of A's estate through forfeiture or merger. If, on the other hand, O could give B a *vested* remainder and at the same time create a condition in favor of C to operate in case B failed to survive A, neither interest would be subject to destruction. Unfortunately, O could not create a condition in favor of C; as we have seen, he could only reserve it to himself. Thus, a transfer in 1500 "to A for life, then to B and his heirs; but if B does not survive A, to C and his heirs" would have given B a vested remainder in fee simple and C nothing. If O does not want B to take unless B survives A, O must use the dangerous contingent remainder construction.

An even more obvious illustration of how O was hobbled in 1500 by his inability to create conditions in strangers was this: O would like to make an effective transfer "to A and his heirs; but if the premises are ever used for the sale of alcoholic beverages, to B and his heirs." The transfer to B will obviously be ineffective, since it is a clear example of an attempt to create a condition in a stranger. But in this case, O does not even have the alternative of the destructible contingent remainder as a device to carry out his purposes. Let us see why: O transfers "to A and his heirs *for so long as* the premises are not used for the sale of alcoholic beverages; then to B and his heirs." Does B have a remainder? No. *A remainder may not be created to follow an estate in fee simple!* The attempted transfer to B is void from the start.

At this point, we must take our usual tour through the Court of Chancery to find the solutions to O's problems. O wants to transfer "to A for life, then to B and his heirs; but if B does not survive A, to C and his heirs." He cannot make this transfer at law, and he is fearful of using contingent remainders at law. Solution? O enfeoffs "T and his heirs to the use of A for life, then to the use of B and his heirs; but if B does not survive A, to the use of C and his heirs." O's intent will be carried out fully. What interests have been created in equity? T owns the legal estate in fee simple, so the seisin remains with him throughout. A has an equitable estate for life. B has an equitable "vested" remainder in fee simple subject to C's interest. Is C's

Equity solution

91. B's remainder would be contingent on his surviving A; C's remainder would be contingent on B's not surviving A.

interest analogous to any interest at law? No. Since it could not be a remainder at law, we cannot call it a remainder in equity. C will get his estate in fee simple by reason of the shifting of B's estate in fee simple to him, so let us call C's interest in this case a *shifting use in fee simple*. Thus, the full label of B's interest is *an equitable "vested" remainder in fee simple, subject to a shifting use in C in fee simple*.

Now for our second problem: O wants to transfer "to A and his heirs; but if the premises are ever used for the sale of alcoholic beverages, to B and his heirs." He cannot do this at law. Nor can he, at law, use a remainder, since a remainder may not follow an estate in fee simple. Solution 1: O enfeoffs "T and his heirs to the use of A and his heirs; *but if* the premises are ever used for the sale of alcoholic beverages, to the use of B and his heirs." T has the legal estate in fee simple; A has an equitable estate in fee simple, subject to a shifting use in B in fee simple.[92] Solution 2: O enfeoffs "T and his heirs to the use of A and his heirs *for so long as* the premises are not used for the sale of alcoholic beverages; then to the use of B and his heirs." Obviously, A again has an equitable estate in fee simple, but what is it subject to? We still cannot call B's interest a remainder, because it is not analogous to the remainder at law. At law, a remainder cannot follow an estate in fee simple. May we call it a shifting use? When we used that label in the preceding paragraph, we applied it to an interest that *cut short* another estate. In this case, B's interest becomes a present estate only when A's estate expires naturally. About the best we can do is to call B's interest a use that takes effect at the expiration of a prior interest. Thus, the full label of A's estate is *an equitable estate in fee simple followed by a use in B in fee simple that takes effect at the expiration of A's estate upon the sale of alcoholic beverages*.[93]

---

92. We shall see in Chapter Four that the creation of this interest in B would violate the Rule Against Perpetuities.

93. B's interest here would also violate the Rule Against Perpetuities. See supra note 92.

Chapter 4

THE STATUTE OF USES AND ITS CONSEQUENCES

SECTION 1. INTRODUCTION

In the preceding chapter, we explored various ways in which transferors could use feoffments to use or bargains and sales to effect transfers that were proscribed at law. By the simple device of dividing ownership of property into *legal* ownership and *equitable* ownership, a transferor could transfer land by will, transfer freeholds without livery of seisin, avoid destructibility, create the equivalent of estates *in futuro*, avoid the Rule in Shelley's Case (and so avoid feudal incidents), make conditions subsequent operate in favor of third persons, and even create interests in third persons to follow a fee simple determinable. The transferor could also use transfers in equity to secure advantages we have not discussed: He could hide his property from his creditors, transfer it to aliens (a practice forbidden at law), and engage in many other forms of good-natured horseplay designed to flout the ancient rules of law that had held feudal society together.

A question we must leave unexplored in this book is why the Chancellor felt constrained to give effect to feoffments to uses that had such tax-avoidance and creditor-avoidance purposes. Perhaps the answer is simply that he focused his attention solely on the moral relationships between the *cestui que use* and the feoffee to uses and so never saw the real-world consequences of the feoffments to use. Perhaps he did see the consequences but thought them beyond his power to prevent.

The real-world consequence most disturbing to King Henry VIII was the depletion of his feudal revenues.[1] Because he lacked popular support in the House of Commons for alternative revenue-gathering proposals,[2] he submitted to Parliament a proposal that had the purpose of restoring to the Crown the feudal incidents lost by feoffments to uses. The proposal went to the heart of the problem: it provided that all equitable estates be converted into legal estates. The proposal was attractive to the common lawyers in the House of Commons because it promised to restore to them the lucrative practice that the practitioners

---

1. See Holdsworth at 153–55.   2. Id.

in Chancery had taken.   The landowners in Commons, who saw
that the proposal would greatly diminish their power to devise
their land,[3] were somewhat less enthusiastic.[4]   Nevertheless,
the proposal was enacted in 1535, to become effective in 1536.
It was, of course, the Statute of Uses.[5]

Let us make clear at the outset that the Statute of Uses was
not intended to abolish the concept of seisin.   On the contrary,
it was intended to restore seisin, by modifying some of its rules,
to the exalted position it had held prior to the development of
the use.   Nor did the statute abolish feoffments to use and bargains and sales.   What the statute did, *and all it did,* was to
execute all equitable estates created by feoffment to use and by
bargain and sale into legal estates.   Here are two easy illustrations of how the statute worked: (1) O enfeoffs "T and his
heirs to the use of O and his heirs."   As soon as the feoffment
is complete, O's *equitable* estate in fee simple is suddenly a *legal*
estate in fee simple.   It has been executed by the statute.   O
is left with exactly the same estate he had before he enfeoffed
T and his heirs.   (2) O bargains and sells "to A and his heirs."
No sooner is the agreement signed and sealed than A's *equitable*
estate in fee simple is executed by the statute into a *legal* estate
in fee simple.[6]

To say that the statute merely executed equitable estates into
legal estates seems to imply that we are back where we were
before the use was developed.   But note that we said the statute
executed *all* such estates.   Does that mean   . . . ?   Yes, it
means precisely that.   Those springing and shifting uses, and
that strange use that follows an expired estate in fee simple
determinable, *may all be created as valid legal estates!*   But if
they are to be executed into legal estates, we can no longer call
them "uses."   They are now *executory interests.*

Let us make one last point before we get to work examining
the consequences of the Statute of Uses.   If springing and shift-

3.   The Statute of Uses abolished all but
one form of devise: the landowner could
still, by careful drafting, create in himself
a "qualified fee" with a power to appoint
his successor by will.   See Megarry, The
Statute of Uses and the Power to Devise,
7 Cam.L.J. 354, 356 (1939).

4.   In fact, the landed gentry, far from
greeting the curtailment of their power to
devise with open arms, met it with arms
of quite a different sort: they sided with
the rebels in an uprising known as the "Pil-
grimage of Grace."   See Holdsworth at
157.   According to one scholar, the pro-

posal "was forced upon an extremely un-
willing Parliament by an extremely strong-
willed king."   Maitland, Equity 35 (1909).

5.   27 Hen. 8, c. 10 (1535).   For a general discussion of the development of the
equitable use and the subsequent enactment of the Statute of Uses, see Holdsworth at 140–75.

6.   The alert reader may have noticed
that the result of this transfer is to give A
a present estate in fee simple *without livery of seisin.*   We shall discuss this phenomenon presently.

ing uses are to be executed into springing and shifting executory interests, what will happen to the rules of seisin?   To some extent the rules will remain the same.   Thus, unless one uses the device of the bargain and sale, feoffment with livery of seisin will still generally be necessary to transfer a present freehold estate.   Moreover, freehold estates will continue to be the only estates capable of carrying the seisin.   The only changes in the rules of seisin that the statute will effect will be to permit the seisin to pass by bargain and sale, to allow it to *spring automatically* out of O, and to let it *shift* from one transferee to another, cutting short the former's estate.

Now we are ready to find out how the statute actually operates in the situations we examined in the preceding chapter.

SECTION 2.   CONVEYANCING PROBLEMS AFTER 1536

We shall take up these problems in the order in which they appear in Chapter Three.   We caution the reader to read the problems with care.

Problem 1: No transfers of land by will

Before 1536, if O wanted to dispose of his land by will, he had merely to enfeoff "T and his heirs, to the use of O and his heirs."   Having done so, he was free to instruct T how he wished the property to be disposed of after his death.   These instructions would be carried out by command of the Court of Chancery. What would happen if O made precisely the same transfer immediately after the Statute of Uses became effective?   He would discover, to his shock, that no sooner did the legal estate in fee simple get into the hands of T than it was back in his own hands again.   At the very moment in which O's equitable estate came into existence, it was executed by the Statute of Uses into a legal estate.   No matter how hard he tried, O could not get the legal title to stay with T: like Sisyphus' stone, it would always return to its starting point.

So distressed was O (and other O's like him) at the loss of his will-making power that he quickly repaired to Parliament to secure its restoration.   His demands were met in 1540 with the enactment of the Statute of Wills.[7]

After the enactment of the Statute of Wills, O could make a will without first transferring *inter vivos* to a feoffee to uses. He had merely to observe the formalities that the statute established.   Moreover, he could devise executory interests (called *executory devises* when created by will) outright; he did not have to devise them as equitable interests for the Statute of Uses to execute into legal interests.   If O wanted to make an *inter*

7.   32 Hen. 8, c. 1 (1540).

vivos transfer of an executory interest, however, he still had to create it first as an equitable estate by feoffment to uses or by bargain and sale. *Only when an* inter vivos *executory interest was so created would the Statute of Uses execute it into a valid legal estate.*[8]

Problem 2: Transfer by livery of seisin

As we have already seen, the Statute of Uses made livery of seisin unnecessary for the transfer of any interest in land. The mere execution by the parties of an agreement of bargain and sale (reciting, of course, the receipt of consideration by the transferor) was effective to transfer the legal estate. The theory was that the bargain and sale still created an equitable estate in the transferee; the Statute of Uses merely executed it into a legal estate at the moment of its creation.

But there was a rub. Anticipating the broad use of the bargain and sale that would follow enactment of the Statute of Uses, and fearful that transfer by bargain and sale would permit secret transfers, Parliament passed a companion statute called the Statute of Enrollments.[9] This statute made bargains and sales of present *freehold estates* invalid unless they were recorded in one of the King's Courts of Record. Recordation also required the payment of a tax.

The common lawyer of 1536 regarded the Statute of Enrollments as just another challenge to his ingenuity; and before long he had come up with a solution. It employed the old lease and release, but with one improvement. Here is the way it worked. O, wishing to transfer his estate in fee simple to A, would *bargain and sell* "to A for one year." This transfer created an equitable estate for one year in A, which, of course, the Statute of Uses executed into a legal estate. The bargain and sale did not have to be recorded, since it did not transfer an estate in freehold. After the Statute of Uses had executed the equitable estate into a legal estate, O had merely to *release* his remaining interest to A. The common-law doctrine of merger did the rest. How was this an improvement over the old lease and release? Since the Statute of Uses *automatically* made A's estate for one year a legal estate, A did not have to enter the land to get legal title.

Problem 3: Destructibility of contingent remainders

When we discussed the destructibility rule as it existed before the Statute of Uses, our classic problem was this: O wishes to

8. Although most jurisdictions accept the Statute of Uses today as a common-law rule, the transferor no longer has to create an equitable estate to be executed into a legal executory interest. He can simply create the executory interest outright, either by *inter vivos* transfer or by will.

9. 27 Hen. 8, c. 16 (1535).

transfer "to A for life; then, if B ever reaches 21, to B and his heirs." O wants B to have the estate even if B reaches 21 after A's death. If O uses purely legal estates to accomplish his aim, he runs the risk that B's contingent remainder will be destroyed if B is only 19 at A's death. And if A's life estate terminates by forfeiture or merger prior to B's reaching 21, B's contingent remainder will be destroyed even if B later reaches 21 before A's death.

The solution prior to 1536 was for O to enfeoff "T and his heirs to the use of A for life; then, if B ever reaches 21, to the use of B and his heirs." As soon as T was enfeoffed, the following interests existed: (1) a *legal* estate in fee simple in T; (2) an equitable estate for life in A; (3) *until A's death*, an equitable contingent remainder in B in fee simple absolute; and (4) *until A's death*, an equitable reversion in fee simple absolute by resulting use in O. Note that up to this point, the interests are precisely the same as those that would have been created had the transfer been made at law. They are simply *enforceable* in equity. Thus, if B died before A and before reaching 21, O would be entitled to possession on A's death just as he would have been at law. The only (and crucial) difference between law and equity came when B was still alive and under 21 at the expiration or termination of A's estate. *At that point*, the labels applied to O's and B's interests changed in equity because they were no longer analogous to legal interests. Thus, B's interest became a *springing use* in fee simple to indicate that if he got possession it would have to *spring* out of O. O's interest, no longer the equivalent of a legal estate in fee simple *absolute*, became a present equitable estate in fee simple by *resulting use*, subject to a *springing use* in B in fee simple. To sum up the whole business, *equity preserved B's contingent remainder from destruction by converting it into a springing use.*

What happens after the Statute of Uses if O enfeoffs "T and his heirs to the use of A for life; then, if B ever reaches 21, to the use of B and his heirs"? All the equitable estates that come into existence *at the moment the transfer is made* are promptly executed into legal estates. T's legal title is gone as soon as he gets it. A has a legal estate for life; he has the seisin. B has a legal contingent remainder in fee simple. O has a legal reversion in fee simple. Now for the real test: if A dies while B is 19, will B's contingent remainder be preserved by being converted into a legal springing executory interest?

Surprisingly enough, *it will not be preserved!* Is this because executory interests are as destructible as contingent remainders? No—they are indestructible. Then why? *Because the courts so decided.* The rule that they announced to produce this result was that if a future interest was so created that it might *under any circumstances* take effect as a remainder, then it would *always* be regarded as a remainder.   It would never be converted into an executory interest.   Thus, since B *could have* reached 21 by A's death, and, consequently, *could have* taken by way of remainder, his interest came within the rule.   Although the rule apparently was applied as early as the sixteenth century, it would ultimately take its name from the 1670 case Purefoy v. Rogers,[10] which gave the doctrine its clearest expression.

The obvious way to avoid the rule of Purefoy v. Rogers is to see to it that the contingent future interest one wishes to create cannot under any circumstances take effect as a remainder.   In other words, the contingent interest must be created so that it can take effect *only as an executory interest*.   Let us recast O's transfer to make sure that B's future interest cannot take effect as a remainder.

The reader will recall that a remainder must be capable of taking the seisin immediately upon, but no sooner than, the natural expiration of all prior particular estates created simultaneously with it.[11]   In order to make sure that B's interest cannot take effect as a remainder, we must create it in such a way that it fails to meet this definitional requirement.   Here is one possible solution: O enfeoffs "T and his heirs to the use of A for life;   then, if B ever reaches 21, to the use of B and his heirs *no sooner than one day after A's death.*"   What *legal* estates come into being by operation of the Statute of Uses?   Let us go at this slowly and carefully, for if we understand this transfer we will have few problems from here on in.   As we commence our analysis, we must bear in mind that one effect the Statute of Uses will have on this transfer will be to bring T's legal estate to an end as soon as it is created.   The moment T gets the seisin from O, he will lose it.   But where will the seisin go?   It must be in someone, since someone must always be seised.   A is the obvious candidate.   The feoffment to T gave A a momentary equitable estate for life that the Statute of Uses immediately executed into a legal estate for life.   Since a present legal estate for life is capable of carrying the seisin, we have no difficulty in concluding that A is seised.

Now that we have found a temporary home for the seisin, we must wonder where it will go when A's legal estate ends.   Let us suppose that B has already reached 21 by the time of A's death.   May the seisin pass to B?   No.   The reason, of course,

---

10.   2 Wms. Saunders 380 (1670).

11.   If the reader should, by some unhappy mischance, fail to recall the relationship between the definition of a remainder and the rules of seisin, we would advise him to review the text accompanying note 70 in Chapter Three.

is that O specified in his transfer to T that B could not get possession sooner than one day after A's death.   Since B cannot take the seisin *immediately* upon A's death, it is clear that B's future interest cannot be a remainder.   B's interest must be an executory interest; we have avoided the rule of Purefoy v. Rogers.

But where *does* the seisin go upon A's death?   The only person available to take the seisin is O.   In order to get to B, the seisin will have to *spring out* of O.   If B is 21 by the time of A's death, the seisin will spring out of O to B one day after A's death.   If B is alive, but not yet 21, at A's death, the seisin will spring out of O to B whenever B does reach 21.   If B never reaches 21, the seisin will stay with O.   Shall we give labels to the legal estates created in A, B, and O by operation of the Statute of Uses?   A has a legal life estate.   O has a *legal reversion in fee simple subject to a springing executory interest in B in fee simple*.   B has a *legal springing executory interest in fee simple* to take effect no sooner than one day after A's death.

O could also avoid the rule of Purefoy v. Rogers by enfeoffing "T and his heirs to the use of A for 200 years if he shall so long live; then, if B ever reaches 21, to the use of B and his heirs." Again, the aim of O's transfer is to give B a future interest that cannot take effect as a contingent remainder.   The transfer to T gives A a momentary *equitable* determinable estate for years, which the Statute of Uses immediately executes into a *legal determinable estate for years*.   Since A does not have a freehold estate, he cannot be seised.   Can A at least hold the seisin for B?   No.   B's future interest is a contingent one, so the termor cannot hold the seisin for him.[12]   The only person left who can take the seisin from T is O.   Since B may never reach 21, O's estate may go on forever.   This means O must have some kind of estate in fee simple.   A remainder may not follow an estate in fee simple, so B's interest cannot be a remainder; once again, O has avoided the rule in Purefoy v. Rogers.   What are the names of O's and B's legal estates in this transfer?   O, by reason of being seised, is said to have a "present" estate despite the occupancy of the termor.[13]   O's estate is called a *"present" estate in fee simple, subject both to a determinable estate for years in A and to a springing executory interest in B in fee simple*.

Remember our problem in which O wanted to give an estate for five years to A, then the estate in fee simple to the heirs of B (a living person)?   Although we did not put O through the

---

12. See supra Chapter Three, note 81 and accompanying text.

13. We note again that we are using quotation marks around "present" as our own mnemonic device—to remind us that O, though seised, is not in physical occupancy of the property.

exercise, he could have accomplished his purpose by enfeoffing "T and his heirs to the use of A for five years, then to the use of the heirs of B." This transfer will also work under the Statute of Uses. A's equitable estate for years is executed into a legal estate for years. Since the seisin cannot be in the termor, it must be in O. O has a "present" estate in fee simple subject to an estate for years in A. The freehold interest of B's prospective heirs is contingent (B's "heirs" cannot be identified until B is dead), so it can never take effect as a remainder: a contingent freehold remainder can never follow an estate for years. So B must have a springing executory interest.[14] The full name of O's interest is a *"present" estate in fee simple, subject both to an estate for years in A and to a springing executory interest in the "heirs" of B.*

What is Purefoy's effect on modern American law? As we observed earlier,[15] the rule of destructibility of contingent remainders has been abolished in all but a few states. Since the Statute of Uses is recognized as a common-law rule in this country, it is possible to use the executory interest to avoid destructibility in the few states that still recognize the doctrine. In those states, it seems possible that Purefoy must still be overcome either by using one of the techniques we have already suggested or, as is more likely to be the case, by using the modern trust device, which we shall be discussing in Section 5 of this chapter and in Part II. As we observed of the Rule in Shelley's Case, the destructibility rule, though possibly supportable by sound policy argument,[16] operates today only to penalize the transferor whose lawyer is not alert to its perils. Anti-destructibility statutes were enacted to protect transferors whose lawyers fail to use, or do not know how to use, executory interests instead of contingent remainders.[17] In a sense, anti-destructibility statutes simply overrule Purefoy v. Rogers for the convenience of conveyancers.

14. Since our discussion of destructibility has once again taken us into springing interests, let us look briefly at the old rule against creating legal freehold estates *in futuro*, a rule that we formerly avoided with a springing use. In our example, O wants to transfer his estate in fee simple "to A and his heirs when A marries B." In equity, he accomplished his purpose by enfeoffing "T and his heirs to the use of A and his heirs when A marries B." What will the Statute of Uses do to the transfer? It will give A a springing executory interest to take effect upon his marrying B. O will keep his estate in fee simple, but it will be subject to the springing executory interest in A. It's as simple as that.

15. See supra Chapter Three, note 46.

16. If, for example, a remainder is contingent because the takers are not identifiable, the destruction of the remainder on the termination of the particular estate will permit earlier alienation of the estate in fee simple. On the other hand, a transfer that results in inalienability of land for a period of time may be perfectly "efficient."

17. Is there any difference between an executory interest and a contingent remainder that is saved from destruction by an anti-destructibility statute? None whatsoever. See Restatement, Property § 240, comment *e* (1936).

Problem 4: The Rule in Shelley's Case

Our discussion of Purefoy v. Rogers in the preceding section also illustrates how transferors could avoid the Rule in Shelley's Case after enactment of the Statute of Uses. The idea, fundamentally, is to make sure that the future interest created in the heirs of A is not a remainder. Thus, if O enfeoffs "T and his heirs to the use of A for 200 years if he shall so long live, then to the use of the heirs of A," the operation of the Statute of Uses will create a springing executory interest in the prospective heirs of A. Why? Note, first, that the prospective heirs' interest is contingent owing to the fact that we do not know who the heirs will be. Their interest could not be a contingent remainder at law, since it followed an estate for years. The seisin, therefore, remains in O. When A's determinable estate for years expires at his death, the seisin will spring from O to the heirs of A. O has from the moment of transfer a *"present" estate in fee simple, subject both to a determinable estate for years in A and to a springing executory interest in the prospective heirs of A in fee simple.*

Similarly, if O enfeoffs "T and his heirs to the use of A for life, then one day thereafter to the use of the heirs of A," it will be impossible for the prospective heirs' future interest to take effect as a remainder. The Statute of Uses will execute A's estate into a legal estate for life. O's equitable reversion, which would have been a reversion in fee simple absolute *at law* prior to the Statute of Uses, is now a reversion in fee simple, subject to a springing executory interest in the heirs of A to take effect one day after A's death. (The idea the reader must try to get is that the operation of the Statute of Uses puts everybody back precisely where they would have been had the transfer been attempted *at law* prior to its enactment—with the one crucial exception that future interests that would have been nullities then, because they violated the rules of seisin, are now given effect. Had O, before enactment of the Statute of Uses, transferred *at law* "to A for life, then one day thereafter to the heirs of A," the heirs would have gotten nothing, and O, at A's death, would have had a present estate in fee simple absolute. That is why we call his estate here an estate in fee simple even though it will last for only one day.)

In Chapter Three we used this technique to avoid the Rule in Shelley's Case: O enfeoffs "T and his heirs *for the life of A* to the use of A for life, then to the heirs of A." The idea was to give an *equitable* estate for life to A and a *legal* remainder to his heirs. Would it work after the Statute of Uses? Possibly not, since the equitable estate in A would be immediately executed into a legal estate for life. That would make both the life estate and the remainder legal estates; hence, the rule might operate. But might it not be argued that for an instant in time A's estate for life *was* equitable—i.e., that measureless moment in which T got and lost the *legal* estate *pur autre vie?* Would we not be in a sorry state if cases were won and lost on arguments like that?

Problem 5: No conditions in third persons

O wishes to make an effective transfer "to A for life, then to B and his heirs; *but if* B does not survive A, to C and his heirs." O could not do this *at law* prior to the enactment of the Statute of Uses because he could not create a condition in a stranger. His only choice *at law* was to give B and C alternative contingent remainders, both of which might be destroyed by premature termination of A's life estate.   Can O, after the Statute of Uses, give B a vested remainder subject to a condition subsequent [18] operating in C's favor?   He can.   O enfeoffs "T and his heirs to the use of A for life; then to the use of B and his heirs; but if B does not survive A, to the use of C and his heirs."   What legal estates do the parties have by operation of the Statute of Uses?   A has his old estate for life.   Under the old law, we would say that B had a vested remainder in fee simple *absolute*, because the attempted transfer to C would be a nullity as an unlawful condition in a stranger.   Now, however, C's interest will be allowed to take effect by cutting short B's vested remainder in fee simple.   B's estate in fee simple will simply *shift* automatically to C if B does not survive A.   Hence, C's interest is a *shifting executory interest* in fee simple absolute.   B's vested remainder must, therefore, be called a *vested remainder in fee simple, subject to a shifting executory interest in C in fee simple absolute.*

Here is another example: O wishes to make an effective transfer "to A and his heirs; but if the premises are ever used for the sale of alcoholic beverages to B and his heirs."   He could not do this *at law* in 1500 because the transfer to B would be regarded as an unlawful condition in a stranger.   Can he do it in 1537?   Yes.   O enfeoffs "T and his heirs to the use of A and his heirs; but if the premises are ever used for the sale of alcoholic beverages, to the use of B and his heirs."   A has a legal *present estate in fee simple, subject to a shifting executory interest in B in fee simple absolute.*   (Today, owing to the Rule

---

18. As we noted earlier, the Restatement of Property limits use of the term "condition subsequent" to language in a conveyance that creates a power of termination in the conveyor.   Restatement, Property § 24 (1936).   We do not so limit it in this book.   The Restatement terms language in a conveyance that creates any kind of executory interest an "executory limitation."   Restatement, Property § 25 (1936).

Against Perpetuities, which we will be considering in section 4 of this chapter, B's interest would fail from the outset.)

Before leaving the shifting executory interest, we must make a final point about it. When we set forth to discuss the possibility of O's creating in 1500 a "condition in a stranger," we imagined that he wished to give to the stranger an interest equivalent to the power of termination that he could retain for himself by transferring subject to a condition subsequent. Is a shifting executory interest a *power of termination created in a stranger?* Conceptually, it is not. When the stated event occurs in the case of a shifting executory interest, the owner of the executory interest *automatically* becomes entitled to possession.[19] If the reader prefers the more common vocabulary, *title* shifts automatically. Despite the automatic shifting of the right to possession, the terminated estate is not thought to *expire*. It is divested or cut short.

One last example: In 1537, O enfeoffs "T and his heirs to the use of A and his heirs *for so long as* the premises are not used for the sale of alcoholic beverages; then to the use of B and his heirs." What legal interests have been created? A's estate is plainly an estate in fee simple determinable. Since B will take only upon the *expiration* of A's estate, B's interest looks like a remainder; but since a remainder cannot follow any estate in fee simple, it cannot be that. It also looks like a possibility of reverter, but we know that such an interest may not be created in a third person. Since it is *not* a remainder, it must be an executory interest. Yet, since it does not cut short A's estate, we cannot call it a shifting executory interest. We are led to call it an executory interest that takes effect upon the expiration of a prior estate. What shall we call A's interest? The "for-so-long-as" language constitutes the special limitation that makes A's estate determinable, but the "then-to-the-use-of-B-and-his-heirs" language constitutes an executory limitation.[20] The full name of A's estate, therefore, is an *estate in fee simple with an executory limitation creating an interest which takes effect at the expiration of a prior interest.* And where have we heard of that before?[21] (Owing to the Rule Against Perpetuities, which we will be examining in section 4 of this chapter, B's interest would fail at the outset.)

---

19. As we noted when we looked at the possibility of reverter, one who "automatically" gets the right to possession will probably have to take precisely the same steps to assert it as must be taken in the case of the "non-automatic" power of termination.

20. As indicated before, the Restatement applies the term "executory limitation" to words creating any executory interest. See note 18 supra.

21. See Chapter Two, note 84 supra, and accompanying text.

SECTION 3. SUMMARY OF THE STATUTE OF USES; THE MODERN EXECUTORY INTEREST

Let us here briefly review what the Statute of Uses accomplished. When we have done so, we shall attempt to place the executory interest in its modern context.

One of its major contributions was its simplification of land transfer. Although it did not bar feoffment with livery of seisin, after its enactment transfer by bargain and sale became the standard way of conveying legal freehold estates. The agreement of bargain and sale, which had, before the statute, left legal title in the transferor and equitable title in the transferee, became in all respects a deed. In the United States today, deeds often contain the ancient formula of bargain and sale as part of the language of transfer. It is, of course, the execution and delivery of the modern deed that constitute the operative elements of transfer—not the Statute of Uses. By its negative influence, the Statute of Uses can also be said to have brought about the legal recognition of testamentary transfer of interests in land. By severely curtailing the power of testamentary disposition that the landowners had been enjoying in Chancery, the Statute of Uses unquestionably accelerated the enactment of the Statute of Wills. In a very real sense, the two statutes may be viewed as companion pieces of legislation.

The most important changes in the law of future interests that the Statute of Uses wrought may be summarized in one sentence. It authorized the creation of legal future interests in transferees that had the capability (theretofore reserved exclusively to the power of termination and, in a restricted sense, the contingent remainder) to divest or cut short vested estates in others. The *springing* executory interest or devise is always a future estate created in a transferee that will, if it vests in possession, divest a present estate in the person who created the executory interest or his successor. (For the purposes of this chapter, we have been treating freehold estates subject to estates for years as "present" estates.)

The *shifting* executory interest or devise is always a future interest created in a transferee that will, if it "vests," divest or cut short a vested estate in a transferee created simultaneously with it. The estate so divested may be either a present estate or a future estate. Thus, if a testator devises "to A for life, then to B and his heirs; but if B dies without issue surviving, to C and his heirs," the shifting executory devise in C will divest B's vested estate whether B's death without issue occurs before or after A's death.

Executory interests may be created today without the necessity of first creating equitable springing or shifting uses to be executed by the Statute of Uses. Thus a transfer today by modern deed "to A for 200 years, if he shall so long live, then to the heirs of A," will create in the heirs of A a springing executory interest.[22] Similarly, O may, by modern deed, transfer "to A and his heirs, but if A dies without issue surviving, to B and his heirs," thereby creating a shifting executory interest in B.

A serious question may be raised at this point whether, in view of the fact that the destructibility doctrine and the Rule in Shelley's Case have been abolished in nearly all states, the conceptual distinction between the executory interest and the remainder is justified. What difference does it make whether an interest is a remainder or an executory interest? Does *calling* an interest a remainder imply that a different set of consequences will flow from that which would flow if the interest were *called* an executory interest? Surely, there is no consequential difference today, at least in states that have abolished destructibility, between these two transfers: (a) "to A for life, then if B survives A, to B and his heirs; otherwise to C and his heirs," and (b) "to A for life, then to B and his heirs; but if B does not survive A, to C and his heirs." And would it matter to the prospective heirs of A in a state that had abolished the Rule in Shelley's Case that they got their future interest by a conveyance "to A for life, then to the heirs of A" rather than by a conveyance "to A for 200 years if he shall so long live, then to the heirs of A"? We should suppose it would not.[23]

As a matter of fact, if we ran down a checklist of characteristics of remainders and executory interests, we would find them practically identical. May remainders be transferred? Yes, and so may executory interests. May remainders be devised? Yes, if they are generally inheritable. The same is true of ex-

22. The Restatement of Property appears to call a contingent freehold future interest that follows an estate for years a contingent remainder. See Restatement, Property § 156, comment *e* (1936). That could be troubling to a conveyancer today who wanted to use a determinable estate for years to avoid the Rule in Shelley's Case or the destructibility rule. What is puzzling is the fact that the Restatement calls an "executory interest" any legal future interest that became possible as a result of the Statutes of Uses and Wills. Id. § 158, comment *c*. The contingent freehold estate following an estate for years *is* a legal estate that became possible as a result of the Statutes of Uses and Wills.

23. It *might* matter to persons *other* than the prospective heirs of A. Assume that O, in a state that has *not* abolished the rule, avoids the rule by conveying "to A for 200 years if he shall so long live, then to the heirs of A." Might a court find that O had become A's landlord? Might a court conclude that O is legally responsible for the payment of real estate taxes during A's life? About all one can say is that one wonders whether consequences like those should result from a mere attempt to avoid the Rule in Shelley's Case.

ecutory interests. May remainders be inherited? Yes, if not measured by decedent's life. That is also true of the executory interest. Are remainders more vulnerable to the Rule Against Perpetuities than executory interests, or is the reverse the case? Generally speaking, the same standards apply to both interests. (We shall discuss this point briefly in our next section and more thoroughly in Part II.) Are owners of executory interests entitled to less or more protection of their possible future possession than owners of remainders? The amount of protection that each receives will depend on the same test: the likelihood or unlikelihood of his getting possession.

But if executory interests and remainders are pretty much the same today, what can possibly justify our having gone through that painful label-making session from which we have just emerged? The purpose of the label-making was not to equip the reader with the workaday vocabulary of the practicing lawyer. If a typical practicing lawyer today were asked to give a precise definition of a springing or shifting executory interest, he would probably only cough and stammer. The reason, of course, is that he has probably not heard those labels mentioned since he left law school. This does not mean that executory interests are not being used today to transmit wealth from generation to generation. They are, in fact, used fairly frequently. What it means is that their *labels* have become functionless.

But why do the law schools still bother with the labels? Why do we bother with them here? One reason, though not our chief one, is that in a few states the distinction between executory interests and remainders is still relevant in practice. Another reason, though still not our main one, is that the reader may be asked to study cases (usually older ones) that use the labels without defining their meaning. But our chief reason for going through the label-making session was to make visible the process through which the executory interest became woven into the syntax of our law of future interests. In a sixteenth-century world that took its definitions and labels seriously, springing and shifting executory interests could be used to do a host of things that remainders could not do. To work, of course, they had to be distinguished from remainders. That distinguishing process resulted in the construction of an elaborate conceptual structure that is almost totally functionless today. How do we define an executory interest? It is a future interest created in a transferee *that is not a remainder.* And what *difference* does it make today whether a future interest is a remainder or an executory interest? So little that one must wonder whether such a definition ought to be part of the stuff of modern law.

SECTION 4. THE STATUTE OF USES AND THE RULE AGAINST PERPETUITIES

The reader is invited, at this point, to re-examine two transfers that we imagined O making in 1537. In one, O enfeoffed "T and his heirs to the use of A and his heirs; but if the premises are ever used for the sale of alcoholic beverages, to the use of B and his heirs." In the other, O accomplished the same purposes by enfeoffing "T and his heirs to the use of A and his heirs for so long as the premises are not used for the sale of alcoholic beverages; then to the use of B and his heirs." The first transfer gave B a shifting executory interest, and the second gave B an executory interest that takes effect on the expiration of a prior estate.

What should be apparent from these transfers is that the Statute of Uses gave to landowners enormous power to control the use of land literally for centuries into the future. The contingent remainder, by reason of its destructibility, was not quite as powerful a device. By an arranged merger, a life tenant and a reversioner could easily destroy the contingent remainder and thereby create a transferable estate in fee simple absolute. But the executory interest was not similarly destructible. Thus, by the careful use of executory interests or devises, a transferor could direct the use of land practically for all time.

Early efforts to curb this power proved ineffective; but in 1681, the famous Duke of Norfolk's Case[24] laid down the outlines of what is today called the *Rule Against Perpetuities*. The rule is far too complex to yield its contents in one neat paragraph. Even the famous "nutshell" into which Professor Leach squeezed the rule ran some 33 pages in length.[25] But for our purposes here, it may suffice to say that the rule makes *void* any *"contingent"* interest *created in a transferee that, viewed from the moment of its creation,* is not *certain* to *"vest"* within the life of a *person living* at the time the interest is *created, plus* 21 years.

The quotation marks around the word "vests" are intended to imply that the word performs a different *function* from that which we have heretofore discussed. The concept of vestedness or non-vestedness of an interest has, up to this point, taken its meaning *solely* from the doctrine of destructibility. That doctrine, as we have seen, related to matters of seisin that are no longer significant in modern law. One would expect, therefore, that the use of the concept of vestedness in a rule that performs the *function* of preventing dead-hand control of property over time might import a different meaning. Sadly, it does not. A

---

24. 3 Ch.Cas. 1 (1681).

25. Leach, Perpetuities in a Nutshell, 51 Harv.L.Rev. 638 (1938).

"vested interest" under the Rule Against Perpetuities is almost precisely what a "vested interest" is under the doctrine of destructibility—that is, an interest that is subject to no condition precedent other than the expiration of estates prior to it in possession and the takers of which are identifiable. Thus, we are sometimes treated to the spectacle of interests being declared void by the Rule Against Perpetuities that are *factually* more certain of becoming present estates than interests that the rule leaves untouched. It is sometimes said that *all* executory interests are deemed "contingent" at the time of their creation. On its face alone, the proposition seems absurd; but we shall leave that discussion to Part II.

Why do our transfers above violate the rule? Simply because there is no certainty that a sale of alcoholic beverages will take place no later than 21 years after the death of a person living at the time the interests were sought to be created. Thus, the attempted transfers to B are void from the moment of their creation. Why don't we wait and see whether such a sale occurs within that period, and then make our decision about the validity of the interests? We shall direct our attention to that question in Part II as well.

SECTION 5. THE MODERN TRUST

In Part II of this book, which covers materials usually reserved for second-year and third-year study at law school, the transfers that will be discussed will often be to trustees who will hold "legal" title to the property—usually cash and corporate securities—for the benefit of others who hold beneficial or "equitable" title. There can be no doubt that the modern law of future interests concerns itself almost exclusively with property in trust. When the reader gets to Part II, which he may wish to defer until it is appropriate to his studies, he will discover that the property with which he is concerned is not likely to be real property. It will more often consist of cash and corporate securities placed in the hands of banks and trust companies for expert administration and investment. Thus, he will not be so much concerned with what happens to Blackacre as with what happens to a *changing fund* in the hands of its professional managers. Because trustees uniformly are given power, within certain limits, to invest and re-invest the assets that comprise the *corpus* of the trust, the problem of alienability is usually not present. What replaces alienability as the focus of social inquiry is the problem of control of the *use* of wealth over time. Although trusts are often created by *inter vivos* transfer, many of the examples used in Part II will involve testamentary transfers.

This too may bring into focus problems that we have avoided in Part I.

We shall say no more of the trust here except to answer a question that may have occurred to the reader during his study of the Statute of Uses. If the Statute of Uses is accepted as a common-law rule of law (it generally is), how can a trust be created today? Why is not a trust created today executed into a legal estate in the hands of its beneficiaries? The actual answer is that society wanted trusts, and got them. But as a footnote to our discussion of the Statute of Uses, we will mention that ways were quickly discovered, after its enactment, to leave legal title in the trustee despite the act. One way was to create a use-on-a-use. O would *bargain and sell* (use number one) to "T and his heirs *for the use of* (use number 2) A for life, etc." The Statute of Uses executed *only the first use*. Thus, legal title moved to T, but did *not* then move to A and the other beneficiaries. The second use was left unexecuted. Hence, the beneficiaries had precisely the same equitable estates they would have had by enfeoffment to uses before enactment of the Statute. Shortly after the Statute's enactment, it was also decided that so-called "active trusts"—i.e., those requiring T to perform affirmative management duties with respect to the property—were not executed by the statute. A third device was simply to transfer personal property, instead of real property, to T. The Statute had no application to such property.

SECTION 6. THE DOCTRINE OF THE WORTHIER TITLE

It has not seemed to us useful to jigsaw this doctrine into our earlier discussion; so we are left with it to discuss now. We shall be brief.

O makes an *inter vivos* transfer "to A for life, then to the heirs of O." What are the consequences today? We should probably expect that A would get an estate for life and the heirs of O a contingent remainder (contingent because they are not yet identified) in fee simple absolute. That may, in fact, be the result in most jurisdictions. But it is possible, *given those words alone*, that a modern court will construe the transfer as giving *no interest whatsoever to the heirs*. If a court so construes the transfer, O will obviously be left with a reversion in fee simple absolute. It may be that his heirs will later get the reversion if O does not transfer it to others either *inter vivos* or by will; but they will have no right to it by reason of being remaindermen. O can do with his reversion what he wants.

The construction of O's transfer so as to create a reversion in O and no interest in his heirs would result from an application of the *Doctrine of the Worthier Title*.   The doctrine is clearly feudal in origin.   Its function during the feudal period was probably to prevent a transferor from making his *own heirs* "purchasers," thereby freeing them from the burdens of the feudal incidents.   After enactment of the Statute of Wills, the doctrine was also applied to cases where one received by will the same quality and quantity of estate that one would have received had one taken as an heir.   Here again, it seems reasonable to suppose that the purpose of the doctrine was to assure mesne lords that they would not be denied the benefits of the incidents by the simple expedient of a tenant's making his own heirs "purchasers" by devise.   In its application to transfers by will, it did not deprive the devisees of the property.   They kept the property, but were simply treated as though they had received it by inheritance.

The application of the doctrine to transfers by will—the so-called testamentary branch of the doctrine—is wholly irrelevant today.   Even if it applied, it would usually produce no consequences worth mentioning.   Heirs and devisees are treated pretty much alike.   But the *inter vivos* branch was given new life in American law by a 1919 decision of Judge Cardozo in the case of Doctor v. Hughes.[26]   In applying the doctrine, Cardozo made clear that it no longer *prohibits* a transferor from creating a valid remainder in his heirs;   it simply requires that his intent to do so be "clearly expressed."   Thus, under Doctor v. Hughes, the doctrine emerges not as a fixed rule of law, but as a constructional preference.   It has also been applied to transfers of personal property.   The reader should note that the doctrine differs from the Rule in Shelley's Case in that the latter applies only to a remainder given to the *life tenant's* heirs.   The Doctrine of the Worthier Title applies only to transfers to the *transferor's* heirs. They were probably both intended originally to prevent incident-avoidance.

---

26.   225 N.Y. 305, 122 N.E. 221 (1919). The *inter vivos* branch serves to further early alienability of land.   O's heirs, being unascertained, cannot transfer their future interest; but O can.

*

Part II

FUTURE INTERESTS: PROBLEMS IN
THE MODERN LAW

INTRODUCTION

The future interest originated as a legal interest in land. Except for reversionary interests under leases, the legal future interest in land is infrequently created today. The lease, of course, is a commercial relationship. Our focus is upon the donative disposition of wealth in which today the future interest is usually an equitable interest under a trust. The property held in trust may be land, but it is more often debt and equity securities, i.e., bonds, stocks, certificates of deposit, because accumulated wealth today is more often held in those forms than in the form of land. This is reflective of the change from a predominantly agrarian economy to an industrial and service economy.

A person who owns land may attempt to control the benefit of that wealth for an extended period of time after his death by the use of the future interest. He could convey the land to A for life, remainder to A's children in fee. This, of course, would create legal present and future interests. This form of divided ownership presents problems with respect to the competent management of the land, its sale if this becomes advisable, and disposition of the proceeds of such sale. The donor's objectives in these respects can be more effectively accomplished by placing the land in trust with a bank or an individual as trustee for the benefit of A for life, with remainder in fee in A's children, as explained in the succeeding paragraphs.

Legal future interests are virtually never created in personal property. Except for certain forms of personal property described as "consumables," legal future interests can be created in personal property. Obviously a legal future interest in a sweater or a football would not be meaningful, since the chattel is bound to be consumed in a short period of time. But there is no reason why a legal future interest cannot be created in personal property which is not consumable in this manner. Legal present and future interests can be created certainly in 100 shares of General Motors common stock—the stock may be held in the names of A for life, remainder to B in fee. But to split

121

ownership in securities in this way creates serious problems. Securities are the subject of frequent trading. In order to sell the complete title (there is no market for anything less), the consent of both A and B will be necessary. In addition, assuming both are willing to sell, there is a problem of valuing the present and future interests in order to allocate the proceeds of the sale. If the proceeds are distributed outright to A and B in the proportion agreed upon, the donor's objective of control of the benefit of the wealth over a period of time is defeated. These matters may be further complicated by the fact that some of the owners of legal present and future interests may be minors, and some of the remaindermen may be unborn.

The goal of control of the benefit of property over an extended period of time is better served by the creation of a trust in which the trustee, skilled in investment management, holds full legal title to the land or securities, with the power of sale over the entire property interest, legal and equitable, and pays the income to A for life, and upon A's death, pays the principal of the trust to B. The trustee holds the legal fee interest; the beneficial or equitable interests are held by A, life income beneficiary, and B, remainderman in fee.

The modern trust almost invariably provides that the trustee has the power to sell and reinvest. Consequently, the property in which A and B have beneficial or equitable interests is a fund whose components change from time to time. The equitable interests of the life income beneficiary and the remainderman attach to the individual property components which comprise the corpus or principal of the trust at any one time; when a share of stock is sold by the trustee, the equitable life and remainder interests attach to the proceeds, and then attach to the securities purchased with the proceeds. The legal fee title of the trustee, of course, attaches as well. The donor's objective of controlling the benefit of the wealth for an extended period can be accomplished more effectively and with greater certainty of result by use of the trust than by use of legal present and future interests.

The vocabulary, definitions and classifications of the historical land law have been applied to the modern equitable future interest in securities. Many of the land law rules have been applied to such modern equitable interests. Property law is history-bound, and its adaptation to current needs and circumstances sometimes seems to take place at a glacial rate. Reverence for history and tradition is nowhere more apparent than in the field of property law.

Chapter 5

CONDITIONS OF SURVIVORSHIP

The question of whether an individual named in a dispositive instrument must survive to a particular time in order to be entitled to take is frequently encountered in the law of future interests. This chapter discusses several important problem areas.

SECTION 1. LAPSE

Let us assume that testator bequeaths $1000 to A. If A was alive at the time the will was executed but predeceased the testator, the bequest to A is said to lapse.[1] This means that the bequest to A is invalid, and the property passes as if there were no bequest to A in the will. The $1000 passes to the residuary legatees in the will, assuming there is a residuary clause, and if not, it passes to the intestate takers. The conceptual explanation for the principle of lapse is that the will is effective as of the date of the testator's death, and the gift cannot be made to one who is not alive to receive it. We shall see, however, in the next section that statutes have been enacted in most jurisdictions which provide for substitutional gifts under certain circumstances in the event of lapse.

The question of lapse may arise in connection with the apparent simultaneous death of the testator and a legatee in an accident. Under the Uniform Simultaneous Death Act, which has been enacted in most states, if there is no sufficient evidence that the testator and the legatee or devisee have died otherwise than simultaneously, the legatee or devisee is treated as having predeceased the testator, unless the will provides otherwise.[2] Uniform Probate Code § 2–601 goes beyond simultaneous death to provide that a legatee or devisee who does not survive the testator for 120 hours is treated as if he predeceased the testator, unless the will provides otherwise. The Uniform Probate Code has been legislated in a minority of states.[3]

The lapsed bequest or devise is to be distinguished from the void bequest or devise. Lapse occurs when an event subsequent to the execution of the will renders the gift ineffective; a void gift is one which would be invalid if the testator died immediately

---

1. The death of the legatee prior to that of the testator is the most common form of lapse. There are, however, other forms including renunciation of the legacy and dissolution of a corporate legatee prior to testator's death. See Atkinson, Wills § 140, at 777 (2d ed. 1953).

2. Uniform Simultaneous Death Act, 8A U.L.A. 557 (1983).

3. Uniform Probate Code, 8 U.L.A. 128 (1983).

upon the execution of the will. A bequest or devise lapses when the legatee was alive at the time the will was executed but predeceased the testator. If the legatee was dead at the time the testator executed the will, the gift is said to be void.[4] The consequences of the void gift and the lapsed gift are the same, except in some states with respect to the application of the lapse statutes discussed in the following section. The incidence of a bequest or devise to one who is dead at the time of the execution of the will is, of course, quite rare, whereas the incidence of the lapsed bequest or devise is not unusual due to the lengthy gap that frequently exists between the execution of the will and the testator's death.

Let us assume that after several specific and general bequests the testator bequeaths and devises all the rest and residue of her property to A. A predeceases the testator. The residuary gift lapses, and the property that otherwise would have gone to A passes to the testator's intestate takers. The lapse is of the entire residuary estate and intestacy is all that remains.

Suppose the testator, after several specific and general bequests, bequeaths and devises all the rest and residue of her property one-half to A and one-half to B. A predeceases the testator but B survives the testator. Does the gift to A lapse and pass to the intestate takers, or does it pass to the other residuary legatee? Some courts have taken the rather mechanical view that after the residue there is only intestacy, and that is the fate of the lapsed fractional residuary gift.[5] Other courts have taken what seems to be a more sensible view, and one which is certainly consonant with the presumption against intestacy, that the gift passes to B, the other residuary legatee.[6] Uniform Probate Code § 2–606 provides that the lapsed residuary gift passes to the other residuary legatees rather than by intestacy, as do the statutes in some states that have not adopted the Code.[7]

Suppose testator bequeaths $100,000 in trust to pay the income to A for life, remainder to B. A survives the testator and

---

4. Equitable Trust Co. v. Smith, 26 Md.App. 204, 337 A.2d 205 (1975); Padgett v. Black, 229 S.C. 142, 92 S.E.2d 153 (1956). Bequests and devises may, of course, be void for other reasons, e.g., violation of the rule against perpetuities, or on a condition that is deemed contrary to public policy.

5. Moffett v. Howard, 392 So.2d 509 (Miss.1981); Dean v. Moore, 380 P.2d 934 (Okl.1963); In re Estate of O'Hara, 549 S.W.2d 233 (Tex.Civ.App.1977). Expression of intent by testator will, of course, result in distributing share of predeceasing residuary legatee among surviving residuary legatees. Bahan v. Citizens and Southern National Bank, 267 S.C. 303, 227 S.E.2d 671 (1976); In re Estate of Kugler, 52 Wis.2d 532, 190 N.W.2d 883 (1971).

6. In re Estate of Jackson, 106 Ariz. 82, 471 P.2d 278 (1970); In re Estate of Frolich, 112 N.H. 320, 295 A.2d 448 (1972); In re Slack Trust, 126 Vt. 37, 220 A.2d 472 (1966).

7. E.g., Md.Est. & Trusts Code Ann. § 4–404; Mass.Gen.Laws Ann. c.191, §§ 1A, 22; N.C.Gen.Stat. § 31–42; Pa.Stat.Ann.tit. 20, § 2514.

B predeceases the testator. The remainder interest lapses, and upon the termination of A's life estate the corpus of the trust passes to the residuary legatees. Of course, if A predeceases the testator and B survives the testator, B is entitled to the corpus upon the testator's death.

It should also be pointed out that if a donor purports to make an inter vivos gift of a present or future interest to one who is dead at the time the transfer is made, such transfer is void. Obviously this is not likely to be a frequent occurrence.

SECTION 2.   LAPSE STATUTES

Most jurisdictions have statutes which provide for substitutional gifts in the event of lapse in certain circumstances. These lapse statutes vary considerably. The principal differences are the definitions of the predeceasing legatees and devisees to whom the statute applies. Uniform Probate Code § 2–605 is limited to the predeceasing legatee or devisee (or one who does not survive the testator for 120 hours) who is a grandparent or a descendant of a grandparent of the testator. The statutes of some states are limited to the predeceasing legatee or devisee who is a descendant of the testator,[8] or a descendant or a sibling of the testator.[9] Some statutes apply to all predeceasing legatees or devisees.[10] Most of the statutes designate the descendants of the predeceasing legatee who survive the testator as the substitutional takers.[11]

Under these statutes, if testator bequeaths $100,000 to his son A, and A predeceases the testator leaving two children who survive the testator, the $100,000 does not pass into the residue but instead passes to the two children of A. If, however, A had no children or grandchildren who survived the testator, the money would pass to the residuary legatees. It should be stressed that the statutes provide for substitutional legatees; the lapsed gift does not pass through the estate of the predeceased legatee. Many lapse statutes, including Uniform Probate Code § 2–605, apply to the void bequest (legatee dead at execution of will) as well as the lapsed bequest.[12]

It should be emphasized that the doctrine of lapse, and the lapse statutes, apply only to the situation of the legatee or devisee

---

8. E.g., Ill.Ann.Stat. ch. 110½, § 4–11; Miss.Code Ann. § 91–5–7; Tex. Probate Code Ann. § 68.

9. E.g., Conn.Gen.Stat.Ann. § 45–276a; N.Y.Est. Powers & Trusts Law § 3–3.3; Pa.Stat.Ann.tit. 20, § 2514.

10. E.g., R.I.Gen.Laws § 33–6–19; Tenn.Code Ann. § 32–306; Va.Code § 64.1–64; W.Va. Code § 41–3–3.

11. E.g., D.C.Code Ann. § 18–308; Ga.Code Ann. § 113–812; Ky.Rev. Stat.Ann. § 394.400; N.H.Rev.Stat. Ann. § 551.12.

12. E.g., Del.Code Ann. tit. 12, § 2313; Ind.Code Ann. § 29–1–6–1; N.J.Stat.Ann. § 3B:3–35; Ohio Rev.Code Ann. § 2107.52; S.D.Comp.Laws Ann. § 29–6–8; Wyo.Stat. § 2–6–106.

who predeceases the testator.   If testator devises Blackacre to
A for life, remainder to B in fee, and B survives the testator but
predeceases A, there is no issue of lapse.   There may possibly
be a question of whether B must survive A in order to take the
remainder, a matter which is discussed later in this chapter, but
this is not a lapse question and the lapse statute has no applicability.

SECTION 3.   CONTROL OF LAPSE BY TESTATOR

The doctrine of lapse, and the application of lapse statutes,
are subject to the control of the testator.   The testator could
bequeath "$10,000 to A, or if he predeceases me, to A's residuary
legatees and devisees who survive me, or if there are none, to
A's intestate takers".   Here testator has circumvented the doctrine of lapse by providing an alternative gift to those who succeed to A's property.   A testator can always provide for alternative gifts in the event a legatee predeceases him, such as "$10,000
to A, or if he predeceases me, to B, or if she predeceases me,
to C".

Testator may bequeath "$10,000 to A if he survives me", with-
out providing for an alternative legatee.   If A predeceases the
testator, the lapse statute is not applicable because the testator
has anticipated that A may predecease him and has provided that
there is to be no gift in that event.[13]   The application of a lapse
statute is subject to the expression of a contrary intent by the
testator.[14]   The theory of lapse statutes is that the provision for
substitutional takers reflects the presumed intent of the testator
had he thought of the possibility that the legatee might predecease him;   consequently, any indication that the testator did not
wish the lapse statute to operate will be controlling.

If the bequest is "$10,000 to A if he survives me, or if he
does not survive me, to B", and both A and B predecease the
testator, there is a lapse of the bequest to B and the gift passes
to B's substitutional takers (assuming B is within the class of
legatees covered by the lapse statute) because there has been
no expression of an intention that the lapse statute is not to be
applied to his gift.

The testator can protect against intestacy resulting from lapse
in the residue by providing in the residuary clause that his prop-

---

13.   In re Estate of Kerr, 433 F.2d 479
(D.C. Cir. 1970);   In re Estate of Evans,
193 Neb. 437, 227 N.W.2d 603 (1975);   In
re Robinson's Will, 37 Misc.2d 546, 236
N.Y.S.2d 293 (1963);   Shalkhauser v.
Beach, 14 Ohio Misc. 1, 233 N.E.2d 527
(1968).   But see Gale v. Keyes, 45 Ohio
App. 61, 186 N.E. 755 (1933).

14.   Unif. Probate Code § 2–603, 8
U.L.A. 130 (1983);   Iowa Code Ann.
§ 633.273;   Or.Rev.Stat. § 112.395;
Tenn.Code Ann. § 32–306;   Vt.Stat.
Ann.tit. 14, § 558;   Wis.Stat.Ann.
§ 853.27.

erty is to go "to A and B in equal parts, or if either A or B predeceases me, then her share to the survivor, or if both A and B predecease me, then to C if she survives me, or if not, to Charity Hospital". The last legatee is bound to be there.

It should be pointed out here briefly that lapse does not occur in the class gift unless all the potential members of the class predecease the testator. If testator bequeaths "$100,000 to my children", and a child predeceases the testator, the entire $100,000 passes to the children who are alive at the testator's death; the legatees are the people who answer the class description at the effective date of the dispositive instrument. The predeceased child had no interest which would lapse. It should be noted, however, that a lapse statute may apply and produce a substitutional gift to the descendants of the predeceased child; this is confusing and apparently inconsistent. A discussion of the relationship of lapse and lapse statutes to class gifts appears in the next chapter.[15]

SECTION 4. SURVIVORSHIP TO DISTRIBUTION: TERMINATION OF PRECEDING INTEREST

Suppose testator bequeaths and devises his residuary estate in trust to pay the income to A for life, principal over to B at A's death. A and B survive the testator but B predeceases A. Who takes the principal on A's death? There is a pervasive constructional preference in property law for vested future interests over contingent future interests and for early vesting over vesting at a later time; this means, in this context, that there is a constructional preference for there being no condition of survivorship of the life tenant.[16] The result is that B's estate takes the corpus of the trust. There is no issue of lapse in this problem since B survived the testator.

Why this constructional preference for vested over contingent? Its explanation is historical. In the earliest phase of English land law, contingent remainders were not recognized as valid interests in land. After the law recognized the contingent remainder, it was not alienable and it was destructible. In order to uphold the grantor's intent, and in order to support the common law policy favoring free alienability of land, the constructional preference for vested over contingent became established. This remains standard doctrine today, although the reasons for its establishment are, for the most part, no longer relevant.[17] The contingent remainder today is, in most jurisdictions, alienable, voluntarily and involuntarily, and it is indestructible. The

15. See infra p. 140.

16. Simes & Smith § 585 (2d ed. 1956).

17. See 5 American Law of Property § 21.6 (Casner ed. 1952).

principal significance today of the vested versus the contingent construction is with respect to the rule against perpetuities, which is discussed in a later chapter.   It can be convincingly argued that a condition of survivorship to the termination of the preceding estate should be the constructional preference, as representing the presumed intent of the testator had he thought of the problem.   It seems a reasonable guess that in many instances the testator envisions a distribution only to the individual remainderman and does not intend a gift to the remainderman's estate.

A most effective and scholarly defense has been made, however, of the constructional preference against implied conditions of survivorship; the essence of the defense is that the implied condition of survivorship tends to disturb orderly and rational dispositive plans.[18]   An implied condition of survivorship can result in the disinheritance of one line of a family, as in a remainder to "children".   Also, if the implied condition of survivorship is applied to a residuary remainder interest, intestacy may result, against which there is a constructional preference.

Suppose testator bequeaths property in trust to pay income to A for life, principal over to "surviving" brothers and sisters of the testator.   What does "surviving" mean in this context? Does it mean that the remaindermen must survive the life income beneficiary, or only survive the testator?   The preferred construction is survivorship of the life tenant,[19] although the preference for the vested construction is so strong that some courts have held that it means survivorship only of the testator.[20]   If the term is construed as survivorship only of the testator, is not the use of the term merely surplusage since the remainderman couldn't take anyhow if he predeceased the testator?   For most purposes this construction would make the survivorship language surplusage, except that it could be meaningful if a lapse statute was applicable to this class gift; this problem will be discussed in the chapter dealing with class gifts.[21]

Let us assume that settlor irrevocably transfers securities inter vivos to a trustee to pay the income to settlor's wife for

---

18.   Halbach, Future Interests: Express and Implied Conditions of Survival, 49 Cal.L.Rev. 297, 304–12 (1961). For other scholarly discussions of this basic question, see Chaffin, Descendible Future Interests in Georgia: The Effect of The Preference For Early Vesting, 7 Ga.L.Rev. 443 (1973); Rabin, The Law Favors the Vesting of Estates.   Why?   65 Colum.L.Rev. 467 (1965).

19.   Dean v. Stuckey, 380 P.2d 824 (Alaska 1980); McVey v. Pfingston, 3

Kan.App.2d 276, 593 P.2d 1014 (1979); In the Matter of Will of Gautier, 3 N.Y.2d 502, 169 N.Y.S.2d 4, 146 N.E.2d 771 (1957); Cal.Prob.Code § 122.   See Restatement, Property § 251 (1940).

20.   Moorman v. Moorman, 156 Ind.App. 606, 297 N.E.2d 836 (1973); Porter v. Porter, 50 Mich. 456, 15 N.W. 550 (1883); Nass's Estate, 320 Pa. 380, 182 A. 401 (1936).

21.   See infra p. 140.

life, and on her death principal over to settlor's nephews and nieces.   At the date of the transfer in trust, settlor had six nephews and nieces;   at the settlor's death prior to his wife's death, only four of the six are living;   at settlor's wife's death, only three of them are living.   Who get the remainder?   The date of the transfer in trust was the date of the creation of the future interest;   applying the judicial preference for the vested construction, the six nephews and nieces alive at the creation of the trust, or their estates, take the remainder.[22]   The date of the settlor's death is irrelevant since it was not a testamentary disposition.   What happens if the nephews and nieces increase in number from the time of the creation of the trust to the time of distribution (settlor's wife's death)?   The additional nephews and nieces are entitled to take, together with those alive at the time of the creation of the trust;   this problem will be taken up in the chapter dealing with class gifts.[23]

Assume the same facts as in the immediately preceding problem, except that the trust is revocable, and the settlor does not revoke during his lifetime.   This power of revocation places the trust corpus completely within the control of the settlor during his lifetime.   Does the fact that the settlor retains such control up to the time of his death cause there to be an implied condition that the members of the class must survive until the settlor's death?   Is the settlor like a testator in this situation?   On substantially these facts it has been held that those members of the class who predecease the settlor do not take, but for those who survive the settlor there is no condition of survivorship to the time of distribution which is the settlor's wife's death.[24]   There are also cases to the contrary which hold that the reservation of the power of revocation by the settlor, or the existence of the power of a life income beneficiary to invade principal, does not cause there to be any implied condition of survivorship to the time of the expiration of the power.[25]

There is no implied condition that the takers in default of an exercise of a power of appointment must survive to the time of distribution.   Testator bequeaths to A for life, remainder to those persons to whom A appoints by will, and in default of appointment, to B;   if B survives testator and predeceases A,

22.   Hinds v. McNair, —— Ind.App. ——, 413 N.E.2d 586 (1980);   Second Bank-State Street Trust Co. v. Second Bank-State Street Trust Co., 335 Mass. 407, 140 N.E.2d 201 (1957).

23.   See infra pp. 144–47.

24.   Old Colony Trust Co. v. Clemons, 332 Mass. 535, 126 N.E.2d 193 (1955).

25.   Breeze v. Breeze, —— Ind.App. ——, 428 N.E.2d 286 (1981);   Detroit Bank & Trust Co. v. Grout, 95 Mich.App. 253, 289 N.W.2d 898 (1980);   First National Bank of Cincinnati v. Tenney, 165 Ohio St. 513, 138 N.E.2d 15 (1956).

and A fails to exercise his power of appointment, then B's estate takes. B's interest is described as a vested remainder subject to divestment by A's exercise of his power; B need not survive to the time of distribution in order to take.[26]

Suppose testator bequeaths in trust to pay income to A for life, principal over to B or the children of B. B survives the testator but predeceases A. B has two children, C1 who survives testator but predeceases A, and C2 who survives testator and A. Who gets the principal? Is there a condition that B must survive A in order to take? This seems to be the purpose of the alternative gift to B's children, and it has been so held.[27] There is some authority, however, to the effect that B has to survive only the testator and that there is no condition of survivorship to the time of distribution.[28] Assuming B's estate is not entitled to take, must the children of B survive A in order to take? There is a constructional preference for early vesting, and accordingly it has been held that there is no condition of survivorship of the life tenant, as far as the children of B are concerned. The estate of C1 takes one-half the corpus, and C2 takes the other half.[29]

Suppose in the preceding example B predeceases A, having survived the testator, and B never has any children. Assuming a jurisdiction in which B would be required to survive A if B had children, does the principal return to the testator's estate under these circumstances, or does it pass to the estate of B? Does the condition of survivorship to distribution apply only if there are children of B entitled to take? Or does B's remainder interest fail in any event if he fails to survive the life tenant? There is authority that in these circumstances B must survive A in order to take even though B never has any children.[30] There is also authority that the condition of survivorship to distribution applies only if there are children of B.[31] The courts which take

26. Restatement Property § 261 (1940).

27. Pate v. Edwards 388 So.2d 544 (Ala.1980); Old Colony Trust Co. v. Barker, 332 Mass. 533, 126 N.E.2d 188 (1955); Browing v. Sacrison, 267 Or. 645, 518 P.2d 656 (1974).

28. Mead v. Close, 115 Conn. 443, 161 A. 799 (1932); In re Will of Walker, 85 Misc.2d 110, 380 N.Y.S.2d 211 (1975); Roberts v. Northwestern Bank, 271 N.C. 292, 156 S.E.2d 229 (1967).

29. In re Estate of Ferry, 55 Cal.2d 776, 13 Cal.Rptr. 180, 361 P.2d 900 (1961); Mueller v. Forsyth, 94 Ill.App.2d 258, 235 N.E.2d 645 (1968); In re Estate of Coe, 77 N.J.Super. 181, 185 A.2d 696 (1962), reversed on other grounds 42 N.J. 485, 201 A.2d 571 (1964); Rennolds v. Branch, 182 Va. 678, 29 S.E.2d 847 (1944). See generally Halbach, Future Interests: Express and Implied Conditions of Survival, 49 Cal.L.Rev. 297, 323–27 (1961).

30. Robertson v. Robertson, 313 Mass. 520, 48 N.E.2d 29 (1943); Carpenter v. Smith, 77 R.I. 358, 75 A.2d 413 (1950); Restatement, Property § 252 (1940). See Simes & Smith § 581 (2d ed. 1956).

31. St. Louis Union Trust Co. v. Hearne, 111 Ill.App.2d 411, 250 N.E.2d 674 (1969); In re Estate of Paulson, 188 Kan. 467, 363 P.2d 422 (1961); Boyd v. Bartlett, 325 Mass. 206, 89 N.E.2d 772 (1950); In re Estate of Blough, 474 Pa. 177, 378 A.2d 276 (1977).

the latter view are likely to describe the interest of B, not as a contingent remainder, but rather as a vested remainder subject to divestment if B predeceases A and has children.

There is a relatively common situation in which an implied condition of survivorship to the termination of the preceding interest is found. Testator bequeaths in trust to pay the income to A for life, principal over to the issue of A. The word "issue" literally includes all descendants of the ancestor, but in this context it has been construed to mean the lineal heirs of the ancestor, with the consequent implication that survivorship of the ancestor is required.[32] Issue who take may be determined on a per stirpital basis, as under the statute of intestacy. In the case of a gift to A for life, remainder to the issue of B, and B predeceases A, it has been held that those who take are the issue of B alive at the time of distribution, i.e., A's death, rather than those issue who are alive at B's death,[33] but there is authority to the contrary.[34] A discussion of the terms "issue" and "heirs" appears in the final chapter of this book.[35]

There are a couple of situations in which some courts, on very questionable grounds, have found an implied condition of survivorship. Suppose testator bequeaths in trust to pay the income to A for life, remainder to the children of A who survive A, or if none survive, then to B. If no children of A survive A, and B predeceases A, does B's estate take, or is there an implied condition that B survive A simply because there is another condition precedent to B's taking, namely, A's death without surviving children? Some courts have held that there is a condition of survivorship as long as there is another condition precedent attached to the future interest which is unsatisfied.[36] In our example, the other condition precedent could not be satisfied until A's death, and therefore the condition of survivorship would continue to A's death. It may well be that there should be a constructional preference for survivorship to the time of distribution in some situations, but to recognize it peculiarly in this situation does not seem to make much sense, and this anomalous rule obtains today in only a few states.[37]

32. Reynolds v. Love, 191 Ala. 218, 68 So. 27 (1915); Clarke v. Clarke, 222 Md. 153, 159 A.2d 362 (1960); In re Estate of Cary, 25 Misc.2d 244, 201 N.Y.S.2d 179 (1960).

33. Altman v. Rider, 291 S.W.2d 577 (Ky.1956); In re Estate of de Florez, 27 Misc.2d 674, 210 N.Y.S.2d 560 (1960). See Jackson v. Riggs National Bank, 314 A.2d 178 (Del.1973). See also Halbach, Future Interests: Express and Implied Conditions of Survival, 49 Cal.L.Rev. 297, 322, 328 (1961).

34. Tuffy v. Nichols, 120 F.2d 906 (2d Cir. 1941); Rennolds v. Branch, 182 Va. 678, 29 S.E.2d 847 (1944).

35. See infra pp. 230–33.

36. Fletcher v. Hurdle, 259 Ark. 640, 536 S.W.2d 109 (1976); Schau v. Cecil, 257 Iowa 1296, 136 N.W.2d 515 (1965); Lawson v. Lawson, 267 N.C. 643, 148 S.E.2d 546 (1966).

37. 5 American Law of Property § 21.25 (Casner ed. 1952); Simes & Smith § 594 (2d ed. 1956).

There is another aberration which must be mentioned. This is the so-called "divide-and-pay-over" rule. Testator bequeaths in trust to pay the income to A for life, and upon A's death, the trustee is to "divide and pay over" the principal of the trust among the children of A. Does the use of the phrase "divide and pay over", in the absence of other language of gift, imply a condition of survivorship in order for the children to take? There have been cases in the past in which the courts have found a condition of survivorship because such donative words were exclusively used.[38] The thinking seemed to be that these words of physical division and payment referred to a future act, and that therefore the gift did not take place until such future time and required that the donees be alive at that time in order to receive the gift. This is unconvincing, and conceptually unsound. At the time for distribution the trustee must make a division and payment, and to attach any significance to the unnecessary statement of this in a will or trust deed is remarkable indeed. To the extent that this rule had significance at one time, it has been whittled away by disingenuous distinctions and qualifications. The outstanding qualification goes like this—if the phrase is used in connection with the creation of a preceding estate, then the phrase does not carry any implication of a condition of survivorship. This just about kills the rule, because such language of division and payment is invariably used following a life interest. Some courts have expressly abolished the rule. It has very little significance today.[39]

Needless to say, any recourse to constructional rules with respect to survivorship is a reproach to the draftsman of the instrument. The instrument should be crystal-clear as to the requirement of survivorship or the absence of any such requirement. The purpose of any discussion such as this is to point out the pitfalls, rather than to suggest rules which the draftsman should employ and rely upon. This discussion is essentially litigation analysis, and under no circumstances is it to be mistaken for instruction for drafting dispositive instruments.

SECTION 5.   SURVIVORSHIP TO DISTRIBUTION: THE AGE CONTINGENCY

The question of survivorship arises principally in three contexts: Survivorship of the testator; survivorship of the preceding interest, usually a life interest; and survivorship to a

---

38. E.g., In re Crane, 164 N.Y. 71, 58 N.E. 47 (1900); Scott's Estate, 301 Pa. 509, 152 A. 560 (1930); In re Estate of Lawrence, 22 Wis.2d 624, 126 N.W.2d 517 (1964).

39. 5 American Law of Property § 21.21, at 160 (Casner ed. 1952); Simes & Smith § 658 (2d ed. 1956); Restatement, Property § 260 (1940).

certain age. We now briefly consider the last of these, which is employed usually to assure that the beneficiary has attained sufficient maturity to handle the funds to be given him.

Suppose testator bequeaths $10,000 to A if A shall attain age 21. Here clearly there is a condition of survivorship to age 21. But suppose the bequest is to "A to be paid to A at age 21"; A survives the testator but dies at age 18. Does the bequest go to the estate of A, or does it pass to the residuary legatees? Was the gift conditional upon A's attaining 21, or was this a vested gift to A with only the time of payment postponed to age 21? There is a constructional rule of thumb in our law, derived from an ancient case, to the effect that the clause "to be paid at age 21" indicates that the gift is vested in A immediately upon the testator's death, assuming of course that A survives the testator, and only the time of payment is postponed.[40]

Suppose the testamentary gift is to "A at age 21"; does this language call for survivorship to age 21? There is another constructional bromide, stemming from the same ancient case, that this language requires survivorship.[41] The omission of the phrase "to be paid" preceding "at age 21" makes the difference. This distinction should raise an eyebrow or two, but it is part of the traditional dogma of future interests.

Suppose the bequest is to A "when he shall arrive at age 21"; if A survives testator but dies at age 18, does A's estate receive the bequest? There is a constructional rule of thumb that this language creates a condition of survivorship to the stated age.[42] But do we have a different result if the language of the bequest is "to be paid to A when A arrives at age 21"? It is said that this language produces a vested gift with only the time of payment postponed.[43] Once again, the use of the language "to be paid" makes the difference.

It seems that slight variations in the language of the will from the pattern just discussed can produce different results, and certainly the structure of the particular will and the relationship of the legatee to the testator will have their effect upon the construction placed upon the words which modify the gift. It goes

---

40. This rule was first articulated in Clobberie's Case, 2 Vent. 342, 86 Eng.Rep. 476 (1677), and has been followed in numerous subsequent decisions down to the present day. See, e.g., Zimmerman v. First National Bank, 348 So.2d 1359 (Ala.1977); In re Will of Mansur, 98 Vt. 296, 127 A. 297 (1925); In re Will of Fouks, 206 Wis. 69, 238 N.W. 869 (1931).

41. Clobberie's Case, supra note 40; see, e.g., Thomas v. Pullman Trust & Sav-

ings Bank, 371 Ill. 577, 21 N.E.2d 897 (1939); Muller v. Cox, 98 N.J.Eq. 188, 130 A. 811 (1925).

42. Allen v. Burkhiser, 125 N.J.Eq. 524, 6 A.2d 656 (1939). Contra, Brizendine v. American Trust & Savings Bank, 211 Ala. 694, 101 So. 618 (1924).

43. See Restatement, Property § 257, comment *d* (1940).

without saying that if there is a gift over to another person upon failure of the first taker to reach a certain age, there is a condition of survivorship; the only issue is whether the age contingency is a condition precedent or a condition subsequent, which question is discussed in the next section.

Of course the age contingency problem can arise following a life estate: Bequest in trust for A for life, remainder to B to be paid at age 21. The principles discussed above are equally applicable to this situation.

If the will provides for payment of the income from the bequest to the legatee prior to his arriving at the stated age, this is some evidence of the testator's intention that there is no condition of survivorship, although it certainly should not be conclusive. If, on the other hand, the will provides for the payment of income to another during the period prior to the legatee's arriving at the stated age, this is some evidence that the gift is contingent upon survivorship to the stated age.[44]

If the gift is vested with time of payment postponed and income is payable to the legatee prior to his attaining the stated age, the death of the legatee prior to his attaining the stated age should cause an immediate payment of the principal sum to his estate.[45]

SECTION 6.   VESTED VS. CONTINGENT

We have been discussing the question of the existence or non-existence of a condition of survivorship, but we have not been concerned with the question of whether the condition of survivorship is precedent or subsequent. This issue has been discussed earlier in this book,[46] but a brief summary in connection with survivorship is called for at this point.

If there is a condition of survivorship and there are no alternative takers, the condition is usually precedent and the interest is contingent. An issue of classification may arise where there is a condition of survivorship and there are alternative takers. If testator devises to A for life, remainder to B, but if B does not survive A, then to C, B has a vested remainder subject to complete divestment, and C has an executory interest which is contingent in nature. If, however, testator devises to A for life, remainder to B if he survives A, but if B does not survive A, then to C, it appears that B and C have alternative contingent remainders. However, the constructional preference for vested

---

44.   See 5 American Law of Property § 21.20 (Casner ed. 1952); Simes & Smith § 588 (2d ed. 1956); Restatement, Property § 257 (1940).

45.   Simes & Smith § 589 (2d ed. 1956).

46.   See supra pp. 66–73.

is so strong in our law that there is authority to the effect that B has a vested remainder subject to complete divestment, and C has an executory interest.[47]   If testator bequeaths to the children of A when they arrive at age 21, but if any child shall die prior to 21, his share to B, the interest of a child at birth may be construed as vested subject to complete divestment.

This is all a matter of words, a matter of form.   At one time the distinction between contingent and vested subject to complete divestment was of considerable significance, but today in most jurisdictions its significance is limited principally to the rule against perpetuities.   The historical problems of destructibility of contingent remainders and inalienability of contingent interests are relevant today in only a few states.[48]

47. Bush v. Hamill, 273 Ill. 132, 112 N.E. 375 (1916); Hersey v. Purington, 96 Me. 166, 51 A. 865 (1902).

48. See 5 American Law of Property § 21.6 (Casner ed. 1952); Halbach, Future Interests: Express and Implied Conditions of Survival, 49 Cal.L.Rev. 431, 461–465 (1961).

Chapter 6

CLASS GIFTS

SECTION 1.   DEFINITION AND SIGNIFICANCE

If testator leaves a will in which he devises Blackacre "to A, B, and C, equally as tenants in common", the devise is not a class gift even though A, B, and C are all children of the testator. It is three individual gifts to those persons.   However, if the same testator devises Blackacre "to my children equally as tenants in common," the devise is a class gift.   What differences in legal result follow from these two forms of devise?   If A, B, and C are the only children testator ever has, and they all survive the testator, then clearly there is no difference in legal result whichever form of devise is used.   If, however, another child, D, is born to the testator, and D survives the testator, then obviously the class gift produces a different result from that of the several gifts to A, B, and C as individuals.   Also, if A should predecease the testator, there may be a different result in the class gift situation from the individual gift situation;   more on this point below.[1]

Suppose in the preceding class devise, D, a child of the testator, was conceived but unborn at the time of the testator's death.   Would D be entitled to a share of the land?   For all class gift purposes, a person is deemed to have been in being from the time of his conception,[2] and therefore D is a member of the class of devisees.

The typical class gift is to "children," "issue," "heirs," "brothers and sisters," "nieces and nephews," "grandchildren."   A class gift is one in which the donor intends to benefit a group or a class of persons, as distinguished from specific individuals;   the class gift donor is said to be "group-minded".   The class gift is one in which the donor intends that the number of donees, from the time of the delivery of the instrument of gift in the case of the inter vivos gift, or from the time of the execution of the will in the case of the testamentary gift, is subject to fluctuation by way of increase or decrease, or by way of increase only, or by way of decrease only, depending on the circumstances of the gift.[3]

---

1.   See infra p. 137.

2.   In re Estate of Walton, 183 Kan. 238, 326 P.2d 264 (1958); Ebbs v. Smith, 59 Ohio Misc. 133, 394 N.E.2d 1034 (1979);

Estate of Trattner, 394 Pa. 133, 145 A.2d 678 (1958).   See Simes & Smith § 650 (2d ed. 1956).

3.   3 Powell, Real Property § 352 (1967).

Fluctuation in the number of donees is the feature which distinguishes the class gift from the individual gift. Presumably if the donor did not intend fluctuation in numbers, he would have named specific individuals as donees rather than employ a group or class designation.

In the case of the devise of Blackacre to A, B and C, as tenants in common, such individuals being the children of the testator, let us assume that A predeceases the testator. Since this is three individual gifts, A's interest lapses, and if the lapse statute is not applicable because A has no descendants, A's interest, which would have been one-third tenant in common in fee, passes to the residuary devisees or to the testator's heirs in the absence of a residuary clause in the will.[4]

Let us assume that the devise of Blackacre is to the "children" of the testator. Testator had three children at the time of the execution of the will, A, B and C, but A predeceased the testator. The members of the class are those who answer the description at the date the will becomes effective, which is the testator's death; this means that the devisees are B and C. There is no question of lapse because A had no interest which could lapse; the only devisees are those members of the group or class who are living at the effective date of the dispositive instrument. The class membership was subject to increase or decrease from the time of the execution of the will. By the use of the term "children" instead of the designation of specifically named devisees, the testator anticipated an increase or decrease in the number of devisees from the number existing at the time of the execution of the will. The members of the class who are alive at the testator's death take the entire devise.[5] However, it should be pointed out that many states have applied the lapse statute to the member of the class who predeceases the testator; this is discussed in the next section. It should also be pointed out that if the class gift is a future interest, members of the class who are born after the testator's death may be included within the class; this is discussed in Section 4 of this Chapter.

Let us modify the examples we have been discussing by making the gifts remainder interests. Testator devises Blackacre to X for life, remainder in fee as tenants in common to A, B, and C, on condition that each takes only if he survives X. Or, testator devises Blackacre to X for life, remainder in fee to testator's children who survive X, as tenants in common. A, B and

---

4. See discussion of lapse supra pp. 123–25.

5. In re Estate of Kalouse, 282 N.W.2d 98 (Iowa 1979); Lichter v. Bletcher, 266 Minn. 326, 123 N.W.2d 612 (1963); Industrial National Bank v. Glocester Manton Free Public Library, 107 R.I. 161, 265 A.2d 724 (1970). See 5 American Law of Property § 22.4 (Casner ed. 1952).

C are the only children testator has.   All three children survive
testator but A predeceases X.   The first remainder to A, B and
C constitutes three individual gifts;   consequently B takes one-
third, C takes one-third, and the one-third that would have gone
to A fails and passes to the residuary devisees, or in the absence
of a residuary clause, to testator's heirs.[6]   The second remainder
to testator's children who survive X is a class gift, and the remaindermen are those who answer the class description.   B and
C are the children who survive X, and each takes one-half.[7]

There should be no mystique surrounding the class gift;   any
legal conclusions concerning a gift to a class, as distinguished
from a gift to several individuals, should reflect what the donor,
or the hypothetical reasonable donor, would have intended had
he focused upon the problem.   Many of the legal conclusions
concerning the effect of class gifts are in the nature of constructional preferences or rules to resolve questions of disposition on
which the instrument is silent.   The reader should adopt a critical
attitude and determine for himself whether the conclusions are
reasonable inferences or merely fossilized legalisms.

Suppose the testator devises Blackacre to "my children, A,
B, and C, as tenants in common".   Is this a class gift or is it
several individual gifts?   It certainly will make a difference if
A predeceases the testator without leaving any descendants of
his own.   There is authority on both sides, but the prevailing
construction is that the gift is not a class gift and the use of the
term "children" is merely descriptive of the individual devisees.[8]

Suppose testator bequeaths "$100,000 to my friend, Mary Smith,
and the children of my brother, John."   Mary predeceased the
testator.   There were four children of John at the time of the
execution of the will, one of whom predeceased the testator.
John did not have any more children after testator executed his
will.   Who gets what?   Does Mary Smith's share lapse and pass
into the residue?   What about the share of the child of John who
predeceased the testator?   Do we have a class gift here?   If so,
who comprise the class?   If Mary and the children constitute
one class, then the three surviving children take the entire

---

6.   See generally 5 American Law of
Property § 21.12 (Casner ed. 1952).

7.   Hitchcock v. Skelly Oil Co., 197 Kan.
1, 414 P.2d 67 (1966);   Percival v. Percival,
526 P.2d 342 (Wyo.1974).   See 5 American Law of Property § 21.12 (Casner ed.
1952).

8.   Brown v. Leadley, 81 Ill.App.3d 504,
36 Ill.Dec. 758, 401 N.E.2d 599 (1980);

South Shore National Bank v. Berman, 1
Mass.App.Ct. 9, 294 N.E.2d 432 (1972);
Weems v. Frost National Bank, 301 S.W.2d
714 (Tex.Civ.App.1957).   See Simes &
Smith § 612 (2d ed. 1956).   Class gift construction: In re Estate of Dumas, 117 N.H.
909, 379 A.2d 836 (1977);   Nolan v. Borger, 32 Ohio Op.2d 255, 203 N.E.2d 274
(1963).

$100,000. There is support for this conclusion, and there is also authority for the construction that Mary takes individually and John's children take as a class.[9]

If Mary and the children constitute one class, how is this rationalized? As far as the children of John are concerned, this is an example of class gift terminology by the use of "children". If the testator had been thinking of a benefit to individuals rather than a class, he would have made gifts to the children of John by naming them individually as legatees. But how does friend Mary fit into the same class with the children of John? Almost invariably a class gift includes people with some common characteristic, and Mary has no common characteristic with the others. If Mary and the children are treated as one class, then it seems that the members of the class in a class gift need not have any common characteristic; a gift will be treated as a class gift if it appears that the conclusions of a class gift were intended by the donor. If it is inferred that the testator would have wanted Mary's share to pass to the children if she predeceased the testator, instead of lapsing and passing to the residuary legatees, then the court calls it a class gift. As with so many legal terms and categories, the class gift label may be applied to rationalize a result which appears reasonable under the circumstances of the particular case.[10]

In this immediately preceding example of a class gift, the class could have increased or decreased from the time of the execution of the will. An example of a class gift in which the class can only decrease is a bequest to the children of a person who is deceased at the time of the execution of the will. An example of a class gift in which the class can only increase would be an irrevocable inter vivos transfer in trust to pay the income to the settlor's wife for her life, and principal over to the settlor's children; here all the children alive at the effective date of the transfer in trust are members of the class, and the class remains open to include later children born before the death of the life income beneficiary, in accordance with principles which are discussed below.[11]

---

9. One class: In re Estate of Kalouse, 282 N.W.2d 98 (Iowa 1979). Individual gift and class gift: Palmer v. Jones, 299 Ill. 263, 132 N.E. 567 (1921); Bradley v. Estate of Jackson, 1 Kan.App.2d 695, 573 P.2d 628 (1977). See Simes & Smith § 615 (2d ed. 1956). If it is one class, Mary and each child share equally; if it is an individual gift and a class gift, the probable result is one-half to Mary and one-half to the children. This question is discussed in 5 American Law of Property § 22.13 (Casner ed. 1952).

10. Horseman v. Horseman, 309 Ky. 289, 217 S.W.2d 645 (1949); Svenson v. First National Bank, 5 Mass.App.Ct. 440, 363 N.E.2d 1129 (1977); Nolan v. Borger, 32 Ohio Op.2d 255, 203 N.E.2d 274 (1963). See Simes & Smith § 612 (2d ed. 1956).

11. See infra pp. 144–47.

SECTION 2. CLASS GIFTS AND LAPSE STATUTES

Suppose testator bequeaths $100,000 to his "nephews". A, a nephew of the testator, was alive at the time of the execution of the will and predeceased the testator; B and C, the other nephews of the testator, survived the testator. Standard class gift doctrine requires that the entire $100,000 pass to B and C; the interest of A does not lapse but rather the gift is to those who answer the class description at the date of death of the testator. But suppose there is a lapse statute in the jurisdiction applicable to nephews and A has children who survive the testator. Do the children of A take his share of the $100,000 as they would if there had been a gift of $33,333 to A individually? Or is the nature of the class gift such as to make application of the lapse statute inappropriate? A majority of American jurisdictions have taken the position that the lapse statute is applicable to the class gift situation.[12] If, however, A has no descendants who survive the testator, thereby preventing the lapse statute from operating for want of substitutional takers, the entire $100,000 passes to the surviving nephews, B and C. The application of the lapse statute to the class gift situation results in a substitutional gift where no lapse has occurred.

A few jurisdictions do not apply the lapse statute to the class gift; this seems to be logically consistent with class gift doctrine.[13] However, the argument for the application of the lapse statute to the class gift is that the purpose of the lapse statute is to implement the presumed intention of the testator to benefit descendants of the predeceased legatee, and that such purpose is as relevant in the case of the class gift as it is in the case of the individual gift. The failure to apply the lapse statute to the class gift can result in the disinheritance of one line of the family of the testator.

Let us assume that testator bequeaths $20,000 to "my sisters who survive me". The testator was survived by three sisters; one sister of the testator was alive at the time of the execution of the will and predeceased the testator leaving children who survived the testator. In addition to the class designation, the testator has expressly made the gift conditional upon survivor-

---

12. The Uniform Probate Code § 2–605, and the lapse statutes in about half the states are expressly applicable to the class gift, e.g., Ill.Ann.Stat. ch. 110½, § 4–11; Mass.Gen.Laws Ann. ch. 191, § 22; N.Y.Est.Powers & Trusts Law § 3–3.3; N.C.Gen.Stat. § 31–42; Wis.Stat.Ann. § 853.27. There is also case authority: In re Steidl's Estate, 89 Cal.App.2d 488, 201 P.2d 58 (1948); Gianoli v. Gabaccia, 82 Nev. 108, 412 P.2d 439 (1966); Hov-

erstad v. First National Bank & Trust Co., 76 S.D. 119, 74 N.W.2d 48 (1956); Burch v. McMillin, 15 S.W.2d 86 (Tex.Civ.App.1929).

13. Johns v. Citizens & Southern National Bank, 206 Ga. 313, 57 S.E.2d 182 (1950); In re Estate of Kalouse, 282 N.W.2d 98 (Iowa, 1979). See Simes & Smith § 662 (2d ed. 1956).

ship.   Assuming a lapse statute applicable to sisters, it will not be applied since the testator has evidenced an intention that it should not be; [14]   this is, of course, analogous to the individual gift with the express condition of survival of the testator.

Suppose testator bequeaths his residuary estate to the "children of A".   A had three children, two of whom survived the testator and one of whom was dead at the time of the execution of the will.   The testator knew that the child was dead at the time he executed his will.   The one who was dead at the time of the making of the will was survived by children who survived the testator.   Does it make good sense to apply a lapse statute in this situation?   It seems not, since under the circumstances "children" could not reasonably be construed to include that child who was known to be dead at the time the testator executed his will.   It does not seem reasonable to infer that the testator would have intended to have any share of the gift pass to such child's descendants.   Uniform Probate Code § 2–605, however, expressly includes the class member who was dead at the execution of the will, as do the lapse statutes of a number of other states, and there are statutes which expressly exclude such person;   in the absence of express statutory provision, the case law is mixed. [15]

SECTION 3.   DETERMINATION OF CLASS MEMBERSHIP: IMMEDIATE GIFTS

Let us assume that testator bequeaths $50,000 to the children of A.   A is alive at the testator's death, and A has four children who are alive at that time.   The bequest, however, is not limited to the children of A who are alive at the testator's death;   it purports to include all children of A.   Do we hold up the payment of the bequest until the death of A so that we can be sure that all possible children of A will receive their shares?   In this situation the law has adopted what is called a rule of convenience. The class is said to "close" at the date of the testator's death; the entire amount of the bequest is divided among those members of the class in existence at the time of the testator's death.   Chil-

14.   In re Holtforth's Estate, 298 Mich. 708, 299 N.W. 776 (1941);   In re Estate of Leuer, 84 Misc.2d 1087, 378 N.Y.S.2d 612 (Sur.Ct.1976);   Cowgill v. Faulconer, 57 Ohio Misc. 6, 385 N.E.2d 327 (1978).   See also discussion of control of lapse by testamentary provision at supra pp. 126–27.

15.   Statutes which include the class member who is dead at the execution of the will: Del.Code Ann.tit. 12, § 2313;   Mass.Gen.Laws Ann. ch. 191, § 22; N.J.Stat.Ann. § 3B:3–35;   Tenn.Code Ann.

§§ 32–305, 32–306.   Statutes which exclude the class member who was dead at the execution of the will: Md.Est. & Trusts Code Ann. § 4–403;   N.Y.Est. Powers & Trusts Law § 3–3.3;   Or.Rev.Stat. § 112.395;   Wis.Stat.Ann. § 853.27. There is case authority for including the deceased class member, Gianoli v. Gabaccia, 82 Nev. 108, 412 P.2d 439 (1966), and for excluding the deceased class member, In re Hutton's Estate, 106 Wash. 578, 180 P. 882 (1919).   See Simes & Smith § 664 (2d ed. 1956).

dren born after the testator's death are not legatees.[16]   If the class were not closed at this time, and afterborn children were includible within the class of legatees, then it would not be possible to distribute to the existing children because one would not know how many ways the gift was to be divided.   So the rule became established that in the case of an immediate gift, a gift of a present interest, the class closes at the date of the testator's death, if there is a person in being entitled to distribution at that time.   This is a rule of construction, not a rule of law, and it yields to evidence of a contrary intention.

This rule of convenience probably coincides with what the testator would have wanted had he thought about the possibility of A being alive at his death and capable of having additional children.   Of course, the testator could have controlled the result by providing that the $50,000 was to go to those children of A who were alive at the testator's death, or by providing that the $50,000 was to go to the children of A whether born prior to or after the testator's death.

Let us further assume in this example that we have been discussing that the parent, A, is a male and is 60 years old at the time of the testator's death.   Instead of closing the class, why doesn't the court require a bond from the four children to assure the return of funds in the unlikely event more children of A are born or adopted.   The law has not seen fit to take this route;   rather than become involved with the expense and practical difficulties of this procedure, it has simply closed the class at the testator's death.   And it should be stressed that the class does not remain open until the termination of the administration of the estate.   Of course, a child of A who was conceived but unborn at the time of the testator's death is included in the class, since such child is deemed to have been in being at the date of the testator's death;[17]   the quest for certainty is compromised in the interest of the fetus.

If the bequest is to the children of A, and A is dead at the testator's death, and four children of A survive the testator, there is no class-closing problem.   Similarly, there is no class-closing problem in the bequest to the children of the testator;   the testator cannot have any children after his death.

Let us assume that testator bequeathed $50,000 to the children of A, and A is alive at the testator's death and has had no children. Do we rigidly apply the principle that in the case of the immediate gift the class closes at the testator's death and therefore the gift

16.   Loockerman v. McBlair, 6 Gill. 177 (Md.Ct.App.1847);   Clarke v. Clarke, 253 N.C. 156, 116 S.E.2d 449 (1960).   See 5   American Law of Property § 22.42 (Casner ed. 1952).

17.   See supra note 2.

fails for want of a legatee? But the class is closed only because that is the time for distribution if there is a member of the class entitled to take. Here, however, there is no one entitled to distribution; there is no reason to close the class. The rest of the testator's estate is administered and distributed and the class gift is held open.[18] But how long does the executor, or someone else appointed by the court for the purpose, hold on to this money? Suppose A has a child three years later—does that child take the entire $50,000 on a "first come, first served" theory? Isn't the birth of the first child the time for distribution and the time for closing the class? It has been maintained that in this situation the class remains open as long as A is alive, despite the fact that the first child to be born is entitled to his share at birth. Does this mean that the entire $50,000 is held back until A's death because it is impossible to determine the share to which the first child is entitled until A's death? It has been maintained that the first child should receive the entire amount subject to partial divestment by the birth of later children.[19] This would be very cumbersome, requiring a bond to secure the obligation to repay. There is little case authority on the matters discussed in this paragraph, and prediction of results is speculative.

It should be noted in this discussion that the traditional common law view is that there is a conclusive presumption that a person is capable of having children up to the time of his death, and that evidence to the contrary is inadmissible.[20] There are some modern cases, however, which hold that the presumption of fertility is rebuttable by medical evidence.[21] The traditional conclusive presumption has special significance in connection with the rule against perpetuities.[22]

In many jurisdictions the adopted child is deemed to be included in the term "children" or other family class terms in dispositive instruments. For class-closing purposes the effective date of adoption is determinative. Assume testator bequeaths $50,000 to the children of A; A survives testator, has one child alive at testator's death, and adopts a two-year old child three

---

18. Simes & Smith § 636 (2d ed. 1956); Restatement, Property § 294(b), and comment o (1940).

19. See 5 American Law of Property § 22.42, at 355 (Casner ed. 1952).

20. Connecticut Bank & Trust Co. v. Brody, 174 Conn. 616, 392 A.2d 445 (1978); Clark v. Citizens & Southern National Bank, 243 Ga. 703, 257 S.E.2d 244 (1979); Walton v. Lee, 634 S.W.2d 159 (Ky.1982); Gettins v. Grand Rapids Trust Co., 249 Mich. 238, 228 N.W. 703 (1930).

21. Fletcher v. Hurdle, 259 Ark. 640, 536 S.W.2d 109 (1976); Citizens National Bank v. Longshore, 304 So.2d 287 (Miss.1974); In re Bassett's Estate, 104 N.H. 504, 190 A.2d 415 (1963); Street v. National Newark & Essex Bank, 121 N.J.Super. 586, 298 A.2d 289 (1972); In re Estate of Weeks, 485 Pa. 329, 402 A.2d 657 (1979). See 4 Scott, Law of Trusts § 340.1 (3d ed. 1967); Restatement, Property § 274 (1940).

22. See discussion infra p. 188.

months after testator's death. The class closes at testator's death and the adopted child is excluded.[23]

The class gift of income requires special analysis. Suppose testator bequeaths $100,000 in trust to pay the income to the children of A for their lives, and upon the death of the last survivor of such children of A, to pay over the principal to B. A is alive at testator's death and has two children who are alive at testator's death. Then five years later A has a third child. Is the third child entitled to receive any income, or did the class close at the testator's death? Clearly the third child cannot claim a share of payments made prior to his birth, but there is no reason why the third child cannot join in the class and share in the subsequent income payments. There is no inconvenience in permitting the class to expand (or contract) when periodic income payments are involved. Income payments are made to those children who are alive at the time each installment of income is due. In a sense the class closes with respect to each installment of income.[24]

SECTION 4. DETERMINATION OF CLASS MEMBERSHIP: POSTPONED GIFTS

Let us assume that testator bequeaths $100,000 in trust to pay the income to A for life, principal over to the children of A. A survived the testator, and at the testator's death A had one child, C1. Then three years later, A had another child, C2. Five years later A died, survived by C1 and C2. Who is entitled to the remainder? Is the class of A's children closed at the testator's death, or is it kept open to a later date? The remainder was to the children of A, without limitation as to when they might be born. We have seen that where the gift is an immediate one, that is, one which is theoretically possessory upon the testator's death, the class closes upon the testator's death if there is someone entitled to take at that time, in order that an effective distribution may presently be made. But why close the class at the testator's death in the instant situation? The distribution is not to be made at the time of the testator's death, but rather at the death of the life tenant. There is no reason to close the class until it is necessary to make a distribution.

---

23. In re Silberman's Will, 23 N.Y.2d 98, 295 N.Y.S.2d 478, 242 N.E.2d 736 (1968). See In re Estate of Markowitz, 126 N.J.Super. 140, 312 A.2d 901 (1973). For discussion of inclusion of adopted children in gift to "children," see infra p. 233.

24. Hamilton National Bank v. Hutcheson, 357 F.Supp. 114 (E.D.Tenn.1973), affirmed mem. sub nom. Hamilton National Bank v. Meadow, 492 F.2d 1243 (6th Cir. 1974); McDowell National Bank v. Applegate, 479 Pa. 300, 388 A.2d 666 (1978); In re Estate of Evans, 274 Wis. 459, 80 N.W.2d 408 (1957), rehearing denied 274 Wis. 459, 81 N.W.2d 489 (1957).

So C2 is entitled to take one half the remainder.[25] There is no premature closing of the class in this situation.

Suppose testator bequeaths $100,000 in trust to pay the income to A for life, principal over on A's death to the children of B. A and B are alive at testator's death. B has one child at testator's death, C1. B then has another child, C2. Then C1 dies. Then A dies. B is alive at A's death. Three years after A's death, B has another child, C3. Who is entitled to the remainder? There is no reason to close the class until A's death; clearly C2 is entitled to share. How about C1? C1 survived the testator; was there any need for C1 to survive the life tenant? Ordinarily in the case of the postponed gift, the future interest, there is no implied condition of survivorship to the time for distribution, and this principle is applicable to class gifts as it is to individual gifts. Consequently, C1's estate is entitled to a share of the remainder.[26] How about C3? The general principle is that the class closes at the time for distribution, and therefore C3 is not entitled to share.

In the case of an immediate gift to a class, the membership is determined at the effective date of the dispositive instrument— in the case of a will, the date of death of the testator. This is, of course, subject to the qualification regarding the absence of any members of the class at that time and the possibility of the birth of members of the class at a later time. In the case of a class gift of a remainder, absent any provision for survivorship of the preceding tenant, the minimum membership is determined at the effective date of the dispositive instrument, and the maximum membership is determined at the time for distribution. The future interest of the member of the class who is alive at the effective date of the instrument is called a vested remainder subject to partial divestment, or subject to open; this means that such member of the class is entitled to a portion of the gift, but such portion is subject to reduction by the birth of additional members of the class prior to the time for distribution.[27]

Obviously the testator can control this situation by providing for payment of income to A for life, remainder to the children of B who are alive at A's death. Here the testator has made his intention clear, and no reliance upon constructional principles

---

25. Zimmerman v. First National Bank, 348 So.2d 1359 (Ala.1977); In re Estate of Doyle, 202 Cal.App.2d 434, 21 Cal.Rptr. 123 (1962); In re Will of Greenwood, 268 A.2d 867 (Del.1970).

26. Hartford National Bank & Trust Co. v. Birge, 159 Conn. 35, 266 A.2d 373 (1970); In re Estate of Coe, 77 N.J.Super. 181, 185 A.2d 696 (1962), reversed on other grounds 42 N.J. 485, 201 A.2d 571 (1964); Everhard v. Brown, 75 Ohio App. 451, 62 N.E.2d 901 (1945). Several states have legislated modifications of this rule as applied to class gifts: Ill.Ann.Stat. ch. 110½, § 4–11; Pa.Stat.Ann.tit. 20, § 2514(5); Tenn.Code Ann. § 32–305.

27. See discussion of remainders supra p. 70.

dealing with survivorship or convenience of distribution is necessary; any child of B must survive the life tenant in order to take, and children of B born after the life tenant's death do not take.

Let us assume a bequest in trust to pay the income to A for life, remainder to the children of B; A and B survive the testator, and B survives A without having had any children at the time of A's death. Does the class remain open? The same principle applies here as in the case of the immediate gift to the children of B where B survives the testator and has had no children; the remainder interest does not fail and pass to the residue or next of kin, but rather is held open until B's death.[28] Of course, if in this situation B had had a child who survived the testator but predeceased the life income beneficiary, the estate of such child would be entitled to take and the class would close upon the death of the life income beneficiary.

Assume a bequest of $50,000 to the children of A to be paid when each reaches age 21. A survives the testator, and A has two children at the date of testator's death, C1 age 16, and C2 age 12. Two years later C3 is born to A. Then three years later C1 arrives at age 21. Then two years later C4 is born to A. Who share in the bequest? The gift appears to be one which is vested with time of payment postponed to age 21.[29] No one was entitled to distribution until C1 arrived at age 21; there was no reason to close the class until that event occurred. In order to determine the share to which C1 is entitled, it is necessary to close the class at that time. Consequently C3 is included within the class of legatees, and C4 is excluded.[30]

Suppose testator bequeaths $60,000 to such children of A who shall attain age 21. A survives the testator, and at testator's death A has two children, C1 age 16, and C2 age 12. Two years later C3 is born to A. Then three years later C1 arrives at age 21. Then C2 dies at age 20. How is the bequest divided? This is a gift in which there is clearly a condition precedent that each member of the class must live to age 21 in order to take. When C1 arrived at age 21, the class closed in order to determine what share C1 was entitled to; C1 got $20,000 at that time.[31] Upon C2's death, the class was reduced to two; at that point C1 became entitled to an additional $10,000. If C3 should survive to age

28. Simes & Smith § 640 (2d ed. 1956); 5 American Law of Property § 22.43 (Casner ed. 1952).

29. See discussion of conditions of survivorship supra pp. 132–34.

30. In re Estate of Winters, 162 So.2d 282 (Fla.Dist.Ct.App.1964); B.M.C. Durfee Trust Co. v. Taylor, 325 Mass. 201, 89 N.E.2d 777 (1950); In re Estate of Murphy, 99 Mont. 114, 43 P.2d 233 (1935); In re Estate of Pergament, 8 Misc.2d 233, 163 N.Y.S.2d 72 (1957).

31. Id.

21, he will then receive his $30,000; if C3 should die under 21, then the remaining $30,000 will go to C1 as the only member of the class.[32]

Assume the same facts as the immediately preceding example, except that C4 is born after C1 arrives at 21 and before C2 dies. Is there any way of sneaking C4 into the class under these circumstances? Why can't C4 take C2's place, assuming of course that he survives to age 21? Would there be any inconvenience involved in this? It would seem not. If C4 had been born after C2's death, there would be inconvenience because the share which had been held back for C2 would have been distributed in part to C1 immediately upon C2's death. But there does not appear to be any authority to support the substitution of C4 for C2 where C4 is born before C2 dies—the standard rule is that the class closes for good when C1 arrives at age 21.

SECTION 5.   PER CAPITA CLASS GIFTS

Testator bequeaths $10,000 to each child of A. Note that this is a different type of gift from those we have been discussing. Here we have a gift of a specific amount of money to each member of a class; in the previous examples we were discussing the gift of an amount which was to be divided among a class. Suppose at testator's death A is alive and has three children. Is the class closed at the testator's death or does it remain open until A dies? The rule is that the class is closed at the testator's death.[33] If the rule were otherwise, the settlement of the estate would have to be delayed until the total number of A's children was determined; it would be impossible to determine how much was distributable to the residuary legatees and how much was to be held back on account of the per capita class gift if the class were not closed at the testator's death. In the case of the bequest of $100,000 to be divided among A's children, A surviving the testator, the class closes at the testator's death because otherwise it would be impossible to determine the shares to which the children then living would be entitled. The reason for closing the class at the testator's death in the case of the per capita gift of a certain amount to each member of the class is different but equally compelling.

Suppose in the preceding per capita class gift example A survived the testator but had no children at the testator's death. Would the gift fail, or would the class remain open until A's death? It has been held that the gift fails.[34] If the result were otherwise

---

32. Simes, Handbook of Law of Future Interests § 102 (2d ed. 1966).

33. Simes & Smith § 648 (2d ed. 1956).

34. Rogers v. Mutch, 10 Ch.D. 25 (1878). See Simes and Smith § 648 (2d ed. 1956); 5 American Law of Property § 22.42 (Casner ed. 1952).

it would be impossible to determine how much to distribute to the residuary legatees and how much to withhold for the class because the class is indefinite in size.   Here we have a different result from the gift of an amount to be divided among the class, A surviving the testator without any children living at the time, because in that situation we know how much to hold back for potential distribution to the class.

Let us assume a bequest of $10,000 to each child of A who reaches age 21.   At testator's death A is living and has two children, C1 age 14, and C2 age 10.   Does the class close at testator's death or does it remain open until there is a child of A entitled to distribution?   The rule is that the class closes at the testator's death although it is not time for distribution.[35]   C1 and C2 are the only potential takers.   If the result were otherwise, it would be impossible for the executor to determine how much to set aside for the class and how much to distribute to the residuary legatees.

35.   Simes & Smith § 648 (2d ed. 1956).

Chapter 7

POWERS OF APPOINTMENT

SECTION 1. INTRODUCTION

The future interest has been defined as an interest (a) which potentially gives the holder the right of possession or enjoyment at some time in the future, and (b) which is regarded as a part of the total present ownership.[1] The creator of the future interest may be the grantor of real property, the settlor of a living trust, or a testator. But the property owner, instead of creating the future interest himself, may choose to delegate the creation of the future interest to another person who will exercise his authority at a later time. This is accomplished by means of the power of appointment. For example, A transfers property to T, in trust, to pay the income to S, A's son, for life, then to pay the income to G, A's grandson, for life, then to pay over the corpus of the trust to such children of G as G shall by will appoint. Another example: A bequeaths property to T, in trust, to pay the income to W, A's wife, for life, then to pay over the principal to such children of A as W shall by will appoint.

In each of the above examples, the owner of property chose to delegate the creation of a future interest to another person who will presumably be in a better position than the property owner to make an intelligent decision as to the ultimate disposition of the property. If the property owner creates the future interest, he makes his decision on the basis of only such information as is available to him at the time of his transfer.

The Restatement of Property has this to say about the usefulness of the power of appointment:

> Owners often wish to control the devolution of their property through two or more generations; and the rule against perpetuities does not prevent an owner who is competently advised from exercising such control for about a century. Plainly no human foresight is adequate to frame in advance dispositions which will meet the exigencies of the maximum period of control or even of the comparatively small fraction thereof commonly utilized by testators and settlors. Births and deaths in varying combinations, the commercial success of some family members and the failure

---

1. Simes & Smith § 1 (2d ed. 1956).

of others, the varying capacities of individuals as to the husbanding of resources, fluctuation in income returns and the value of the monetary unit, legislative action and constitutional amendment reflecting social and political change— all these are factors whose unpredictability indicates the folly of rigid predetermined future limitations and the desirability of gifts containing a substantial element of flexibility. The power of appointment, particularly the special power, is the most efficient device yet contrived by which an owner may obtain such flexibility while still controlling the general purposes to which his property shall be devoted. . . .[2]

The power of appointment had its origins in medieval land law. Prior to the English Statute of Wills in 1540, land was generally not transferable by will. However, A, the owner of fee simple absolute in Blackacre, could enfeoff B and his heirs to the use of A and to the use of those whom A might designate in his will.[3] The will was available for the disposition of personalty, and it could be used to transmit use interests in land. After land became generally devisable, it was no longer necessary to use this device. The power of appointment remained, however, as a means of creating interests in land. As a sophisticated technique of property settlement, it was not widely used in this country until the twentieth century,[4] and the law relating to it is still extremely thin in many problem areas.

It should be pointed out that the owner of property may reserve to himself a power of appointment. For example, A irrevocably transfers property to T, in trust, to pay the income to A for life, then to pay over the corpus of the trust to such persons as A shall by will appoint, and in default of appointment, to the children of A. In this situation A has postponed his final decision as to the disposition of the remainder interest to a later time. The purpose here is clearly different from what it is in the situation in which the power is given to another to be exercised at some time following the death of the creator of the power. Here the property owner may be attempting to avoid estate administration expenses and delay, and possibly claims of his surviving spouse for her statutory forced share or claims of his creditors. He will not avoid estate taxes by this means, he may not have put his property beyond the reach of his creditors, and he may not have placed the property beyond the reach of his surviving spouse.[5]

2. Restatement, Property, Introductory Note Ch. 25, at 1808–09 (1940).

3. See 5 American Law of Property § 23.2 (Casner ed. 1952).

4. Id.

5. See infra pp. 172–75.

The power of revocation reserved by a settlor, and a discretionary power in a trustee to distribute principal or to allocate income among beneficiaries, are similar to the power of appointment, but for pedagogical purposes such powers are generally treated separately from powers of appointment, and this pattern is followed here.[6]   Discussion of such powers is left to the subject of trusts.

SECTION 2. DEFINITIONS

The subject of powers of appointment has its special vocabulary.   The owner of property who creates the power of appointment with respect to it is called the "donor" of the power. The person who is to exercise the power is called the "donee" of the power.   The property interest which is the subject of the power is called "the appointive property."   The persons to whom the appointive property may be appointed are called the "objects of the power" or "permissible appointees".   The persons to whom the appointment is actually made are called the "appointees". Those persons whom the donor designates to receive the appointive property if the donee fails to exercise her power are called the "takers in default".   Needless to say, this vocabulary is not exclusive, and other terms and phrases are sometimes used.

Powers of appointment are characterized by (a) the nature of the objects of the power, and (b) the time when the power can be exercised.   If the power can be exercised in favor of the donee, the donee's creditors, the donee's estate, or the creditors of the donee's estate, the power is called a "general power of appointment".   If the power can be exercised only in favor of a group or class of persons, not including the donee, her estate, her creditors, or the creditors of her estate, the power is called a "special power of appointment".   If a power can be exercised in favor of anyone except the donee, her estate, her creditors, or the creditors of her estate, is it a special power?   It does not fit the traditional definition because the objects of the power are not a specified group or class,[7] but for most analytical purposes it fits the special power category.[8]

The donor may also control the time of exercise of the power. It is common to limit the time of exercise to the date of death of the donee, and to require that the power be exercised by will, in which case the power is said to be a "testamentary power",

6. Restatement, Second, Property, Donative Transfers § 11.1 (Tent. Draft No. 5, 1982) defines the power of appointment to include the power of revocation and the fiduciary discretionary power, but this definition is unusual.

7. See Simes & Smith § 875 (2d ed.

1956); 5 American Law of Property § 23.12 (Casner ed. 1952).

8. Restatement, Second, Property, Donative Transfers § 11.4 (Tent. Draft No. 5, 1982) breaks powers down into general powers and non-general powers; the latter includes any power that is not general.

or a "power exercisable by will". If the donor permits the donee to exercise the power at any time during the donee's lifetime, the power is said to be "presently exercisable", or "inter vivos". The presently exercisable power is invariably required to be exercised by an instrument in writing, and consequently this power is frequently referred to as a power exercisable by deed. The presently exercisable power may be exercisable both during the donee's lifetime and at his death, in which case it is commonly referred to as a "power exercisable by deed or will". It is possible to create a power which is exercisable by deed only after a certain date or event occurs, in which case the power is not presently exercisable; this type of power is apparently uncommon and in this discussion a reference to a power exercisable by deed or to an inter vivos power means that the power is presently exercisable.

So there may be a general testamentary power, a general power exercisable by deed, and a general power exercisable by deed or will. And there may be a special testamentary power, a special power exercisable by deed, and a special power exercisable by deed or will.[9]

A bequeaths $100,000 to T, in trust, to pay the income to W, A's wife, for her life, and upon W's death, to pay over the principal of the trust to such persons as W shall by will appoint. W is authorized to appoint to anyone, without limitation. When the donor places no limitation upon the permissible appointees, it has been generally held that the donee may appoint to herself or her estate, thereby making the power a general power.[10] The time at which W may exercise the power is the date of her death, and the exercise must be by will. This is a general testamentary power.

A bequeaths $100,000 to T, in trust, to pay the income to C, A's child, for his life, and upon C's death to pay over the principal of the trust to such issue of C as C shall at any time appoint by

---

9. Powers are occasionally given the additional labels of collateral, in gross, or appendant. A collateral power is one held by a donee who has no interest of any kind in the assets subject to the power. A power in gross is one held by a donee who has an interest in the assets subject to the power which cannot be affected by the exercise of the power, e.g., a life tenant with a power over the remainder. A power appendant is one held by a donee who owns the property interest in the assets subject to the power which can be divested by the exercise of the power; it seems that the power appendant adds nothing to the ownership and is generally not recognized today as a power. See Restatement, Second, Property, Donative Transfers § 12.3 (Tent. Draft No. 5, 1982). These several classifications are seldom used today and do not have much analytical usefulness. See 5 American Law of Property §§ 23.12, 23.13 (Casner ed. 1952); Simes & Smith § 876 (2d ed. 1956).

10. Wilson v. United States, 254 F.Supp. 822 (E.D.Pa.1966), reversed and remanded on other grounds 372 F.2d 232 (3d Cir. 1967); In re Jackson Trust, 351 Pa. 89, 40 A.2d 393 (1945); Restatement, Second, Property, Donative Transfers § 12.2 (Tent. Draft No. 5, 1982).

deed or will.   C may appoint only to his issue.   C may exercise
the power during his lifetime or at his death by will.   This is a
special power exercisable by deed or will.   It should be noted
that C's power of appointment is over only the remainder interest;
the appointive property is a future interest.   C could have been
given a presently exercisable power to appoint principal to his
issue which would call for distribution of principal to the appointees at the time of the appointment.   This would be a power
over a present fee interest.   Such an appointment would result
in the partial or total termination of the trust prior to C's death.

A bequeaths $100,000 to T, in trust, to pay the income to W,
A's wife, for life, and to pay over the principal of the trust, or
any part thereof, during the lifetime of W or after W's death,
to such persons as C, A's son, shall from time to time appoint
by deed or will.   C may appoint to anyone, including himself,
at any time.   This is a general power exercisable by deed or
will.   C may at any time vest in himself absolute title in the
trust corpus.   All that stands between C and full ownership is
the formality of execution and delivery of a piece of paper.   It
should be noted that in this situation C, the donee, could have
been given a presently exercisable power over the principal of
the trust following W's life interest—that is, a power presently
exercisable over only the remainder interest in the trust.   This
would give C, the donee, the equivalent of ownership during the
life tenant's life of the remainder interest in the trust;   in other
words, C could appoint the remainder to himself and then proceed
to sell or otherwise transfer such interest.

How close to ownership is the general testamentary power?
A bequeaths $100,000 to T, in trust, to pay the income to B for
life, and upon B's death, to pay the principal of the trust to such
persons as B shall by will appoint.   B can exercise his power
only at his death;   B cannot enjoy the principal or dispose of the
remainder interest during his lifetime.   B cannot make the remainder interest his own during his lifetime, although he can
appoint to his estate or to his creditors at his death.   The general
testamentary power, when combined with the life income interest
in the donee, approaches ownership but is not the equivalent of it.

Although the donee is empowered to appoint, he cannot be
compelled to appoint and he may fail to appoint.   To provide for
this contingency, it is customary for the donor of the power to
set forth in the creating instrument the persons who shall receive
the property in the event the donee, for whatever reason, fails
to exercise the power.

Let us assume that A conveys Blackacre to B for life, remainder to such persons as B shall by will appoint, and in default
of appointment, to the children of B who shall survive B.   Who

has title to the property if B fails to appoint and no children of B survive B? The interest of the takers in default was in the nature of a contingent remainder which did not vest; the donor designated the future interest in the event the donee failed to do so, but the condition precedent to taking did not materialize.[11] A had a reversion, and fee simple absolute in possession is vested in A or A's assigns, or A's heirs or devisees. Needless to say, if A did not set forth any takers in default in the creating instrument and if B died intestate, then the property would similarly revert to A or his successors.

It should be emphasized that the power of appointment, whether general or special, is personal to the donee; the donee cannot transfer or assign his power to appoint to another person.[12] As we shall see, the donee may be able to create further powers in the exercise of a power in certain circumstances, but this has been distinguished from the direct transfer of the power as such.[13]

SECTION 3. EXCLUSIVE AND NON-EXCLUSIVE SPECIAL POWERS

Suppose A is given a power to appoint "among A's children". A has three children. Can A appoint all the appointive property to one child? Or must the donee appoint some part of the appointive property to each of the children? If the donee must appoint some part to each, is there a minimum amount which must be appointed to each child? A special power in which the donee is required to appoint some part to each of the members of the class is described as a "non-exclusive" power; a special power in which the donee may appoint to some member of the class and exclude others is called an "exclusive" power. In the above example, the donor's intent is less than clear, and the courts have adopted constructional preferences to resolve the difficulty.

The donor can, of course, make it clear that the donee can appoint and exclude a member of the class of permissible appointees; a power to appoint to "such of A's children as donee shall select" would be a clear case of an exclusive power. The donor can make it clear that the power is non-exclusive by creating a power to appoint "to each child of A such share of the appointive property as donee shall designate". If there is ambiguity, as in the case of the power to appoint "among the children of A", some courts have adopted a constructional preference for

---

11. In this situation there will be no condition of survivorship of the life tenant in the absence of an express provision therefor. See supra p. 127.

12. De Charette v. De Charette, 264

Ky. 525, 94 S.W.2d 1018 (1936); Boston Safe Deposit & Trust Co. v. Prindle, 290 Mass. 577, 195 N.E. 793 (1935). See Simes & Smith § 943 (2d ed. 1956).

13. See infra pp. 157–60.

the "non-exclusive" power,[14] while others have adopted a constructional preference for the "exclusive" power,[15] the latter being probably the prevailing construction.

If it is assumed that a special power is non-exclusive, is it possible to satisfy the requirements of such a power by a nominal appointment to one or more members of the class? Let us assume that A has a non-exclusive power to appoint among his children, of which there are three, and that the appointive property has a value of $50,000. Can A appoint $10 to one child, $10 to another child, and $49,980 to the third child? Or must A appoint a "substantial" amount to each member of the class? Some courts have adopted the "illusory" doctrine—that is to say, a nominal or "illusory" appointment is not compliance with the strictures of the non-exclusive power.[16] Other courts have held that an appointment of any amount, however small, or nominal, constitutes compliance with the limitations of the non-exclusive power.[17] To recognize a power as non-exclusive, and then to permit a nominal appointment to constitute compliance, does not make much sense.

It should also be pointed out that if the donee of a non-exclusive power appoints in a manner inconsistent with the principles of the non-exclusive power, the appointment is invalid in toto,[18] and the property passes to the takers in default, or if there are no takers in default provided for, the appointive property passes in equal parts to the class of permissible appointees as discussed below.[19]

Obviously the issue of "exclusive" and "non-exclusive" has nothing to do with general powers.

SECTION 4. PROPERTY INTERESTS WHICH MAY BE CREATED BY APPOINTMENT

In the exercise of the donee's power of appointment, what interests in the appointive property can he create? Must the

14. In re Sloan's Estate, 7 Cal.App.2d 319, 46 P.2d 1007 (1935); Hopkins v. Dimock, 138 N.J.Eq. 434, 48 A.2d 204 (1946), affirmed 140 N.J.Eq. 182, 52 A.2d 853 (1947). See 5 American Law of Property § 23.57 (Casner ed. 1952).

15. Harlan v. Citizens National Bank, 251 S.W.2d 284 (Ky.1952); Moore v. Emery, 137 Me. 259, 18 A.2d 781 (1941); Frye v. Lorin, 330 Mass. 389, 113 N.E.2d 595 (1953). Restatement, Second, Property, Donative Transfers § 21.1 (Tent. Draft No. 6, 1983) provides that the power is exclusive unless the donor has specified the minimum share which an object must receive.

16. Barrett's Executor v. Barrett, 166 Ky. 411, 179 S.W. 396 (1915). See Frye v. Loring, 330 Mass. 389, 113 N.E.2d 595 (1953).

17. Hawthorn v. Ulrich, 207 Ill. 430, 69 N.E. 885 (1904); Hodges v. Stegall, 169 Tenn. 202, 83 S.W.2d 901 (1935). See Simes & Smith § 982 (2d ed. 1956).

18. Barrett's Executor v. Barrett, 166 Ky. 411, 179 S.W. 396 (1915); 5 American Law of Property § 23.57, at 621 (Casner ed. 1952).

19. See infra p. 165.

donee appoint only a legal fee simple absolute, or can the donee create equitable and legal present and future interests? Can the donee create a power of appointment in the exercise of his power of appointment?

Let us first consider these questions with respect to the presently exercisable general power. The donee can at any moment vest in himself the total ownership of the property interest which is the subject of the power. There is no reason why there should be any limitation upon such donee's power to create any interests of any kind, subject of course to the limitations of the rule against perpetuities.[20]

But suppose the donor purports to limit such donee's power to create future interests, or to create a trust, or to create a power of appointment in the exercise of the power—is this restriction effective? It seems it should not be binding because the donee can unquestionably accomplish the circumvention of the restriction by appointing to himself and then disposing of the property as he sees fit. The donee of the general power exercisable by deed, or by deed or will, has the substantial equivalent of absolute ownership in the property interest which is the subject of the power, and his power of disposition should be equivalent to that of a fee owner in every respect.[21] It is not clear, however, that such restrictions are invalid.[22]

Does the donee of a general testamentary power have complete freedom in the creation of property interests? This power is not the equivalent of absolute ownership of the appointive property interest, but as of the donee's death he has the power to appoint to his estate—it is the equivalent of ownership at death insofar as one can be thought to have ownership at the time of his death. Can the donee dispose of the property as if he were disposing of his own property? It is generally accepted that he can,[23] although with respect to the rule against perpetuities there are differences between the disposition of owned property and the disposition of property subject to a general testamentary power.[24]

But suppose the donor purports to limit the exercise of the general testamentary power to the appointment of a legal fee

---

20. See infra p. 203.

21. See Simes & Smith § 976 (2d ed. 1956); Restatement, Second, Property, Donative Transfers § 19.1 (Tent. Draft No. 6, 1983).

22. See cases cited infra note 26.

23. First National Bank of Arizona v. First National Bank of Birmingham, 348

So.2d 1041 (Ala.1977); Lamkin v. Safe Deposit & Trust Co., 192 Md. 472, 64 A.2d 704 (1949); Massey v. Guaranty Trust Co., 142 Neb. 237, 5 N.W.2d 279 (1942); In re Hart's Will, 262 App.Div. 190, 28 N.Y.S.2d 781 (1941). See Simes & Smith § 976 (2d ed. 1956).

24. See infra pp. 201–203.

interest only—would this be an effective restriction? Since the donee has the power to appoint to his estate and then dispose of the property as he sees fit, there doesn't seem to be sound reason to hold the restriction effective.[25] There is, however, some authority that such a restriction is effective.[26]

So the better view is that the donee of the general power, under any circumstances, can appoint Blackacre to A for life, then to B for life, remainder to C in fee. Or the donee can appoint to T, in trust, to pay the income to A for life, remainder to such persons as A shall by will appoint. But, in the latter appointment, has the donee attempted to assign or delegate his power, which, of course, is not permitted?[27] The generally accepted view is that it constitutes a permissible exercise of a general power rather than an improper delegation or assignment.[28] If the donee can appoint the fee to a person, then he should be able to give that person a power of appointment; also if the donee can appoint to himself or his estate and then create the power, he should be permitted to create the power directly.[29]

It is clear that a donor of a special power can place whatever restrictions he wishes upon the nature of the interests which the donee can appoint. The donor of the special power can effectively limit the donee to the appointment of a legal fee interest only, or prohibit the donee from creating a power of appointment.[30] The reasoning which denies validity to such restrictions in the case of the general power is not applicable to the special power.

In the absence of any explicit restriction, is there any reason why the donee of a special power cannot appoint such legal and equitable present and future interests as she wishes? There is no reason why this cannot be done, so long as the appointees are

---

25. See Restatement, Second, Property, Donative Transfers § 19.1 (Tent. Draft No. 6, 1983); Simes & Smith § 976 (2d ed. 1956).

26. See Equitable Trust Co. v. James, 29 Del.Ch. 166, 47 A.2d 303 (1946); Massey v. Guaranty Trust Co., 142 Neb. 237, 5 N.W.2d 279 (1942); Marx v. Rice, 1 N.J. 574, 65 A.2d 48 (1949).

27. See supra p. 154.

28. Lamkin v. Safe Deposit & Trust Co., 192 Md. 472, 64 A.2d 704 (1949); Garfield v. State Street Trust Co., 320 Mass. 646, 70 N.E.2d 705 (1947); In re Wildenburg's Estate, 174 Misc. 503, 21 N.Y.S.2d 331 (Surr.Ct.1940). But see De Charette

v. De Charette, 264 Ky. 525, 94 S.W.2d 1018 (1936), where the appointment of a special testamentary power in the exercise of a general testamentary power was held to be an improper delegation.

29. Restatement, Second, Property, Donative Transfers § 19.2 (Tent. Draft No. 6, 1983).

30. Union & New Haven Trust Co. v. Taylor, 133 Conn. 221, 50 A.2d 168 (1946); Loring v. Karri-Davies, 371 Mass. 346, 357 N.E.2d 11 (1976); In re Kennedy's Will, 279 N.Y. 255, 18 N.E.2d 146 (1938); Restatement, Second, Property, Donative Transfers § 19.3, 19.4 (Tent. Draft No. 6, 1983).

all objects of the special power.[31]   Let us assume that A has a
special power to appoint among his descendants.   A wishes to
have the benefits extend for more than one generation—A appoints to T, in trust, to pay the income to C, a son of A, for life,
then to pay the income to G, a grandson of A, for life, then to
pay over the principal to the children of G who survive G and
reach age 21.   The donee of the special power has created present
and future equitable interests and all the beneficiaries are within
the class of permissible appointees.   It should be pointed out
that if a trust is created in the exercise of a special power, the
trustee need not be within the class of permissible appointees;
the trust beneficiaries are the appointees.[32]

Suppose A, the donee of a special power to appoint among
A's children, appoints to C, A's son, for life, remainder to such
persons as C shall by will appoint.   Here A has appointed a
limited interest to C, an object of the power, and has appointed
to such object a general testamentary power.   Is such an appointment by A a valid exercise of A's special power?   A could
have appointed a fee simple absolute to C;   instead he appointed
a life estate and a general power exercisable only at C's death.
This is not the same as fee ownership, but it approaches it.   We
have stated above that a donee of a power cannot assign or delegate the exercise of his power to another person;   the power
of appointment is said to be personal to the donee.   Has A in
the preceding example delegated his power to C?   A did not
assign to someone the power to select among A's children;   rather
A gave C, an object of the power, a limited interest plus a general
testamentary power.   It seems that the better view is that this
exercise of a special power is valid,[33] but there is some authority
for the proposition that such exercise is an improper delegation
of the power.[34]   If it is held that the power in C is improper,
there is no reason why the appointment of the life interest in C
should not be upheld.[35]

31.   See Equitable Trust Co. v. Foulke,
28 Del.Ch. 238, 40 A.2d 713 (1945);   In re
Estate of Spencer, 232 N.W.2d 491 (Iowa,
1975);   Loring v. Karri-Davies, 371 Mass.
346, 357 N.E.2d 11 (1976);   National State
Bank v. Morrison, 9 N.J.Super. 552, 75
A.2d 916 (1950);   annot., 94 A.L.R.3d 895,
899 (1979).

32.   Simes & Smith § 976 (2d ed. 1956).

33.   See Stone v. Forbes, 189 Mass. 163,
75 N.E. 141 (1905);   National State Bank
v. Morrison, 9 N.J.Super. 552, 75 A.2d 916
(1950);   Restatement, Second, Property,
Donative Transfers § 19.4 (Tent. Draft No.

6, 1983);   Simes & Smith § 977 (2d ed.
1956).

34.   Union & New Haven Trust Co. v.
Taylor, 133 Conn. 221, 50 A.2d 168 (1946);
Thayer v. Rivers, 179 Mass. 280, 60 N.E.
796 (1901).

35.   First National Bank of Arizona v.
First National Bank of Birmingham, 348
So.2d 1041 (Ala.1977);   In re Estate of
Spencer, 232 N.W.2d 491 (Iowa, 1975);
Thayer v. Rivers, 179 Mass. 280, 60 N.E.
796 (1901);   In re Cary's Will, 44 Misc.2d
929, 255 N.Y.S.2d 419 (1965).

Suppose A, a donee of a power to appoint among A's issue, appoints to T, in trust, to pay the income to C, A's son, for life, then to pay over the principal to such of C's children as C shall by will appoint. Is this a valid exercise of A's special power? The life interest of C is clearly within the power. The objects of the special power given to C are also within the scope of A's power. C is given the discretion by A to choose, at C's death, the members of the class of A's permissible appointees who are to receive the property. Does this constitute an improper delegation of A's power? The exercise by A seems reasonable, although it is clearly a form of delegation of discretion which the donor of the power vested in A. It is arguable that the special power in C created by the exercise of the special power in A constitutes an invalid delegation by A.[36] Nevertheless, the better view is that this is a valid exercise of A's power in all respects.[37]

Suppose A, a donee of a special power to appoint among A's children, appoints to T, in trust, to pay the income to C, A's son, for life, then to pay over the principal to such children of C as C shall by will appoint. Is this a valid exercise of A's power? C is a member of the class of permissible appointees, but C's children are not. If C were given a general power by A, as in a previous example, there would be little trouble in upholding A's exercise since C, an object of A's power, has been given something which approaches fee ownership.[38] But here C can appoint only to individuals who are not members of the group included within A's special power. A could not have appointed a remainder to C's children; A cannot appoint a special power to C to be exercised only in favor of C's children.[39]

What happens to the life interest appointed to C in the preceding example? That aspect of A's exercise is within the scope of A's power. There is no reason why the trust for C's life should not be given full effect. A had the power to appoint a fee to C; it is not essential, however, that he appoint a fee. It is permissible for A to exercise his power partially by appointing less than the totality of the property interest subject to the power,[40] unless the donor of the special power has expressly required that the appointment be of the entire property interest.[41]

36. See Simes & Smith § 977 (2d ed. 1956).

37. In re Finucane's Will, 199 Misc. 1069, 100 N.Y.S.2d 1005 (Surr.Ct.1950); In re Lewis' Estates, 269 Pa. 379, 112 A. 454 (1921); Conn.Gen.Stat.Ann. § 45–123a; Va.Code § 55–25.1; Restatement, Second, of Property, Donative Transfers § 19.4 (Tent. Draft No. 6, 1983).

38. See supra p. 158.

39. In re Cary's Will, 44 Misc.2d 929, 255 N.Y.S.2d 419 (1965); Restatement, Second, Property, Donative Transfers § 19.4 (Tent. Draft No. 6, 1983).

40. See cases cited supra note 35.

41. See cases cited supra note 30.

Continuing our discussion of the preceding example, where does the property go on C's death? To the takers in default set forth in A's instrument exercising his power, provided they are within the class of permissible appointees, or if such default clause does not exist, to the takers in default set forth in the instrument executed by the donor of A's power. In the absence of any provision for takers in default in the donor's instrument, the property will go in equal parts to the children of A, the objects of A's special power, on the basis of principles discussed below.[42]

Suppose A, the donee of a special power to appoint among his descendants, appoints to C, A's son, for life, remainder to such issue of A as W, A's wife, may by deed or will appoint. The persons who can receive the property are all members of the class of permissible appointees. However, the "sub-power", as it is sometimes called, created by A in the exercise of his power, is in W, a non-object of the power, to appoint among A's issue. Previously, we have seen that the designation of an object of the original power as the donee of a "sub-power" may be a proper exercise by A. Does it make any difference that W, who could not receive any of the appointive property, is given discretion to appoint? Or is this an improper delegation of A's power? Judicial authority on this point is sparse, but the Restatement upholds this power in W.[43]

It is generally accepted that the donee of a power may exercise it partially by appointing a limited interest only in all the appointive property,[44] or by appointing a fee interest in only a part of the appointive property.[45] For example, A, donee of a general power, appoints to T, in trust, to pay the income to B for life, and no further provision for disposition is made by A. There is no reason why the partial appointment should not be valid, the property after the appointee's death passing to the takers in default, or, in the absence of such provision, to the donor or her estate. Another example: A, donee of a general testamentary power over property of a value of $200,000, appoints $100,000 to B, and makes no disposition of the remaining $100,000. There is no reason why the appointment of the $100,000 should not be valid, the remaining unappointed property passing to the takers in default, or in the absence of any provision therefor, to the donor or her estate. It is recognized, however, that if the donor of a special power expressly requires the donee to make an ap-

---

42. See infra p. 165.

43. Restatement, Second, Property, Donative Transfers § 19.4 (Tent. Draft No. 6, 1983).

44. Welch v. Morse, 323 Mass. 233, 81 N.E.2d 361 (1948). See annot., 94 A.L.R.3d 895 (1979).

45. In re Baird's Estate, 120 Cal. App. 2d 219, 260 P.2d 1052 (1953). See Simes & Smith § 976 (2d ed. 1956).

pointment of the entire interest, such requirement will be effective;[46] but it has been maintained that any such restriction on the exercise of the general power should be ineffective.[47]

SECTION 5.　IMPLIED EXERCISE OF POWERS

In the case of a testamentary power, the question may arise as to whether the donee has exercised his power in his will. Let us assume that A, donee of a general testamentary power, dies leaving a will in which he "bequeaths and devises all my property, real and personal, to B", but makes no reference to any power of appointment. Has A exercised his power? The question of whether the power has been exercised is, at least in theory, one of the testator's intent, but in this situation there often is little or no evidence of intention. A may have considered his power to be his property; A may simply have forgotten about his power; A may have been aware of his power but deliberately did not exercise it. In the face of such an ambiguous situation, the court must indulge in some kind of presumption, and the usual presumption at common law has been that the power was not exercised.[48]

Courts, however, have sometimes inferred an intention to exercise when the will is silent, and the following have been standard, but not exclusive, indicia of intention to exercise: (a) reference in the will to the power; (b) reference in the will to the appointive property; (c) ineffectuality of dispositive provisions in the will if the will does not exercise the power.[49] As an example of (a), the donee-testator may make reference to his power of appointment in connection with certain administrative provisions of the will. As an example of (b), the testator who is the donee of a power of appointment over Blackacre may purport to devise Blackacre to X. Certainly this should constitute an exercise of the power in favor of X.[50] As an example of (c),

46. See 5 American Law of Property § 23.48 (Casner ed. 1952); Restatement, Second, Property, Donative Transfers § 19.3 (Tent. Draft No. 6, 1983).

47. See 5 American Law of Property § 23.48 (Casner ed. 1952); Restatement, Second, Property, Donative Transfers § 19.1 (Tent. Draft No. 6, 1983).

48. Morgan Guaranty Trust Co. v. Huntington, 149 Conn. 331, 179 A.2d 604 (1962); May v. Citizens & Southern Bank, 223 Ga. 614, 157 S.E.2d 279 (1967); Bussing v. Hough, 237 Iowa 194, 21 N.W.2d 587 (1946); Republic National Bank v. Fredericks, 155 Tex. 79, 283 S.W.2d 39 (1955).

49. Blagge v. Miles, 3 F.Cas. 559 (C.C.Mass.1841) (No. 1479); DiSesa v. Hickey, 160 Conn. 250, 278 A.2d 785 (1971); DePass v. Kansas Masonic Home Corp., 132 Fla. 455, 181 So. 410 (1938); Emery v. Emery, 325 Ill. 212, 156 N.E. 364 (1927); In re Proestler's Will, 232 Iowa 640, 5 N.W.2d 922 (1942).

50. Cathell v. Burris, 21 Del.Ch. 233, 187 A. 9 (1936); Hopkins v. Fauble, 47 Ill.App.2d 263, 197 N.E.2d 725 (1964); Osburn v. Murphy, 135 Ind.App. 291, 193 N.E.2d 669 (1963); Restatement, Second, Property, Donative Transfers § 17.4 (Tent. Draft No. 6, 1983).

the donee of a general testamentary power may leave a net probate estate of $20,000 and a will in which he bequeaths $10,000 to X, $5,000 to Y, and the residue of his estate in trust to pay income to Z for life, remainder over to Z's children; the appointive property has a value of $100,000. It is apparent that the will would not be effectual unless it is construed to exercise the power. In such circumstances, it seems reasonable to conclude that the donee-testator intended his will to exercise the power, at least if his financial situation was not radically different at the time of execution of the will from what it was at the time of his death.[51]

More than half the states now have statutes dealing with the question of the implied exercise of a power by a residuary clause or general disposition of the testator's entire estate. A number of the statutes, including those based on the Uniform Probate Code § 2–610, adopt the presumption that the power is not exercised unless there is evidence of an intention to exercise it.[52] Some of the statutes adopt the contrary presumption that the power is exercised unless there is evidence of an intention not to exercise it;[53] many of these statutes are limited to general powers.[54]

Let us look at a refinement of this problem. Suppose A, donee of a general testamentary power, expressly exercises his power in his will in favor of B, but the exercise is invalid because the appointee predeceased the donee; lapse in appointment is discussed below. A subsequent residuary clause in the will disposes of all the donee's property, real and personal, to C. Does the residuary clause constitute an exercise of the power? Does it follow that because the specific exercise is invalid, the donee intends that the benefit accrue to the residuary legatee? If the donee's intent is our guide, then this is another case of reading the mind of a dead man who obviously did not focus upon the problem, a rather speculative undertaking at best. On the basis

---

51. Hartford-Connecticut Trust Co. v. Thayer, 105 Conn. 57, 134 A. 155 (1926); Illinois State Trust Co. v. Southern Illinois National Bank, 29 Ill.App.3d 1, 329 N.E.2d 805 (1975); Bar Harbor Banking & Trust Co. v. Preachers' Aid Society of the Methodist Church, 244 A.2d 558 (Me.1968); Hood v. Francis, 137 N.J.Eq. 200, 44 A.2d 182 (1945). See Restatement, Second, Property, Donative Transfers § 17.5 (Tent. Draft No. 6, 1983).

52. E.g., Alaska Stat. § 13.11.265; Fla.Stat.Ann. § 732.607; Mass.Gen.Laws Ann. ch. 191, § 1A; Or.Rev.Stat. § 112.410. This is the position of Restatement, Second, Property, Donative Transfers § 17.3 (Tent. Draft No. 6, 1983).

53. E.g., Ky.Rev.Stat.Ann. § 394.060; N.Y.Est. Powers & Trusts Law § 10–6.1; Okla.Stat.Ann. tit. 60, § 299.10; S.D.Comp.Laws Ann. § 29–5–24.

54. E.g., N.C.Gen.Stat. § 31–43; Pa.Stat.Ann. tit. 20, § 2514 (13); R.I.Gen.Laws § 33–6–17; Va.Code § 64.1–67. For a thorough discussion of the implied exercise statutes, see French, Exercise of Powers of Appointment: Should Intent To Exercise Be Inferred From A General Disposition of Property?, 1979 Duke L.J. 747.

of the fictitious presumed intent of the donee, it has been held that the residuary clause does exercise the power.[55]   Of course, if a lapse statute applies to the predeceased appointee, the legal result may be different;   this question is discussed below.[56]

Let us assume that A, donee of a general testamentary power, leaves a will which provides that he "bequeaths, devises, and appoints all my property, real and personal, including all property with respect to which I have a power of appointment, to my friend, B."   This language, in which the donee appears to treat his owned property and the appointive property alike as one fund, has been called a "blending clause."   B predeceases A, thereby invalidating the testamentary disposition and the appointment. Does it necessarily follow that the appointive property passes to the takers in default, if provision was made therefor, or to the donor or his estate?   Should the court in this situation find an implied exercise in favor of the estate of the donee?   Is it significant whether or not there is provision for takers in default in the donor's instrument creating the power?   The case law is quite thin, but there is authority that there is an implied exercise in favor of the estate of the donee even where there is provision for takers in default.[57]   The theory is that when a donee uses a blending clause he indicates an intention to dispose of his owned property and appointive property in the same way, and consequently if the appointment fails the appointive property passes to the donee's estate for all purposes;   if the estate is solvent, the property passes to the donee's intestate takers.   It is sometimes said that by the use of a blending clause the donee "captures" the appointive property for his estate.   This legal phenomenon is sometimes referred to as the doctrine of capture.

The doctrine of capture has also been applied in the case of an express and specific appointment in trust, without any blending clause, in which the trust failed.   The trustee was deemed to hold the appointive property on resulting trust for the donee's estate.   The creation of the trust, the holding of title by the trustee, was considered to take the property from the donor or his successors for all purposes.   If the doctrine of capture is

---

55.   Van Wagenen v. Fox, 22 N.Y.S.2d 803 (Sup.Ct.1940);   Jull Estate, 370 Pa. 434, 88 A.2d 753 (1952).   In both New York and Pennsylvania a residuary clause was presumed to exercise the general power.   See Logan v. Harris Trust & Savings Bank, 8 Ill.App.2d 61, 130 N.E.2d 211 (1955).

56.   See infra pp. 165–67.

57.   Fiduciary Trust Co. v. Mishou, 321 Mass. 615, 75 N.E.2d 3 (1947);   Bradford v. Andrew, 308 Ill. 458, 139 N.E. 922 (1923);   Restatement, Second, Property, Donative Transfers § 23.2 (Tent. Draft No. 7, 1984).   But see Bundy v. United States Trust Co., 257 Mass. 72, 153 N.E. 337 (1926), in which the provision for takers in default precluded the implied appointment to the estate of the donee.

based on the presumed intent of the donee, then this result is somewhat difficult to justify.[58]

Let us assume that A, donee of a general testamentary power, leaves a will which makes no reference to any power of appointment and disposes of all of A's real and personal property to B who predeceases A, thereby invalidating the disposition to B. All of A's owned property passes by intestacy. Has A exercised his general testamentary power? If so, by what reasoning, and who are the appointees? If the jurisdiction is one which presumes that the will exercises the power although no mention is made of the power, then it may be contended that there is an implied blending clause, the attempted exercise in favor of B "captured" the appointive property, and there is an implied appointment in favor of A's estate.[59]

If there is a blending clause in the will in which the donee of the power treats his owned property and the appointive property as a unit, and the terms of the disposition and appointment are effective, the appointive property does not become part of the estate of the donee of the power for purposes of the surviving spouse's forced share or for purposes of estate administration generally.[60]

Suppose there is neither an express nor an implied exercise of a general power by the donee—to whom does the appointive property pass? The property passes to the takers in default if the donor has so provided, or if not, then to the donor or his estate.

The implied exercise does not fit easily into the concept of the special power. For one thing, the donee of a special power cannot appoint to his estate; so the doctrine of capture has no application. In other respects there is no reason why there cannot be an implied exercise of a special power.[61] However, the clause in the will which exercises the power by implication

---

58. Talbot v. Riggs, 287 Mass. 144, 191 N.E. 360 (1934); Marx v. Rice, 3 N.J.Super. 581, 67 A.2d 918 (1949); Restatement, Second, Property Donative Transfers § 23.2 comment b (Tent. Draft No. 7, 1984); Restatement, Second, Trusts § 426 (1959). The Talbot case indicates that there would be no implied appointment if there had been provision for takers in default. In Northern Trust Co. v. Porter, 368 Ill. 256, 13 N.E.2d 487 (1938), the doctrine of capture was not applied where there was a provision for takers in default.

59. Old Colony Trust Co. v. Allen, 307 Mass. 40, 29 N.E.2d 310 (1940); Restatement, Second, Property, Donative Trans-

fers § 23.2 comment d (Tent. Draft No. 7, 1984). See Simes & Smith § 974 (2d ed. 1956). In the Old Colony Trust Co. case, there was no provision for takers in default.

60. In re Breault's Estate, 29 Ill.2d 165, 193 N.E.2d 824 (1963); Harlan National Bank v. Brown, 317 S.W.2d 903 (Ky.1958); Kates' Estate, 282 Pa. 417, 128 A. 97 (1925); Rhode Island Hospital Trust Co. v. Anthony, 49 R.I. 339, 142 A. 531 (1928). However, Restatement, Second, Property, Donative Transfers § 22.1 provides in this circumstance that the appointive assets are ratably applied to debts and administration expenses.

must dispose of the property to the objects of the power, and probably to the objects alone; inclusion of a non-object probably would have the effect of negating any intention on the part of the donee to appoint.[62]

Suppose there is neither an express nor an implied exercise of a special power by the donee; to whom does the appointive property pass? The property passes to the takers in default if the donor has so provided in the instrument creating the power. If there is no provision for takers in default, then it might be expected that the appointive property would pass to the donor or his estate, but in these circumstances the courts generally have directed the disposition of the property equally among the members of the appointive class.[63] There are two theories employed to support such a result: (a) implied gift in default of appointment to the members of the appointive class in equal parts,[64] and (b) donee's special power was "in trust" and the court will see that the "trust" is carried out despite the failure of the "trustee" to do so. The donee, of course, is not a trustee in any real sense, but this construct has been used to rationalize the result.[65] It seems that what the courts are saying is that it is more in keeping with the donor's purpose to dispose of the property to the members of the class equally than to let the property fall to the donor's heirs or residuary legatees. The concept of an "implied gift in default" seems to be more realistic than the "trust".

SECTION 6. LAPSE IN APPOINTMENT

If a testator bequeaths or devises property to a legatee or devisee who predeceases the testator, the bequest or devise is said to "lapse" and is ineffective. Many jurisdictions have enacted statutes which provide that in the case of a lapse of a bequest or devise to a descendant or other defined relation of the testator, the bequest or devise shall pass instead to the des-

61. Fiduciary Trust Co. v. First National Bank, 344 Mass. 1, 181 N.E.2d 6 (1962); In re Biddle's Estate, 333 Pa. 316, 5 A.2d 158 (1939). See statutes cited supra note 53.

62. MacLean v. Citizens Fidelity Bank & Trust Co., 437 S.W.2d 766 (Ky.1969); Chase National Bank v. Chicago Title & Trust Co., 155 Misc. 61, 279 N.Y.S. 327 (Sup.Ct.1935), affirmed 246 App.Div. 201, 284 N.Y.S. 472 (1935), affirmed 271 N.Y. 602, 3 N.E.2d 205 (1936); In re Biddle's Estate, 333 Pa. 316, 5 A.2d 158 (1939).

63. Oglesby v. Springfield Marine Bank, 385 Ill. 414, 52 N.E.2d 1000 (1944); First Portland National Bank v. Rodrique, 157 Me. 277, 172 A.2d 107 (1961); Daniel v. Brown, 156 Va. 563, 159 S.E. 209 (1931). Restatement, Second, Property, Donative Transfers § 24.2 supports this result. See 1 Scott, The Law of Trusts § 27.1 (3d ed. 1967).

64. In re Estate of Spencer, 232 N.W.2d 491 (Iowa, 1975); Bridgewater v. Turner, 161 Tenn. 111, 29 S.W.2d 659 (1930).

65. Oglesby v. Springfield Marine Bank, 385 Ill. 414, 52 N.E.2d 1000 (1944); First-Mechanics National Bank v. First-Mechanics National Bank, 137 N.J.Eq. 106, 43 A.2d 674 (1945); In re Will of Seidman, 88 Misc.2d 462, 389 N.Y.S.2d 729 (Surr.Ct.1976), decree modified 58 A.D.2d 72, 395 N.Y.S.2d 674 (1977); Daniel v. Brown, 156 Va. 563, 159 S.E. 209 (1931).

cendants of such predeceased legatee or devisee who survive the testator. The testator may protect against lapse and the application of the lapse statute by providing expressly that the gift will fail or pass to another person, if the legatee or devisee predeceases the testator. This subject of lapse is discussed in some detail in the section dealing with conditions of survivorship.[66]

Does the doctrine of lapse, and the lapse statute, have any bearing upon the exercise of the testamentary power of appointment? Suppose that A, donee of a general testamentary power, appoints to B who predeceases A. Applying the doctrine of lapse to the testamentary appointment, by way of analogy to the testamentary disposition of owned property, the courts hold that the appointment to B is ineffective.[67] Is the lapse statute applicable, assuming B is one of the class of "legatees" covered by the statute? Although the statutes usually do not specifically deal with the question of lapse in the testamentary appointment,[68] the courts have held that the statute applies to the lapsed appointment under a general power.[69] It should be emphasized that for the statute to apply the appointee must have the requisite relationship to the donee of the power.[69a]

Do the same principles apply in the case of the special testamentary power? Suppose A, donee of a special testamentary power to appoint among his children, appoints to his son, B, who predeceases A. The doctrine of lapse is applied and the appointment to son B is ineffective. Does the lapse statute apply? If it were to apply, the result would be an appointment to a nonobject of the power; the grandchildren of A are not objects of the power. Consequently, the lapse statute has been held to be inapplicable in this situation.[70] But suppose the appointive class included grandchildren of A—would the lapse statute then be applicable? There is authority that it is applicable,[71] but it

---

66. See discussion supra pp. 123–27.

67. Dow v. Atwood, 260 A.2d 437 (Me.1969); In re Sears' Estate, 29 Misc.2d 234, 215 N.Y.S.2d 859 (1961); In re Newlin Estate, 72 Pa.D. & C. 446 (1950). See Restatement, Second, Property, Donative Transfers § 18.5 (Tent. Draft No. 6, 1983).

68. Several statutes provide for substitutional takers in the event of lapse in appointment: Cal.Civ.Code § 1389.4; Mich.Stat.Ann. § 556.130; Wis.Stat.Ann. § 853.27.

69. Newton v. Bullard, 181 Ga. 448, 182 S.E. 614 (1935); Thompson v. Pew, 214 Mass. 520, 102 N.E. 122 (1913); In re Goodman, 155 N.Y.S.2d 424 (Sup.Ct. 1956). See Restatement, Second, Property, Donative Transfers § 18.6 (Tent. Draft No. 7, 1984).

69a. However, Restatement, Second, Property, Donative Transfers § 18.6 provides that the statute applies if the appointee has the requisite relationship to either the donor or the donee of the power, but there is no authority for this.

70. Daniel v. Brown, 156 Va. 563, 159 S.E. 209 (1931). See 5 American Law of Property § 23.47 (Casner ed. 1952). But Restatement, Second, Property, Donative Transfers § 18.6 provides that substituted takers should be regarded as objects of the power.

71. In re Grubb's Estate, 36 Pa.D. & C. 1 (1940). But see Dow v. Atwood, 260 A.2d 437 (Me.1969).

has been maintained that the donor of a special power intends that the donee personally make the selection of the appointees, and that the statute should not be a substitute for such exercise of discretion.[72]

It should be emphasized that lapse has no application to this situation: A, donee of a general testamentary power, appoints to B for life, remainder to C. C survives A, but predeceases B. C's interest has not lapsed; C's estate will take the remainder. Lapse is concerned with the death of a legatee or appointee prior to the testator or donee of a testamentary power.

Let us assume that A bequeaths property to T, in trust, to pay the income to B for life, remainder to such children of B as B shall by will appoint, and in default of appointment, to the children of B in equal parts. At A's death, B has three children, C, D, and E. C predeceases B. At B's death the appointive assets have a value of $50,000. B appoints $20,000 to C, $15,000 to D, and $15,000 to E. The appointment to C is ineffective due to lapse. But can C's estate take under the default clause? The default clause contained no condition of survivorship of B, the life tenant, and generally none is implied.[73] The default gift to C did not lapse because C survived A. The default takers have an interest which is generally described as a vested remainder subject to divestment by the exercise of the power, assuming of course that there is no express condition that the default takers survive the preceding life estate. So it seems that C's estate will take one-third of the appointive property which the donee attempted to appoint to C; D and E will each be entitled also to one-third of the unappointed property as takers in default. The appointment to D and E is probably not affected by the lapsed appointment to C.[74]

SECTION 7. RELEASE OF POWERS

Can a donee of a general power divest himself of the power during his lifetime? Of course, the donee cannot be compelled to exercise his power, but for the donee affirmatively to dispose of his power is quite a different thing. Courts have held and many statutes provide that the donee of any general power can

---

72. See Simes & Smith § 984 (2d ed. 1956).

73. See supra p. 129.

74. Graham v. Whitridge, 99 Md. 248, 57 A. 609 (1904); Busch v. Dozier, 375 S.W.2d 27 (Mo.1964); In re Sessions' Estate, 217 Or. 340, 341 P.2d 512 (1959); Restatement, Second, Property, Donative Transfers § 24.3 (Tent. Draft No. 7, 1984). See also 5 American Law of Property § 23.64 (Casner ed. 1952). If the partial invalidity of appointment seriously distorts the donee's apparent intent, the appointment may fail in toto. 5 American Law of Property § 23.50 (Casner ed. 1952).

release his power at any time.[75] If, however, the donor of a general power provides that the donee may not release, this constraint is effective under a number of statutes.[76]

Can a donee of a special power release his power? The case law is thin and inconclusive,[77] but there are statutes in some states which permit such release, and the Restatement supports this position.[78] If, however, the donor provides that the donee may not release, this constraint is effective under some statutes.[79]

It should be noted that the cases, statutes and the Restatement permit the partial release of a power.[80] This can take the form of a reduction of the persons in whose favor the power may be exercised, or the reduction of the property over which the power may be exercised.

SECTION 8. CONTRACTS TO APPOINT; IMPROPER EXERCISE OF SPECIAL POWER

Can the donee of a general power contract to exercise his power in a particular manner? This depends on the nature of the general power. The presently exercisable general power is tantamount to ownership of the property interest to which it pertains; the donee can vest the property interest in himself at any time, and consequently there is no reason why the donee should not be permitted to enter into an enforceable contract for its exercise. The case law is thin, but the commentators and the Restatement support this position.[81]

But the general testamentary power is a little different. The donor has authorized the donee to exercise the power only at the time of his death; the contract to exercise, if enforceable, is like an inter vivos exercise. But we have seen that the donee of a general testamentary power can release his power during his

75. E.g., McLaughlin v. Industrial Trust Co., 28 Del.Ch. 275, 42 A.2d 12 (1945); Lyon v. Alexander, 304 Pa. 288, 156 A. 84 (1931); Ala.Code § 35–4–302; Iowa Code Ann. § 559.1; Ky.Rev. Stat.Ann. § 386.095; Ohio Rev.Code Ann. § 1339.16; Or.Rev.Stat. § 93.220; Restatement, Second, Property, Donative Transfers § 14.1 (Tent. Draft No. 5, 1982).

76. E.g., Conn.Gen.Stat.Ann. § 45–120; Mass.Gen.Laws Ann. ch. 204, § 27; Minn.Stat.Ann. § 502.79; R.I.Gen.Laws § 34–22–3; Wis.Stat.Ann. § 702.09.

77. 5 American Law of Property § 23.27 (Casner ed. 1952); Simes & Smith §§ 1055, 1056 (2d ed. 1956).

78. E.g., Fla.Stat.Ann. § 709.02; Ill.Ann.Stat. ch. 30, § 178; Ind.Code Ann. § 32–3–1–1; N.J.Stat.Ann. §§ 46–2A–1, 46–2A–2; Restatement, Second, Property, Donative Transfers § 14.2 (Tent. Draft No. 5, 1982).

79. E.g., Md.Est. & Trusts Code Ann. § 11–108; Miss.Code Ann. § 91–15–5; Tex.Rev.Civ.Stat.Ann. art. 7425c; Va.Code § 55–279.

80. Central Hanover Bank & Trust Co. v. Hutchinson, 22 N.J.Super. 78, 91 A.2d 654 (1952); Weston v. South Carolina Tax Commission, 212 S.C. 530, 48 S.E.2d 504 (1948); Restatement, Second, Property, Donative Transfers §§ 14.1, 14.2 (Tent. Draft No. 5, 1982). See statutes cited supra notes 75 and 78.

81. Restatement, Second, Property, Donative Transfers § 16.1 (Tent. Draft No. 5, 1982); 5 American Law of Property § 23.34 (Casner ed. 1052); Simes & Smith § 1012 (2d ed. 1956).

lifetime, and such release is like an inter vivos exercise. It seems inconsistent to permit a release of a general testamentary power and to prohibit the donee of such a power to contract as to its exercise, but that is the direction the law has taken. The courts have said that the donor wanted the donee to reserve his discretion up until the last moment, and the contract defeats this purpose. The contract to appoint is simply void, and the estate of the donee is not liable for damages, although there may be liability for the consideration paid by the promisee.[82] If, however, the donee does exercise the power in accordance with the terms of the contract, there is no reason why the appointment should not be effective.[83]

If the donee of a special testamentary power contracts to appoint in a particular manner, the contract is void as in the case of the general testamentary power.[84] If the donee of a special power presently exercisable contracts to appoint, it seems that the contract is valid.[85] However, the contract to appoint in the case of the special power raises the question of the exercise of the special power which benefits a non-object; such an exercise of a special power is frequently referred to as a "fraudulent exercise", but the issue is actually not concerned with fraud but rather the benefiting of someone whom the donor did not intend to be benefited, regardless of the mala fides or bona fides of the donee.

Suppose the donee of a special power over property valued at $100,000 appoints to an object of the power in consideration of $10,000 paid or to be paid to the donee. Or suppose the donee appoints to an object of the power on the understanding that the appointee will hold the property in trust for the benefit of the donee's son, a non-object, or make certain payments to the donee's wife, a non-object. Clearly these constitute appointments for the benefit, in part, of a non-object of the power; such appointments are generally held to be void in toto.[86]

---

82. Northern Trust Co. v. Porter, 368 Ill. 256, 13 N.E.2d 487 (1938); O'Hara v. O'Hara, 185 Md. 321, 44 A.2d 813 (1945); United States Trust Co. v. Montclair Trust Co., 133 N.J.Eq. 579, 33 A.2d 901 (1943); Farmers' Loan & Trust Co. v. Mortimer, 219 N.Y. 290, 114 N.E. 389 (1916); Restatement, Second, Property, Donative Transfers § 16.2 (Tent. Draft No. 5, 1982).

83. In re Rogers' Estate, 168 Misc. 633, 6 N.Y.S.2d 255 (Surr.Ct.1938). See Ingalls Iron Works Co. v. Ingalls, 177 F.Supp. 151 (N.D.Ala.1959), affirmed 280 F.2d 423 (5th Cir. 1960); Northern Trust Co. v. Porter, 368 Ill. 256, 13 N.E.2d 487 (1938); 5 American Law of Property § 23.35 (Casner ed. 1952).

84. Pitman v. Pitman, 314 Mass. 465, 50 N.E.2d 69 (1943). See authorities cited supra note 82.

85. See Restatement, Second, Property, Donative Transfers § 16.1 (Tent. Draft No. 5, 1982); Simes & Smith § 1011 (2d ed. 1956); 5 American Law of Property § 23.34 (Casner ed. 1952).

86. In re Buck Trust, 301 A.2d 328 (Del.Ch.1973); Chenoweth v. Bullitt, 224 Ky. 698, 6 S.W.2d 1061 (1928); Hughes v. McDaniel, 202 Md. 626, 98 A.2d 1 (1953); In re Carroll's Will, 274 N.Y. 288, 8 N.E.2d 864 (1937); Restatement, Second, Property, Donative Transfers § 20.2 (Tent. Draft No. 6, 1983).

There are, of course, subtle ways of benefiting a non-object by the use of a special power. An elderly donee may obtain certain care and support from children or grandchildren who are objects by virtue of the control of wealth represented by the special power to appoint among them. Indeed, this may have been a purpose which the donor had in mind; an argument certainly can be made that in this indirect way the donee was, in a sense, an object of the power. There is also the actual sordid case of the father-donee of a special power to appoint among his children exercisable by deed or will who appointed to his sick son who, the father thought, would die in a short time and the father would succeed to his property; this appointment was held to be invalid.[87]

But suppose the donee of a special power appoints, in good faith, one half of the appointive assets to an object and one half to a non-object of the power. There is no agreed exchange collateral to the appointment—simply a misunderstanding as to the scope of the power. It is generally held that the appointment to the object is valid,[88] but there is authority that if partial invalidity distorts the donee's dispositive plan, the entire appointment fails.[89]

It is possible, of course, that the consideration for the contract to appoint to an object may be a benefit to another object of the special power. For example, the donee may appoint the entire property to one object of the power in consideration for his agreement to finance the college education of another object of the special power. There is no reason why such a contract to appoint by a donee of a special power which is presently exercisable should not be valid.[90] A contract to appoint a presently exercisable special power is likely to involve a "fraudulent" exercise, but it is not necessarily so.

SECTION 9. MARSHALING OF APPOINTED ASSETS

Suppose testator, who is donee of a general testamentary power, executes a will in which the opening clause is a blending clause wherein the testator states that his will disposes of all his owned and appointive property as one fund. The will then provides

87. Wellesley v. Morrington, 2 Kay & J. 143 (1855).

88. First National Bank of Arizona v. First National Bank of Birmingham, 348 So.2d 1041 (Ala.1977); Cathell v. Burris, 21 Del.Ch. 233, 187 A. 9 (1936); Old Colony Trust Co. v. Richardson, 297 Mass. 147, 7 N.E.2d 432 (1937); Busch v. Dozier, 375 S.W.2d 27 (Mo.1964).

89. Parker v. MacBryde, 132 F.2d 932 (4th Cir. 1942); In re Trowbridge's Estate, 124 Misc. 317, 208 N.Y.S. 662 (Surr.Ct.1924). See Restatement, Second, Property, Donative Transfers §23.1 (Tent. Draft No. 7, 1984).

90. See Simes & Smith § 1011 (2d ed. 1956).

for three bequests of $50,000 each to A, B, and C, and a residuary clause which establishes a trust to pay income to D for life, remainder over to the children of D who shall survive D. The appointive property has a value of $100,000, and the owned property has a value of $200,000. We shall see in our discussion of the rule against perpetuities that in the exercise of a general testamentary power the appointment is read back into the instrument of the donor creating the power and the period of perpetuities is calculated as if the donor had designated the appointive interests in the instrument creating the power.[91] Let us further assume that the remainder interest of D's children would be invalid as violative of the rule against perpetuities with respect to the appointive property, but valid with respect to the owned property.

In the case of a blending clause of this kind, normally it is considered that owned property and appointive property are to be applied pro rata among the dispositive provisions of the will.[92] If this is followed in this case, then the appointive property which would have passed to the remaindermen, specifically $50,000, will pass to the donee's intestate takers, or possibly to the donor's takers in default. In this situation, however, the courts have saved the appointment by allocating all the appointive property among the pecuniary legatees, and allocating $50,000 of owned assets among the pecuniary legatees, and the rest of the owned assets to the residuary trust.[93] This is sometimes referred to as "marshaling" of assets to maximize the effectiveness of the terms of the will.

Suppose we have the same facts as above except that the blending clause is used only with respect to the residuary disposition. Can the appointive assets be allocated to the preceding pecuniary legacies? This appears to be a strained result which conflicts with the express provisions of the will, but there is authority for it.[94] Certainly a convincing argument can be made for the proposition that the appointive assets be allocated to the payment of debts, taxes, and administration expenses which ordinarily are satisfied first out of the residuary estate.[95]

91. See infra p. 201.

92. See Simes & Smith § 975, at 438 (2d ed. 1956); Restatement, Second, Property, Donative Transfers § 22.1 (Tent. Draft No. 7, 1984).

93. E.g., Minot v. Paine, 230 Mass. 514, 120 N.E. 167 (1918); In re Fuller's Will, 131 N.Y.S.2d 402 (Surr.Ct.1954). Restatement, Second, Property, Donative Transfers § 22.1 supports this result.

94. In re Wall's Trust, 177 N.Y.S.2d 284 (Sup.Ct.1958); In re Jackson, 337 Pa. 561, 12 A.2d 338 (1940); Restatement, Second, Property, Donative Transfers § 22.1. Contra: Slayton v. Fitch Home, 293 Mass. 574, 200 N.E. 357 (1936). See Simes & Smith § 975 (2d ed. 1956).

95. See Restatement, Second, Property, Donative Transfers § 22.1.

SECTION 10.   CREDITORS' RIGHTS IN POWERS OF APPOINTMENT

Can creditors of a donee reach his power?   Is the power of appointment to be considered "property" for this purpose, or something in the nature of an agency for the donor?   Clearly the property subject to a special power is not the property of the donee in any sense, and it cannot be subject to the claims of the donee's creditors.[96]   But the same result does not necessarily follow with respect to creditors' rights in property subject to a general power.

The rule at common law has been that property subject to a general power is not subject to the claims of the donee's creditors so long as the power is not exercised by the donee.[97]   However, there are statutes in several states which subject property covered by a general power to the claims of the donee's creditors,[98] and it appears that property subject to a presently exercisable general power is included in the bankruptcy estate of a donee.[99] It has also been held in the absence of statute, that the creditors of the donee can reach the assets subject to an unexercised general power in the following circumstances: A irrevocably transfers property to T, in trust, to pay the income to A for life, remainder to such persons as A shall by will appoint, and in default of appointment, to B.   Here, A is donor and donee of the power, and he is also the life income beneficiary.   A's creditors can reach the principal of the trust during A's lifetime as well as at A's death, despite the fact that the trust is irrevocable and the power is only testamentary.[1]   It makes sense that A cannot reserve this much use and control of the property and keep it beyond the reach of his creditors.

At common law the prevailing view has been that creditors of the donee can reach property subject to a general power which

---

96.   Restatement, Second, Property, Donative Transfers § 13.1 (Tent. Draft No. 5, 1982) so provides, "except as required by the rules relating to fraudulent conveyances".   This exception refers to the situation in which the donor owned the property and transferred it in fraud of creditors, reserving to himself as donee a special power.   The entire transfer, including the special power, is subject to the claims of prior creditors.

97.   Gilman v. Bell, 99 Ill. 144 (1881); Irwin Union Bank & Trust Co. v. Long, 160 Ind.App. 509, 312 N.E.2d 908 (1974); Quinn v. Tuttle, 104 N.H. 1, 177 A.2d 391 (1962);   Arnold v. Southern Pine Lumber Co., 58 Tex.Civ.App. 186, 123 S.W. 1162 (1909);   Restatement, Second, Property,

Donative Transfers § 13.2 (Tent. Draft No. 5, 1982).

98.   E.g., Cal.Civ.Code § 1390.3; Mich.Stat.Ann. § 556.123; Minn.Stat.Ann. § 502.70.

99.   11 U.S.C.A. § 541 (Bankruptcy Code of 1978).

1.   United States v. Ritter, 558 F.2d 1165 (4th Cir. 1977);   Nolan v. Nolan, 218 Pa. 135, 67 A. 52 (1907);   Bank of Dallas v. Republic National Bank, 540 S.W.2d 499 (Tex.Civ.App.1976);   Restatement, Second, Property, Donative Transfers § 13.3 (Tent. Draft No. 5, 1982).   See Scott, The Law of Trusts § 156 (3d ed. 1967).

has been exercised.[2]   For example, A, donee of a general testamentary power, dies with debts in excess of his probate assets,
leaving a will which exercises his general power.   The creditors'
claims in excess of the "owned" assets can be satisfied from the
appointive assets;   the claims are first satisfied from probate
assets, and after they are exhausted, the appointive assets are
applied to satisfy the creditors.[3]   If the probate assets are $50,000,
debts are $60,000, and appointive assets are $100,000, the donee's
appointment is effective as to $90,000.   It should be emphasized,
however, that if A does not exercise his testamentary power,
the appointive property will pass to the takers in default, or to
the donor or his estate, free from the donee's creditors' claims,
in the absence of a statute to the contrary.

With respect to the general power which is exercisable by
deed, it seems that the principle that the donee's creditors can
reach the property subject to the exercised general power will
have application only to the so-called fraudulent conveyance.
That is to say, if the owned assets of the donee after the donative
inter vivos exercise are sufficient to satisfy the creditors, then
the exercise of the power will not subject the appointive property
to the claims of the creditors;   if, on the other hand, the owned
assets of the donee are inadequate to satisfy creditors' claims
after the exercise of the power, then the transfer resulting from
the exercise is likely to fall into the category of the fraudulent
conveyance and the creditors will be able to reach the appointive
property in the hands of the appointee.[4]   This discussion is, of
course, a gross oversimplification of the law dealing with fraudulent conveyances, but it points up the fact that the donative
inter vivos appointment by the solvent donee is not going to
subject the appointive property to the claims of the donee's creditors.   If the donee is solvent after he has made his inter vivos
appointment, the appointive property generally will remain free
of the donee's creditors' claims although the donee becomes in-
solvent several years later.

It is strange indeed that the law should distinguish between
the exercise and non-exercise of a general power for the purpose

2. In re Breault's Estate, 63 Ill. App. 2d
246, 211 N.E.2d 424 (1965);   State Street
Trust Co. v. Kissel, 302 Mass. 328, 19
N.E.2d 25 (1939);   Fiske v. Warner, 99
N.H. 236, 109 A.2d 37 (1954);   Seward v.
Kaufman, 119 N.J.Eq. 44, 180 A. 857 (1935);
Restatement, Second, Property, Donative
Transfers § 13.4 (Tent. Draft No. 5, 1982).
Contra: Johnson v. Shriver, 121 Colo. 397,
216 P.2d 653 (1950);   St. Matthew's Bank
v. De Charrette, 259 Ky. 802, 83 S.W.2d
471 (1935).

3. In re Breault's Estate, 63 Ill. App. 2d
246, 211 N.E.2d 424 (1965);   Tuell v. Hur-
ley, 206 Mass. 65, 91 N.E. 1013 (1910);
Seward v. Kaufman, 119 N.J.Eq. 44, 180
A. 857 (1935).

4. See Restatement, Second, Property, Donative Transfers § 13.5 (Tent.
Draft No. 5, 1982);   Simes & Smith § 945
(2d ed. 1956).

of creditors' rights. It would make as much sense to distinguish between testacy and intestacy for the purpose of determining the priority of creditors' claims to those of intestate and testate takers. The justification for holding the appointive property beyond the donee's creditors is that the property belongs to the donor and not the donee; the courts which have permitted creditors to reach the property when the power is exercised have done so on the equitable ground that the donee should not be allowed to benefit non-creditor appointees when he has debts which are unsatisfied. The appointive property functionally is the property of the donee and should be treated as such for purposes of creditors' claims.

SECTION 11. RIGHTS OF SPOUSE

It has been held that the general power is not subject to the dower interest of the spouse or to the statutory forced share of the surviving spouse, regardless of whether the power is exercised or unexercised.[5]

The traditional statutory forced share of the surviving spouse has been limited to the probate estate of the decedent, although some courts have included certain thin inter vivos trusts despite the statutory language. The Uniform Probate Code § 2–202 expands the forced share by the "augmented estate" concept which subjects a number of transfers made by the decedent during the marriage to the surviving spouse's claim. Included in the augmented estate is property transferred by the decedent during the marriage to the extent that the decedent retained at his death a power to dispose of the property for his own benefit. This subjects to the forced share the general power with respect to which the decedent was both donor and donee. A number of states now have such a statutory provision,[6] and the Restatement (Second) of Property, Donative Transfers §13.7 supports this result. It should be emphasized that this provision is not applicable if the decedent held a general testamentary power received from another.[7]

5. Harlan National Bank v. Brown, 317 S.W.2d 903 (Ky.1958); Kates' Estate, 282 Pa. 417, 128 A. 97 (1925). But see Sullivan v. Burkin, 390 Mass. 864, 460 N.E.2d 572 (1984).

6. E.g., Colo.Rev.Stat. § 15–11–201; Me.Rev.Stat.Ann.tit. 18A, §§ 2–201, 2–202; Minn.Stat.Ann. § 525.213; N.Y.Est. Powers & Trusts Law § 5–1.1; Pa.Stat.Ann.tit. 20, § 2203; Utah Code Ann. §§ 75–2–201 to 207.

7. For a thorough discussion of the augmented estate concept, see Kurtz, The Augmented Estate Concept Under the Uniform Probate Code: In Search of an Equitable Elective Share, 62 Iowa L.Rev. 981 (1977). For a thorough discussion of the history and judicial treatment of the traditional forced share, see MacDonald, Fraud on the Widow's Share (1960). For a policy analysis of the forced share, see Haskell, Restraints Upon the Disinheritance of Family Members, which appears in Death, Taxes and Family Property 105 (Halbach ed. 1977).

The so-called "pretermitted" child is not able to treat the appointive property under a general testamentary power of which his parent was donee as part of such parent's estate.[8] The augmented estate concept of the Uniform Probate Code is not applicable to the claim of the pretermitted child.

That the general testamentary power should be beyond the reach of close family under a statutory system established to protect against disinheritance is evidence of the rigid conceptual tradition in the field of property.

SECTION 12.   FORMAL REQUIREMENTS;   CAPACITY; REVOCATION

The formal requirements of creation, exercise, and release of powers require brief comment.   The general rule is that the power can be created by compliance with the formalities required for the transfer of the property which is the subject of the power. That is to say, the power may be created by the due execution of a will, or, with respect to real property, by the execution and delivery of a deed sufficient to transfer title to real property, or, with respect to personal property, by the execution and delivery of an instrument in writing which need not in all respects conform to the technical requirements for the transfer of an interest in real property.[9]   Similarly, a power can be exercised by compliance with the formalities required for the transfer of the property subject to the power.[10]   It appears that the donor of the power may prescribe more stringent formal requirements.[11]

The formal requirements for the release of a power appear to be the execution of an instrument in writing delivered to one who will benefit from the release, such as a taker in default, or

---

8. Sewall v. Wilmer, 132 Mass. 131 (1882); Fiske v. Warner, 99 N.H. 236, 109 A.2d 37 (1954);   Rhode Island Hospital Trust Co. v. Anthony, 49 R.I. 339, 142 A. 531 (1928)   But see In re Pomeroy's Estate, 338 Pa. 443, 13 A.2d 5 (1940);   In re Shoch's Estate, 271 Pa. 158, 114 A. 502 (1921).

By statute in most states certain children who are omitted from their parent's will may be entitled to take their intestate share unless there is evidence that they were intentionally disinherited.   See Atkinson, Wills § 36 (2d ed. 1953).

9. See Restatement, Second, Property, Donative Transfers § 12.1 (Tent. Draft No. 5, 1982);   Simes & Smith § 891 (2d ed. 1956).

10. D.C.Code Ann. § 45–117; Minn.Stat.Ann. § 502.64;   Okla.Stat.

Ann. tit. 60, § 299.3;   Va. Code § 64.1– 50; Wis.Stat.Ann. § 702.05(2);   Restatement, Second, Property, Donative Transfers § 18.2 (Tent. Draft No. 6, 1983).

11. National Shawmut Bank v. Joy, 315 Mass. 457, 53 N.E.2d 113 (1944);   Holzbach v. United Virginia Bank, 216 Va. 482, 219 S.E.2d 868 (1975);   Restatement, Second, Property, Donative Transfers § 18.2 (Tent. Draft No. 6, 1983).   See First National Bank of Arizona v. First National Bank of Birmingham, 348 So.2d 1041 (Ala.1977);   Leidy Chemicals Foundation v. First National Bank, 276 Md. 689, 351 A.2d 129 (1976).   A few states have statutes to the contrary: e.g., Ky.Rev.Stat.Ann. § 394.070;   N.Y.Est. Powers & Trusts Law § 10–6.2(a)(2); N.C.Gen.Stat. § 31–4.

to one interested in the property such as a trustee who holds legal title to the appointive property.[12]

Brief reference should be made to the capacity to create or exercise a power. Clearly the capacity required to transfer an interest in property is required to create a power of appointment.[13] It also stands to reason that the capacity required to transfer an interest in property should be required for the exercise of a power of appointment.[14]

The donor of a power cannot revoke the power that he has given the donee unless he has expressly reserved that right of revocation in his creating instrument;[15] this is likely to occur in connection with the creation of a revocable trust. The donee of a power cannot revoke his appointment unless he has reserved that right;[16] obviously this relates only to the inter vivos power and not to the testamentary power. Also, if the donor of the special power has expressly prohibited a revocable exercise of the power, such prohibition will be effective, but it has been maintained that any such restriction on the general power should be ineffective.[17]

SECTION 13.   TIME OF EXERCISE

It appears as a truism that an appointment cannot be made until the power has been created, but difficulties may be encountered in the application of this obvious principle. Let us assume that A executes a will on March 1 in which A gives B a testamentary power of appointment. B is advised of the power and on March 10 B executes a will in which she purports to exercise the power. On March 20 B dies; on March 25 A dies.

12.   District of Columbia v. Lloyd, 160 F.2d 581 (U.S.App.D.C.1947);   In re Haskell's Trust, 59 Misc.2d 797, 300 N.Y.S.2d 711 (Sup.Ct.1969);   Del.Code Ann. tit. 25, § 502;   Ky.Rev.Stat.Ann. § 386.095; N.C.Gen.Stat. § 39–33, 39–34;   Ohio Rev.Code Ann. § 1339.16, 1339.17; R.I.Gen.Laws § 34–22–4.   See Restatement, Second, Property, Donative Transfers § 14.3 (Tent. Draft No. 5, 1982). Some statutes require filing of release with recorder of deeds if real property is involved.

13.   Restatement, Second, Property, Donative Transfers § 12.1 (Tent. Draft No. 5, 1982).

14.   Holt v. National Bank, 351 So.2d 1370 (Ala.1977); O'Leary v. McCarty, 492 S.W.2d 124 (Mo.App.1973);   Cal.Civ.Code § 1384.1;   Minn.Stat.Ann. § 502.66; Okla.Stat.Ann.tit. 60, § 299.5;   Restate-

ment, Second, Property, Donative Transfers § 18.1 (Tent. Draft No. 6, 1983).

15.   Restatement, Second, Property, Donative Transfers § 15.1 (Tent. Draft No. 5, 1982);   Ala.Code § 35–4–301;   N.Y.Est. Powers & Trusts Law § 10–9.1; Wis.Stat.Ann. § 702.11.

16.   Rice v. Park, 233 Ala. 317, 135 So. 472 (1931);   Wilmington Trust Co. v. Wilmington Trust Co., 21 Del.Ch. 102, 180 A. 597 (1935);   Central Trust Co. v. Watt, 139 Ohio St. 50, 38 N.E.2d 185 (1941);   Restatement, Second, Property, Donative Transfers § 15.2 (Tent. Draft No. 5, 1982).

17.   See Restatement, Second, Property, Donative Transfers § 15.2 (Tent. Draft No. 5, 1982);   Simes & Smith § 985 (2d ed. 1956);   5 American Law of Property § 23.51 (Casner ed. 1952).

Does B's will exercise the power?   It cannot because this would result in the exercise occurring prior to the creation of the power which was at the date of A's death.   A's will created no power in B until the will became effective upon A's death.[18]   If, however, A had died on March 19, B's will would constitute an exercise of the power;   the donee's exercise of her power occurs at the date on which the donee's will is effective, the date of the donee's death.   A donee also exercises her power in the following situation: B executes a will which purports to exercise all powers which she may hold at her death;   later A executes a will giving B a testamentary power;   A dies leaving that will;   and later B dies leaving her will.   The general principle is that if a testator dies leaving a will which purports to exercise, expressly or by implication, any testamentary power which she may hold at her death, such will exercises powers acquired after the will was executed.[19]

18.   Restatement, Second, Property, Donative Transfers § 18.4 (Tent. Draft No. 6, 1983);   Simes & Smith § 979 (2d ed. 1956).

19.   California Trust Co. v. Ott, 59 Cal.App.2d 715, 140 P.2d 79 (Dist.Ct.App.1943);   In re Buck Trust, 277 A.2d 717 (Del.Ch.1971);   In re Smith's Will, 279 App.Div. 140, 108 N.Y.S.2d 290 (1951), affirmed 304 N.Y. 612, 107 N.E.2d 92 (1952);   Restatement, Second, Property, Donative Transfers § 17.6 (Tent. Draft No. 6, 1983).

Chapter 8

RULE AGAINST PERPETUITIES

SECTION 1.   INTRODUCTION

The rule against perpetuities is the principal means which the Anglo-American system of law has employed to limit the power of an individual to control the disposition of his wealth after his death.   The classical statement of the rule is brief and deceptively simple: No interest is good unless it must vest, if at all, not later than 21 years after some life in being at the creation of the interest.[1]   But there is little doubt that in the vast field of property, the body of law involving the rule against perpetuities is the most complex and the least understood.   John Chipman Gray, the scholar who did more to bring order to the subject of the rule against perpetuities than anyone else, had this to say about the rule:

> There is something in the subject which seems to facilitate error.   Perhaps it is because the mode of reasoning is unlike that with which lawyers are most familiar.   .   .   .
> A long list might be formed of the demonstrable blunders with regard to its questions made by eminent men, blunders which they themselves have been sometimes the first to acknowledge;   and there are few lawyers of any practice in drawing wills and settlements who have not at some time either fallen into the net which the Rule spreads for the unwary, or at least shuddered to think how narrowly they have escaped it.[2]

Another scholar who spent a substantial part of an academic lifetime attempting to bring order and add sense to the rule, W. Barton Leach, described the rule as a "technicality-ridden legal nightmare" and a "dangerous instrumentality in the hands of most members of the bar".[3]

It is not clear whether the above comments constitute an indictment of the rule or an indictment of the bar.   The members of the bar, as a class, certainly are substantially above average in intelligence and are trained to cope with logical and verbal complexity;   if the rule gives this group serious trouble, then it

---

1.   Gray, The Rule Against Perpetuities § 201 (4th ed. 1942).

2.   Id. at xi.

3.   Leach, Perpetuities Legislation, Massachusetts Style, 67 Harv.L.Rev. 1349 (1954).

seems that the rule is unjustifiably abstruse. The bar and the legal academicians may be deserving of criticism for permitting this monster to grow and thrive; fortunately, there have been reforms in a number of jurisdictions in recent years which are all to the good,[4] but the rule remains as a monument to modern man's capacity to complicate his existence.

The rule had its origin in the musty atmosphere of seventeenth century land law. Land was wealth, and the landowner frequently wished to assure himself that his wealth would remain in the family for many generations; as a consequence various ingenious and complex forms of land settlement involving future interests were employed to accomplish this end. This "dead hand" control had the effect of restricting the alienability of land and such restriction presumably had adverse sociological and economic consequences. Mention has been made previously of the traditional common law bias in favor of free alienability of land. It has been pointed out that the contingent remainder was at one time destructible; consequently that form of future interest did not pose a threat to the alienability of land since there were means available to do away with it. However, when it was decided that the executory interest was not destructible, it appeared that this device was available as a means to control or fetter the disposition of land in perpetuity.

The development of the rule against perpetuities was an ad hoc common law process beginning in the seventeenth century and finally achieving its modern form in the nineteenth century.[5] Initially it was aimed at the indestructible executory interest, but it became applicable to the contingent remainder as well. For reasons which are more historical than rational, it was not made applicable to the possibility of reverter or the right of entry.[6]

Although the rule originated as a means of solving certain problems dealing with the peculiarities of English land law with its medieval overtones, it was applied lock, stock and barrel to modern equitable future interests in choses in action, stocks and bonds. Little thought appears to have been given to the question of the appropriateness of its application to these modern circumstances.

---

4. See discussion infra pp. 213–21.

5. The rule in modern form was first stated in Cadell v. Palmer, 1 Cl. & F. 372 (1833). For a discussion of the historical development of the rule see Simes & Smith §§ 1211–21 (2d ed. 1956).

6. Schaefers v. Apel, 295 Ala. 277, 328

So.2d 274 (1976); Commercial National Bank v. Martin, 185 Kan. 116, 340 P.2d 899 (1959); City of Laurel v. Powers, 366 So.2d 1079 (Miss.1979); County School Board v. Dowell, 190 Va. 676, 58 S.E.2d 38 (1950). See Restatement, Second, Property, Donative Transfers § 1.4 comment c (1983).

The rule against perpetuities in its common law form is in effect in many jurisdictions. It has been modified in minor respects in some states and substantially in others; these changes are discussed in Section 11 of this chapter. Even where changes have been made, the common law rule remains the basis of the law as modified. Most of this chapter is accordingly devoted to the rule in its common law form. The complexity of the common law rule remains despite the modern reforms.

SECTION 2. REMOTENESS OF VESTING

The phrase "rule against perpetuities" does not describe what the rule actually accomplishes. The rule does not attempt directly to limit the number of successive future interests that can be created; the rule does not attempt directly to limit the duration of a trust; the rule does not attempt directly to limit the period of time between the creation of a future interest and its realization as a present or possessory interest; the rule does not attempt directly to limit the period of time within which absolute title to property is incapable of being transferred. What the rule does is to limit the period of time between the creation of a contingent future interest and its vesting in interest. If it is possible that a contingent future interest may vest in interest after the time limitation established by the rule, then such interest is void. It is by this rather indirect means that the several objectives which are mentioned above as those which the rule does not directly accomplish, are, for the most part, accomplished.

A brief review of the distinction between vesting in interest and vesting in possession is called for at this point.[7] If testator devises Blackacre to A for life, remainder to B in fee, and A and B are alive at testator's death, B's remainder is vested in interest, but it will not become vested in possession until A's death. If testator devises Blackacre to A for life, remainder to B in fee if B attains 21, and A and B are alive at testator's death and B is 18, B's remainder is contingent; if B attains 21 while A is still alive, then B's remainder becomes vested in interest because he has satisfied the condition precedent, but his interest will not be vested in possession until A's death. If testator devises Blackacre to A for life, remainder to B in fee if B survives A, and A and B survive testator, B's remainder is contingent until A's death, and by the nature of the contingency it cannot vest in interest before it vests in possession. The rule against perpetuities requires that the contingent future interest vest in interest within the time limit of the rule, and the time of vesting in possession is irrelevant. If the future interest is vested in

7. See discussion supra pp. 66–70.

interest at the time of its creation, the rule against perpetuities does not affect it; the rule is concerned only with future interests which are contingent at the time of their creation.

The contingent future interest, if it is to be valid, must of logical necessity vest in interest, if it vests at all, within the lifetime of some person who was alive at the time of the creation of the future interest plus 21 years after such person's death. It need not be demonstrated that it has to vest, but if it should vest it must occur within the period of the rule. The time of the creation of the future interest is the date of the testator's death in the case of the testamentary disposition, and the date of the delivery of the deed or other instrument of gift in the case of the irrevocable inter vivos transfer.[8] The determination of whether or not the future interest complies with the rule is made prospectively from the time of the creation of the interest; it is not a question of whether the interest in fact vests in interest within the time limit, but rather whether or not it was possible that it might vest in interest after the expiration of the time limit. Viewed from the time of the creation of the contingent future interest, if it is possible that it might vest in interest too remotely, however likely it is that it will vest within the time limit as a practical matter, the interest is void. Undoubtedly this is scarcely comprehensible to the reader at this point; the principal purpose of this chapter is to make the contents of this paragraph intelligible and meaningful.

SECTION 3. MEASURING LIVES; 21 YEARS

The statement of the rule provides that the contingent interest must vest, if at all, within some life in being at the time of the creation of the interest plus 21 years thereafter. It is not necessary, however, that one specific person alive at the time of the creation of the interest be singled out as the measuring life, as long as it can be demonstrated that the interest must vest within the life of one person, that is, the survivor, among a definable group of persons reasonable in number, plus 21 years thereafter.[9] The group of persons is frequently called the "measuring lives".

Suppose testator bequeaths $100,000 in trust to accumulate the income and to pay over the accumulated income and principal to such grandchildren of testator as are alive 21 years following the death of the last survivor of testator's sons John, Charles

8. Deeds: Second National Bank v. Harris Trust & Savings Bank, 29 Conn.Sup. 275, 283 A.2d 226 (1971); Clarke v. Clarke, 121 Tex. 165, 46 S.W.2d 658 (1932). Wills: In re Estate of Unitt, 197 Neb. 713, 250 N.W.2d 644 (1977); Joyner v. Duncan, 299 N.C. 565, 264 S.E.2d 76 (1980).

9. Fitchie v. Brown, 211 U.S. 321, 29 S.Ct. 106, 53 L.Ed. 202 (1908); Dickson v. Renfro, 263 Ark. 718, 569 S.W.2d 66 (1978); Wing v. Wachovia Bank & Trust Co., 35 N.C.App. 346, 241 S.E.2d 397 (1978). See Simes & Smith § 1223 (2d ed. 1956).

and Thomas.   John, Charles and Thomas are alive at the testator's death.   The future interests of the grandchildren are
contingent because of the condition of survivorship to the time
of distribution.   The interests cannot vest in interest before they
vest in possession because of the nature of the contingency.   Will
the interests vest in time?   Must the vesting occur within the
lifetime of some person who was alive at the creation of the
interest, plus 21 years thereafter?   The answer is that the vesting must occur within the period of the rule.   But who is the
"life in being"?   Can you point to one person and say, at the
time of the creation of the interest, the date of the testator's
death, that this specific person is that "life in being"?   One
person cannot be singled out in this fashion, but the rule does
not require this;   it is clear that it is one of those three sons,
John, Charles and Thomas, that is, the last to die, who will
constitute that "life", and this is sufficient to satisfy the rule.[10]
Those three sons are the "measuring lives".

It should be noted that the statement of the rule provides
that the interest "must vest, if at all" within the period.   What
is the significance of the phrase "if at all"?   In the preceding
example, it is possible that there will be no grandchild of the
testator who will survive to the time of distribution, which is 21
years following the death of the surviving son of the testator.
This fact does not invalidate the future interest.   It is not in-
evitable that any of the future interests will vest, but if any is
to vest, then the vesting must occur within the period of the
rule.   This is the significance of the phrase "if at all".[11]   The
meaning would probably be clearer if the phrase were "if it ever
does vest".

Frequently the measuring life or lives will be the beneficiary
or beneficiaries of a preceding interest.   Testator bequeaths
$100,000 in trust to pay the income to A for life, and upon A's
death to pay the income to B for life, and upon the death of the
survivor of A and B, to pay the principal to the children of B
then living.   A and B are alive at the testator's death.   Clearly
the interests of the children of B must vest, if at all, within the
period of the rule, A and B constituting the measuring lives.[12]
Of course, there is no reason why the measuring life or lives need

---

10.   Fitchie v. Brown, 211 U.S. 321, 29
S.Ct. 106, 53 L.Ed. 202 (1908);   Friday's
Estate, 313 Pa. 328, 170 A. 123 (1933);   Otterback v. Bohrer, 87 Va. 548, 12 S.E.
1013 (1891).

11.   First Alabama Bank v. Adams, 382
So.2d 1104 (Ala.1980);   Joyner v. Duncan,
299 N.C. 565, 264 S.E.2d 76 (1980);   Fink-

beiner v. Finkbeiner, 111 OhioApp. 64, 165
N.E.2d 825 (1959).   See Simes & Smith
§ 1228, at 123 (2d ed. 1956).

12.   First Alabama Bank v. Adams, 382
So.2d 1104 (Ala.1980);   Donahue v. Watson, —— Ind.App. ——, 411 N.E.2d 741
(1980).

be a beneficiary or beneficiaries in the dispositive instrument, but since future interests often are for the benefit of succeeding generations, it is common that the measuring life will be found among the prior beneficiaries of the property disposition.

In the preceding examples, the measuring lives were specifically mentioned in the bequest. However, specific mention of the measuring lives is not necessary. Suppose testator bequeaths $100,000 in trust to pay over $10,000 to each of the first ten grandchildren of the testator who live to age 21. At testator's death he has four children and no grandchildren. Do the interests of the unborn grandchildren violate the rule? The interests are obviously contingent. Who are the measuring lives? There is no specific reference in the will to any group from which that "life in being" can be selected. However, the testator was dead and could have no more children. Each grandchild who lives to age 21 must accomplish this feat within the lifetime of the survivor of the children of the testator plus 21 years thereafter. The measuring lives are the children of the testator, and the specific life is to be found within that group; clearly every grandchild's interest must vest, if at all, within a period measured by the life of the last child of testator to die plus 21 years thereafter. Consequently the future interests of the grandchildren are valid.[13] It should be stressed that it is possible that none of the grandchildren's interests will ever vest, but if any does it must occur within the time limit of the rule.

There is a famous case which deals with the question of the permissible size of the group of measuring lives. In 1926, testator bequeathed a sum to be divided among the testator's descendants who were alive 21 years after the death of all descendants of Queen Victoria who were living at the time of the testator's death. There were 120 descendants of Queen Victoria living at the testator's death. The gift was held to be valid.[14] How large can the group be which constitutes the class of measuring lives? The problem seems to be one of administrative practicality and certainty. Conceivably a testator could leave a fund to his descendants who are alive 21 years after the death of all persons who were living on earth at the time of the testator's death; there would be considerable difficulty in determining the time of distribution and the takers, and certainly this bequest would be invalid. The class of measuring lives must be reasonable in number and the death of the survivor must be capable of ascer-

13. B.M.C. Durfee Trust Co. v. Taylor, 325 Mass. 201, 89 N.E.2d 777 (1950); Lux v. Lux, 109 R.I. 592, 288 A.2d 701 (1972).

14. In re Villar, [1929] 1 Ch. 243.

tainment without unusual difficulty;[15] the Queen Victoria case probably represents the outer limit of permissible lives.[16] Where the group of measuring lives is unreasonably large, there is some difference of view as to whether the gift is invalid because it is violative of the rule against perpetuities or invalid because of indefiniteness.[17]

Suppose the testator bequeaths in trust to pay the income to A for life, then to pay the income to the children of A for their lives, and upon the death of the survivor of A's children, to pay over the principal to B. A and B are alive at the testator's death. Are the interests of A's children valid? Their interests are equitable life income interests only. The only condition to vesting is birth; all children will, of course, meet this condition not later than A's death. Prior to birth the unborn child has a contingent interest; after birth the interest is vested subject to partial divestment, or subject to open. It follows that the interests of all A's children must vest, if at all, within the period of the rule.[18] It is possible that the equitable life income interests of the children of A will last beyond the period of perpetuities, but this is immaterial; all that matters is that the future interest vest in interest within the period of the rule, which is necessarily the case here. A may have a child who is born after the testator's death, and such child may be receiving income after the expiration of the period of the rule, that is, more than 21 years after the death of A, B, and the children of A who were alive at the testator's death, but his interest will have vested not later than A's death. This example is illustrative of the fact that the rule against perpetuities has nothing to do with the duration of a trust.

What about the remainder to B? Is this valid? It is a vested remainder at the time of the creation of the interest. There is no condition precedent to B's taking; there is no express condition of survivorship, and we have seen that ordinarily no condition of survivorship will be inferred.[19] So B's interest may vest in possession after the expiration of the period of the rule,

---

15. Fitchie v. Brown, 211 U.S. 321, 29 S.Ct. 106, 53 L.Ed. 202 (1908). In an early expression of this rule Lord Eldon held that the only limitation on the number of measuring lives is that it must not exceed that "to which testimony can be applied, to determine when the survivor of them drops." Thellusson v. Woodford, 11 Ves. 112, 145 (1805). The "reasonable number of lives" rule has been legislated in several states: Cal.Civ.Code § 715.2; Fla.Stat.Ann. § 689.22(1); N.Y.Est. Powers & Trusts Law § 9–1.1(b); Wyo.Stat. § 34–1–139.

16. Simes & Smith § 1223, at 110–11 (2d ed. 1956).

17. Simes & Smith § 1223, at 112 (2d ed. 1956).

18. Turner v. Safe Deposit & Trust Co., 148 Md. 371, 129 A. 294 (1925); Lowry v. Murren, 195 Neb. 42, 236 N.W.2d 627 (1975); Joyner v. Duncan, 299 N.C. 565, 264 S.E.2d 76 (1980); Sellers v. Powers, 426 S.W.2d 533 (Tex.1968).

19. See discussion of implied conditions of survivorship, supra pp. 127–32.

that is, after the death of A, B, and all the children of A who were alive at the testator's death, plus 21 years, but it is vested in interest from its inception. If B dies two days after the testator's death, B's estate will receive the corpus of the trust upon the death of the survivor of A and A's children.

Suppose the remainder interest to B had provided that it was contingent upon B's survivorship to the time of distribution. Would this condition render the remainder too remote for the purposes of the rule? It would not. B was alive at the testator's death, and the interest of B must vest, if at all, during a life which was in being at the time of the creation of the interest; that life in being is B.

Suppose testator bequeathed in trust to pay the income to A for life, then to pay the income to the children of A for their lives, and then upon the death of the last surviving child of A, to pay over the corpus of the trust to the grandchildren of A.[20] A is alive at the testator's death. As we have seen above, the interests of A's children are within the rule. But what about the interests of A's grandchildren? We shall see that if the interest of any member of a class, in the case of a class gift, is violative of the rule against perpetuities, then the entire class gift is considered to be violative of the rule.[21] Taking this principle as given for the moment, is the gift to the grandchildren invalid? Is there any possibility that the interest of any potential grandchild will vest too remotely? It should be reiterated that the interest of an unborn person is necessarily contingent,[22] that there is no implied condition of survivorship to distribution,[23] and that the interest of a grandchild at birth is vested subject to partial divestment.[24] The last surviving child of A may be a person who was not alive at the death of the testator, and he may have a child who is born beyond the period of the rule. In view of this possibility, viewed from the time of the testator's death, the remainder interest to the class of grandchildren as a whole is invalid as violative of the rule.[25] Can one point to any person or group of persons on this earth who were alive at the testator's death and say that that grandchild must necessarily be born within his or their lives and 21 years thereafter? The answer is no.

20. Note that no part of the corpus is distributed until the death of the survivor among A's children. As each child dies, the income shares of the survivors increase. The children of A have, by implication, cross-remainders for life.

21. See discussion infra pp. 190–93.

22. See discussion supra p. 73.

23. See discussion supra p. 127.

24. See discussion supra p. 70.

25. Connecticut Bank and Trust Co. v. Brody, 174 Conn. 616, 392 A.2d 445 (1978); Rogers v. Rooth, 237 Ga. 713, 229 S.E.2d 445 (1976); Safe Deposit & Trust Co. v. Sheehan, 169 Md. 93, 179 A. 536 (1935); Sellers v. Powers, 426 S.W.2d 533 (Tex.1968).

It should be noted in the immediately preceding example that the trust may last beyond the period of perpetuities, but the life income interests of the children of A must vest within the period. The court will strike the invalid remainder in the grandchildren, but the interests of A and his children remain intact; after the death of the survivor of A's children, the corpus of the trust passes to the testator's residuary legatees or to the next of kin of the testator.[26]

Let us assume that settlor irrevocably transfers inter vivos in trust to pay the income to the children of the settlor for their lives, and upon the death of the survivor of settlor's children, to pay over the principal to the grandchildren of the settlor. There is no problem with the life income interests of the children of the settlor because the interests of all the members of that class must vest within the lifetime of the settlor. But what about the remainder interests of the grandchildren of the settlor? Must the interests of all grandchildren of settlor vest within some life in being at the time of the creation of the interest plus 21 years? If the settlor had a child who was born after the transfer in trust, that child could have a child who was born beyond the period of the rule. This would result in the remote vesting of the interest of a member of the class, and consequently the entire class gift would fail.[27] The settlor cannot serve as the measuring life, nor can the children of the settlor serve as the measuring lives, since there could be children born after the creation of the future interest in the grandchildren.

If the immediately preceding disposition had been by will rather than an irrevocable inter vivos transfer, then the remainder interest in the grandchildren would be valid; the testator's children would be the measuring lives because there could not be any additional children of the testator after his death.[28]

It should be emphasized that the time limit of the rule is some life in being at the creation of the interest, plus 21 years, and the 21 years cannot precede the measuring life. In other words, the measuring life cannot be one that comes into being within 21

26. Rogers v. Rooth, 237 Ga. 713, 229 S.E.2d 445 (1976); Sellers v. Powers, 426 S.W.2d 533 (Tex.1968); Hagemann v. National Bank & Trust Co., 218 Va. 333, 237 S.E.2d 388 (1977). There is also authority that the otherwise valid prior interests are also stricken if their retention is not consistent with the apparent testamentary plan. Connecticut Bank and Trust Co. v. Brody, 174 Conn. 616, 392 A.2d 445 (1978); Taylor v. Dooley, 297 S.W.2d 905 (Ky. 1956). This is sometimes referred to as a form of "infectious invalidity." See discussion infra p. 210.

27. Mounts v. Roberts, 388 S.W.2d 117 (Ky.1965); Ryan v. Ward, 192 Md. 342, 64 A.2d 258 (1949); Hassell v. Sims, 176 Tenn. 318, 141 S.W.2d 472 (1940).

28. First Alabama Bank v. Adams, 382 So.2d 1104 (Ala.1980); Donahue v. Watson, — Ind.App. —, 411 N.E.2d 741 (1980); Lux v. Lux, 109 R.I. 592, 288 A.2d 701 (1972).

years after the creation of the interest.[29]   Also, the rule allows
for the use of 21 years as the time limit without regard to any
life in being at the creation of the interest.[30]   As an example,
testator may bequeath a sum of money to be divided among all
his descendants of whatever degree who are living 21 years after
the testator's death, and the interests of the class of legatees
would be valid.

The period of the rule as we have been discussing it is also
supplemented by actual periods of gestation.   A person conceived at the creation of the interest can be a measuring life;
a person conceived at the expiration of the measuring life is
considered to be in existence at the death of that life in being;
a person conceived at the expiration of the measuring life plus
21 years is considered to be in existence at the expiration of the
period of the rule.   In other words, a person who is conceived
and unborn is deemed to be in existence for all purposes of the
rule.[31]   For example, testator bequeaths in trust to pay the income to his children for their lives, and upon the death of the
survivor, to pay over the principal to testator's grandchildren
who live to age 21.   At testator's death he has no children alive
but his wife is pregnant and gives birth six months after testator's
death;   at the death of that one child, such child has no children
but his wife is pregnant and gives birth six months after his
death and such child lives to be 21.   The grandchild of the testator takes the remainder.   The actual elapsed time from the
creation of the interest, in terms of perpetuities, is one life plus
21 years plus two partial gestation periods of 6 months each.
The time limit for vesting under the rule, to be precisely accurate
about it, is a life in being plus 21 years plus actual periods of
gestation.

SECTION 4.   CERTAINTY OF VESTING

For a contingent future interest to be valid under the rule
against perpetuities, it must be logically demonstrable that, viewed
from the time of the creation of the interest, the interest will
vest, if at all, within the time limit.   Probabilities are irrelevant;

---

29.   Fidelity & Columbia Trust Co. v. Tiffany, 202 Ky. 618, 260 S.W. 357 (1924); Thomas v. Harrison, 24 Ohio Op.2d 148, 191 N.E.2d 862 (1962).

30.   Magee v. Estate of Magee, 236 Miss. 572, 111 So.2d 394 (1959);   Closset v. Burtchaell, 112 Or. 585, 230 P. 554 (1924); Henderson v. Moore, 144 Tex. 398, 190 S.W.2d 800 (1945).

31.   Equitable Trust Co. v. McComb, 19 Del.Ch. 387, 168 A. 203 (1933);   Warner v. Whitman, 353 Mass. 468, 233 N.E.2d 14 (1968);   Will of Pratt, 94 Misc.2d 1020, 405 N.Y.S.2d 995 (1978);   Lux v. Lux, 109 R.I. 592, 288 A.2d 701 (1972).

all that matters is what conceivably can happen, no matter how
far-fetched.   And this idea has been carried to absurd extremes.

Suppose testator bequeaths in trust to pay the income to A
for her life, then to pay the income to the children of A for their
lives, and upon the death of the survivor of such children, to pay
the principal to the grandchildren of A.   At the time of the
testator's death A is 79 years old, and she has two children.
Believe it or not, it has been held that the remainder to the
grandchildren of A is violative of the rule against perpetuities
and invalid.[32]   The law adopted the conclusive presumption that
every person is capable of having children until the day he or
she dies, as far as the rule against perpetuities is concerned.
Consequently, A could have an additional child who would not
be a life in being at the testator's death, and that child could
have a child who would be born beyond the permissible period.
The result of this hypothesis is to invalidate the remainder to
the grandchildren.   This situation is sometimes referred to as
the case of the "fertile octogenarian."   Remember that the class
gift is invalid if it is possible that the interest of any one member
of the class can violate the rule.   The interest of a grandchild
is vested subject to open upon the birth of such grandchild, but
of course prior to birth the interest is still contingent.   If the
law took the rational position that the presumption of fertility
is rebuttable, then the children of A could be the measuring lives
and the remainder to the grandchildren would be valid.   In a
few states the conclusive presumption has been abolished for
perpetuities purposes.[33]   Even with the conclusive presumption,
invalidity may be avoided by a constructional device, discussed
in Section 10 of this Chapter.

Let us take another absurd example.   Testator bequeaths
$50,000 to such issue of his as are living when all his debts, taxes,
and administration expenses are paid and his estate is finally
settled.   Issue, of course, includes descendants of whatever degree—it is not limited to children of the testator.   If the gift
were to children of the testator there would be no problem since
the children would be the measuring lives.   But this bequest
goes beyond children and includes people who may not be born
at the death of the testator.   Is it possible that the interests of
the issue may not vest within the period of the rule?   How do
we know that the estate may not be finally settled for 40 years,
or, for that matter, 22 years?   We don't know it, as a matter
of logical necessity, but it is rare indeed that an estate takes

---

32.   Connecticut Bank and Trust Co. v.
Brody, 174 Conn. 616, 392 A.2d 445 (1978);
Gettins v. Grand Rapids Trust Co., 249
Mich. 238, 228 N.W. 703 (1930);   Turner
v. Turner, 260 S.C. 439, 196 S.E.2d 498
(1973);   Crockett v. Scott, 199 Tenn. 90,
284 S.W.2d 289 (1955).

33.   See discussion infra p. 221 and accompanying notes 18 and 19.

longer than 21 years to settle. It has been held that the gift is violative of the rule.[34] There is also contrary case authority to the effect that the fiduciary obligation to administer the estate expeditiously precludes such an extraordinary delay.[35] Several states have also enacted statutes which have the effect of validating interests which are contingent in this manner.[36]

Here is another strange one. Testator bequeaths in trust to pay the income to A for life, then to pay the income to A's widow for her life, then to pay over the principal to A's children who are then living. A is 40 years old at the testator's death, and is married and the father of two children. A may, of course, have more children, and A may divorce his present wife, or his present wife may die, and A may remarry. The widow is the person who is the decedent's wife at his death. The point is that A's present wife may not be his widow; also, A may have more children after the testator's death. There is no problem with the interest of the widow since her interest clearly must vest within a life in being at the creation of her future interest, namely A's life. But how about the interests of the children of A? Remember that if the class gift is bad as to one member of the class, the entire class gift fails. Can't we say that the interests of all possible children of A must vest within the time limit of the rule because the vesting must occur immediately upon the death of A or his widow, both of whom are lives in being at the creation of the children's interests? But do we know as a certainty that A's widow will be someone who was alive at the testator's death? Isn't it possible that A's present wife will die or be divorced, and A will marry someone who was not alive at the time of the testator's death? Isn't it possible that A may marry someone who is more than 40 years his junior? Of course it is. So the interests of A's children have been held to be invalid in this situation.[37] This situation is sometimes referred to as the case of the "unborn widow." There are statutes, however, in several states which validate such contingent interests by presuming that A's widow was intended to be a person who was living at the testator's death.[38] Absent a statute, invalidity may be avoided by a constructional device, discussed in Section 10 of

---

34. Prime v. Hyne, 260 Cal.App.2d 397, 67 Cal.Rptr. 170 (1968); Ryan v. Beshk, 339 Ill. 45, 170 N.E. 699 (1930). See Simes & Smith § 1228, at 120 (2d ed. 1956).

35. Belfield v. Booth, 63 Conn. 299, 27 A. 585 (1893); Asche v. Asche, 42 Del.Ch. 545, 216 A.2d 272 (1966).

36. Fla.Stat.Ann. § 689.22(5)(c); Ill.Ann.Stat.ch. 30, § 194(c); N.Y.Est. Powers & Trusts Law § 9–1.3(d).

37. Dickerson v. Union National Bank, 268 Ark. 292, 595 S.W.2d 677 (1980); Lanier v. Lanier, 218 Ga. 137, 126 S.E.2d 776 (1962); Perkins v. Iglehart, 183 Md. 520, 39 A.2d 672 (1944); Brookover v. Grimm, 118 W.Va. 227, 190 S.E. 697 (1937).

38. Cal.Civ.Code § 715.7; Fla.Stat. Ann. § 689.22(5)(b); Ill.Ann.Stat.ch. 30, § 194(c)(1); N.Y.Est.Powers & Trusts Law § 9–1.3(d).

this Chapter. Of course, if there were no condition of survivorship attached to the children's gift, then the gift would be valid since the interests of all members of the class must vest not later than A's death, and A is the measuring life.

Another situation which illustrates the rule as to certainty of vesting is that of the bequest to such children of A as reach age 25, and at the testator's death A, a woman, is 45, widowed, and the mother of two children, ages 23 and 21. Is there a possibility that the interest of a member of the class will vest too remotely? There is, if A marries and becomes pregnant prior to the time her first child reaches age 25. When the first child becomes 25, the class closes. It is possible that the interest of a member of the class will vest too remotely—that child conceived in the next two years would have a contingent interest which could vest beyond any life in being plus 21 years. Experience tells us that it is unlikely that the events which could defeat the class gift will occur, but there is no question that the gift to the children of A is invalid.[39]

SECTION 5. CLASS GIFTS

There are two points to keep in mind with respect to the relationship of the rule against perpetuities to class gifts of future interests: First, if the interest of one potential member of the class violates the rule, the entire class gift is deemed to violate the rule;[40] and secondly, standard class-closing principles are applicable in the determination of the membership in the class for the purposes of the rule against prepetuities.[41] Many future interests are class gifts, and consequently the perpetuities rules applicable to them are very significant.

Testator bequeaths in trust to pay the income to A for life, then to pay the income to the children of A for their lives, and upon the death of the survivor of A's children, to pay over the principal to the grandchildren of A.[42] A is alive at the testator's death. Note that there is no condition of survivorship attached to the gift to A's grandchildren. The life income interests of A's children are valid because such life interests are vested at birth and all interests of that class must vest not later than A's death. The remainder interests in A's grandchildren are invalid.

---

39. See Simes & Smith § 1265 (2d ed. 1956).

40. In re Estate of Ghiglia, 42 Cal.App.3d 433, 116 Cal.Rptr. 827 (1974); Beverlin v. First National Bank, 151 Kan. 307, 98 P.2d 200 (1940); Crockett v. Scott, 199 Tenn. 90, 284 S.W.2d 289 (1955); Hagemann v. National Bank & Trust Co., 218 Va. 333, 237 S.E.2d 388 (1977).

41. See Simes & Smith § 1270 (2d ed. 1956). See discussion of class-closing supra pp. 144–47.

42. It is reiterated that no part of the principal is distributed until the death of the survivor among A's children. As each child dies, the income shares of the survivors increase. A's children have cross-remainders for life, by implication.

The interest of a grandchild is vested at birth subject to partial divestment, or subject to open, by the birth of later grandchildren; prior to birth, obviously the interest of a grandchild is contingent. A may have a child after the testator's death, that child may survive A and all the other children of A, and that child may have a child of his own long after the period of perpetuities has run. The class of grandchildren does not close until the death of the last surviving child of A; the class gift to A's grandchildren violates the rule and is void.[43]

Suppose testator bequeaths the residue of his estate in trust to pay the income to A for life, remainder to such children of A as shall attain age 21. A is alive at the testator's death and has no children. The gift to the children of A is valid; A is the measuring life and the interests of all members of the class must vest, if at all, within 21 years after A's death.[44]

Let us assume the testator bequeaths $100,000 to such of his children as shall attain age 25. At his death the testator has four children, ages 12, 8, 5, and 2. The gift does not violate the rule because there can be no additional members of the class after the testator's death; the interest of all members of the class must vest, if at all, within their own lives, that is to say, within the lifetime of the survivor of them. The members of the class are the measuring lives; the fact that the interest of one member of the class cannot vest within 21 years is not significant.

Suppose testator bequeaths in trust to pay the income to A for life, remainder to such children of A as shall attain age 25. A is alive at the testator's death and has no children. The remainder interest violates the rule because it is possible that the interest of a member of the class may vest beyond the period. At A's death he may be survived by two children, ages 8 and 2; the interest of the younger child may not vest in interest within any life in being at the testator's death plus 21 years.[45]

Suppose settlor irrevocably transfers inter vivos in trust to pay the income to A for life, remainder to such children of A as shall attain age 30. At the date of the transfer in trust, A is,

43. Connecticut Bank and Trust Co. v. Brody, 174 Conn. 616, 392 A.2d 445 (1978); Rogers v. Rooth, 237 Ga. 713, 229 S.E.2d 445 (1976); Mounts v. Roberts, 388 S.W.2d 117 (Ky.1965); New England Trust Co. v. Sanger, 337 Mass. 342, 149 N.E.2d 598 (1958); Turner v. Turner, 260 S.C. 439, 196 S.E.2d 498 (1973).

44. Willis v. Hendry, 127 Conn. 653, 20 A.2d 375 (1940); Donahue v. Watson, — Ind.App. —, 411 N.E.2d 741 (1980);

Lux v. Lux, 109 R.I. 592, 288 A.2d 701 (1972); Otterback v. Bohrer, 87 Va. 548, 12 S.E. 1013 (1891).

45. Thomas v. Pullman Trust & Savings Bank, 371 Ill. 577, 21 N.E.2d 897 (1939); Gettins v. Grand Rapids Trust Co., 249 Mich. 238, 228 N.W. 703 (1930); Kates v. Walker, 82 N.J.L. 157, 82 A. 301 (1912); Parker v. Parker, 252 N.C. 399, 113 S.E.2d 899 (1960).

of course, alive, and A has one child who is 31, another child who is 24, and a third who is 19. Is the remainder interest valid? When does the class close? The class closes at the death of A; the fact that A now has one child who is 31 does not close the class since the date of the transfer in trust is not the time for distribution. So it is possible that next year A will have another child and then immediately after that A may die; this results in a member of the class whose interest may not vest within the time limit of the rule. Consequently the remainder to the class of children of A is invalid in its entirety.[46] Of course, it is immaterial that in fact A never has any additional children; recalling the conclusive presumption of fertility, it is also immaterial that it was highly unlikely, or impossible, that A would have any additional children after the creation of the trust.

Let us take a bequest of $100,000 to such children of A as shall attain age 25, and analyze it on the basis of several different assumptions. Assumption (a) is that A is dead at the testator's death and has two children alive at the testator's death, C1 age 12, and C2 age 2. Assumption (b) is that A is alive at the testator's death and has two children at that time, C1 age 12, and C2 age 10. Assumption (c) is that A is alive at the testator's death and has two children, C1 age 27, and C2 age 2. With respect to assumption (a), there can be no additional members of the class after the creation of the interest; the interest of all members of the class must vest within their lives. The age contingency presents no problem and the class gift is valid. With respect to assumption (b), the class will not close until a member of the class is entitled to distribution. There may be additional members of the class born after the testator's death, and the interest of one such afterborn member may not vest within the time limit. For example, A has a child one year after the testator's death, and then the next day A, C1, C2, and, if you will, everyone else in the world who was alive at the testator's death, die. Then the third child survives to age 25, which vesting occurs beyond the period of the rule. The entire class gift is invalid. With respect to assumption (c), the class closes at the testator's death because there is a member of the class entitled to distribution. So the only members of the class are C1 and C2. C2's interest will vest, if it vests at all, more than 21 years after the creation of his interest, but the vesting must occur during his life. Although A is alive and can have more children, the class of children is limited to C1 and C2 under class-closing principles.[47]

---

46. Pitzel v. Schneider, 216 Ill. 87, 74 N.E. 779 (1905); In re Koellhoffer's Estate, 20 N.J.Misc. 139, 25 A.2d 638 (1942).

47. 6 American Law of Property § 24.25, at 80 (Casner ed. 1952); Simes & Smith § 1270, at 203 (2d ed. 1956).

Let us assume testator bequeaths his residuary estate to such of his nephews and nieces as shall attain age 21. At the testator's death, if there is a member of the class who is 21, then the class closes and the only members of the class are those nephews and nieces who are alive at the testator's death; it follows that all interests must vest within the period because the potential takers are the measuring lives. But if we assume that there is no member of the class who is 21 at the testator's death, our analysis is different since the class does not close at the testator's death. If the parents of the testator are dead at the time of the testator's death, then there can be no additional brothers or sisters of the testator, and the existing brothers and sisters can constitute the measuring lives; it follows that the interests of all members of the class must vest, if at all, within the lifetime of the survivor of the brothers and sisters of the testator, plus 21 years thereafter. The class gift is valid under these circumstances. But suppose we assume that the parents of the testator are alive at the death of the testator, and there is no member of the class who is 21 at the testator's death. All the brothers and sisters of the testator who are alive at the testator's death, and all nephews and nieces alive at the testator's death, may die the next day. Then the testator's parents have a son a year later. Then the parents of the testator die. Then that brother of the testator who was not alive at the testator's death, has a child who survives to age 21; under the bequest he is entitled to take and the vesting will have occurred beyond any life in being at the creation of the interest plus 21 years. So the gift to the class of nephews and nieces, where the testator's parents are alive and there are no members of the class entitled to take at the testator's death, is invalid under the rule.[48]

Several of the preceding examples deal with gifts in which the attainment of a certain age is a condition precedent to taking; as we have seen in the chapter dealing with conditions of survivorship, frequently the postponed gift to a certain age constitutes a vested gift at birth with enjoyment, or payment, postponed to the designated age. Suppose testator bequeaths in trust to A for life, remainder to the children of A to be paid to them at age 25. This language is conventionally construed to create a vested gift at birth of the child with payment postponed to the designated age.[49] Clearly the interests of all members of the class must vest in interest within the period of the rule; A is the measuring life and the future interest of all members of the class must vest in interest not later than A's death. The

---

48. See 6 American Law of Property § 24.25, at 79, case 35 (Casner ed. 1952).

49. See discussion of conditions of survivorship supra p. 133.

fact that the gift may not vest in possession, or enjoyment, within
the period of the rule is, of course, irrelevant.[50]

It should be mentioned at this point that there is a traditional
preference for the vested construction over the contingent construction, which preference can save a future interest from destruction by the rule against perpetuities.

Here is a tricky class gift problem dealing with the vested
gift with payment postponed.   Suppose testator bequeaths the
residue of his estate in trust to pay the income to A for life,
remainder to the grandchildren of B to be paid to them at age
25.   At testator's death, A and B are alive, and B has one grandchild who is age 10.   The language of the remainder is conventionally construed as creating a vested remainder at birth with
enjoyment postponed.   Is the remainder valid?   When does the
class close?   The class must close at A's death or 15 years after
testator's death, whichever occurs last.   The ten year old grandchild of B has a vested interest and he will be entitled to distribution at age 25, or if he should die prior to that age, when
he would have arrived at that age, but, of course, in no event
prior to A's death.   Only such grandchildren as are born prior
to the time for distribution will comprise the class, and the interests of such grandchildren would be vested within the period
of the rule.[51]   But suppose that at the testator's death B has
only one grandchild who is one year old, all other facts remaining
the same.   Is the remainder good?   That grandchild's interest
is vested, but when does the class close?   It closes at A's death
or 24 years after testator's death, whichever occurs last.   One
year after testator's death, B may have another child, and immediately following the birth of that child, A, B, all B's children
(other than that last child), and the one granchild previously
referred to, may die.   Then 22 years later that one child gives
birth to a child;   the interest of that grandchild of B vests at
birth which is beyond the period of the rule.   The remainder is
invalid as a consequence.[52]

The idea that the class gift is invalid in its entirety if it is
invalid in part is clearly a gloss on the rule against perpetuities
as stated in the opening section of this chapter.   The effect of
this principle is to invalidate the interest of a member of the
class which must vest in interest within the period of the rule

50.   Zimmerman v. First National Bank,
348 So.2d 1359 (Ala.1977);   Hill v. Birmingham, 131 Conn. 174, 38 A.2d 604
(1944);   De Ford v. Coleman, 348 Mass.
299, 203 N.E.2d 686 (1965);   Joyner v.
Duncan, 299 N.C. 565, 264 S.E.2d 76 (1980).

51.   See Gray, The Rule Against Perpetuities § 638 (4th ed. 1942).   If A should

die before the oldest grandchild reaches
25, and that grandchild dies under 25, it
would seem improper to distribute at such
grandchild's death and close the class at
such time.

52.   See Simes & Smith § 1270, at 206
(2d ed. 1956).

because of the fact that it may be subject to partial divestment by the interest of another member of the class which is remote. This does not fit into the broad statement of the rule against perpetuities.   It seems that it is only the remote divesting interest which is invalid.   It has been argued, however, that the vested interest subject to partial divestment is vested with respect to the individual but contingent as to the quantity;   this contingency has to do with the potential shares of the members of the class whose interests are remote.   In other words, the precise quantity to be taken by the members of the class will be determined only after the period of the rule.   The "all-or-nothing" rule, as it has been labeled, has been also defended on the ground that the donor's plan would be disturbed if the class gift were valid in part and invalid in part;   the donor's plan or intention is supposedly better served if none of the class members receive anything than if some receive the whole or a part of the whole.[53]   This may be so in some situations and not in others. Certain statutory reforms in recent years have, in effect, modified the "all-or-nothing" rule for the better, and certain constructional means have been employed by the courts to this end; more about this later in Sections 10 and 11 of this Chapter.

There are a couple of common law qualifications to the "all-or-nothing" class gift rule.   One qualification has to do with "sub-classes", and another has to do with the per capita class gift. First, the sub-class situation.   Suppose testator bequeaths $100,000 in trust to pay the income to A for life, then to pay the income to the children of A for their respective lives, and upon the death of each child of A, to pay to the children of such child a percentage of the principal equal to the percentage of the income which the parent was entitled to.   A survives the testator.   The testator has created separate sub-classes among the granchildren of A.   This is not a case of one class consisting of all the grandchildren of A, but rather one or more classes each of which consists of the children of a child of A.   Let us assume A had one child, C1, who was living at the testator's death, and a second child, C2, born three years after testator's death.   The interests of all the children of C1 obviously must vest not later than C1's death, which is within the rule.   The amount which each child of C1 will take will be determined at C1's death if C1 outlives A;   if A outlives C1, the amount which each child of C1 will take will be determined at A's death, as described in the next paragraph.   A, of course, is also a life in being at the testator's death.   In either case, the amount will be determined within the

<hr/>

53. Restatement, Property § 371, comment *a* (1944).   It has been argued that there is no rational basis for the "all

or nothing" rule.   Leach, The Rule Against Perpetuities and Gifts to Classes, 51 Harv.L.Rev. 1329 (1938).

period of the rule. The remainder to the children of C1 is valid. The interests of C2's children would be invalid because children of C2, who is not a measuring life, may be born after the period of the rule. So $50,000 would pass to the children of C1, and the $50,000 intended for the children of C2 would pass to the residuary legatees, or in the absence of a residuary clause, to the testator's intestate takers.[54]

If C1 predeceases A, the determination of the quantity that C1's children take is not made at C1's death, but rather at A's death, because A could have additional children after C1's death which would reduce the total amount to be divided among C1's children. A was a life in being at the testator's death, and the determination of the quantity is made within the period of the rule. It follows that the measuring life which validates the interests of C1's children is the survivor of C1 and A.

The sub-class result may be summarized as follows: The remainder to the children of any child of A who was living at the testator's death is valid, and the remainder to the children of any child of A who was born after the testator's death is invalid.

This sub-class disposition is substantively different from the three-generation disposition of a similar nature which we have previously discussed: Testator bequeaths in trust to pay the income to A for life, then to pay the income to the children of A for their lives, and upon the death of the survivor of such children, to pay over the principal to the grandchildren of A. Note that in this disposition the surviving child of A receives all the income, and that there is no distribution of principal until the death of that survivor. The ultimate remainder is in one class, all the grandchildren of A. The surviving child of A may not have been alive at the testator's death. Clearly there may be grandchildren of A born after the period of the rule, and as a result the remainder to the grandchildren of A is invalid.

Now the per capita class gift qualification to the "all-or-nothing" class gift rule. The per capita class gift is one in which a specific amount is given to each member of a class, as distinguished from the ordinary class gift in which a specific amount is to be divided among the members of the class. In the per capita class gift the amount which a member of the class receives does not vary in accordance with the number of members of the class, whereas in the ordinary class gift the amount each member

54. American Security & Trust Co. v. Cramer, 175 F.Supp. 367 (D.D.C.1959); First Alabama Bank v. Adams, 382 So.2d 1104 (Ala.1980); Second Bank-State St. Trust Co. v. Second Bank-State St. Trust Co., 335 Mass. 407, 140 N.E.2d 201 (1957); Harrah Estate, 364 Pa. 451, 72 A.2d 587 (1950).

receives does vary with the membership in the class.   Testator bequeaths $1,000 to each grandchild of testator who lives to age 30.   Testator is survived by his only child and two grandchildren, ages 6 and 2.   Under standard class-closing principles, the membership in the class is determined at the testator's death in the case of a per capita gift of this nature, and consequently the interests of the two grandchildren are valid since they must vest within their own lives.   This example involves no qualification of the all-or-nothing rule;   it is merely the consequence of class-closing principles otherwise applicable.[55]   But suppose the bequest had been $1,000 to each grandchild of testator who lives to age 30, whether born prior or subsequent to testator's death, and the executor is directed in the will to set aside a reasonable fund for this purpose.   Testator is survived by his only child and two grandchildren, ages 6 and 2.   The class-closing principle is only a rule of construction and can be negated by express language in the will.   In this case the testator made it clear that he intended that future grandchildren were to be included, and consequently the class remains open until the testator's child's death.   The testator's child may die survived by a child of his who is under 9 years of age and was not alive at testator's death; it seems that the interest of such grandchild would vest too remotely and the application of the all-or-nothing rule would result in the invalidity of the entire class gift.   But the all-or-nothing rule has been qualified in this situation to the effect that the gifts of the fixed amount to the grandchildren living at the testator's death are valid, and the gifts to grandchildren born after the testator's death are invalid as violative of the rule against perpetuities.[56]

In the per capita class gift, the amount to be received by the members of the class whose interests must vest within the period of the rule is not dependent in any way upon the number of members of the class whose interests may vest beyond the period of the rule.   In other words, the interest of the class member which must vest within the period of the rule is also fixed as to quantity within the period of the rule.   This differentiates it from the ordinary class gift in which the amount to be received by the member of the class whose interest must vest within the period of the rule is dependent upon the number of members of the class whose interests may vest beyond the period of the rule. This is the basis for the different treatment of the per capita class gift.

---

55.   See supra pp. 147.

56.   Restatement, Property § 385 (1944);   6 American Law of Property § 24.28 (Casner ed. 1952);   Simes & Smith § 1266 (2d ed. 1956).

SECTION 6.   POWERS OF APPOINTMENT

In the analysis of the relationship between the rule against perpetuities and powers of appointment, it is necessary to consider (a) the validity of the power, and (b) the validity of the appointed interests.

First, the validity of the power.   With respect to special powers of appointment and general testamentary powers of appointment, the power is void under the rule if it is possible for it to be exercised beyond the period of the rule as measured from the time of the creation of the power.   With respect to general powers of appointment exercisable by deed or will, that is, presently exercisable general powers, the power is valid if it must be acquired, that is, be exercisable, within the period of the rule, as measured from the time of the creation of the power;   it makes no difference that the power is exercisable beyond the period of the rule, provided it is necessarily exercisable within the period of the rule.

Suppose testator devises and bequeaths his estate in trust to pay the income to A for life, remainder to such children of A as A shall by deed or will appoint.   Here we have a special power exercisable by deed or will, and it cannot be exercised beyond the period of the rule.   A was alive at the testator's death.   A is the measuring life and the power is exercisable only during his life or immediately upon his death by his last will.[57]   It should be stressed that we are not now concerned with the interests which are created by the exercise of the power but only with the validity of the power itself.

Similarly, if testator bequeathed in trust to pay the income to A for life, remainder to such persons as A shall by will appoint, the power would be valid.[58]   This is, of course, a general testamentary power.

Suppose testator bequeaths $250,000 in trust to pay the income to A for life, then to pay the income to the children of A for their respective lives, and upon the death of each child of A to pay over the percentage of the corpus equal to the percentage of income that such child was receiving to such persons as such child shall by will appoint.   A was alive at the testator's death and had no children at that time.   The powers are general testamentary powers.   The only measuring life is A, and clearly

---

57.   See Bartlett v. Sears, 81 Conn. 34, 70 A. 33 (1908);   Thomas v. Harrison, 24 Ohio Op.2d 148, 191 N.E.2d 862 (1962);   Lewis Estate, 349 Pa. 571, 37 A.2d 482 (1944).

58.   Lamkin v. Safe Deposit & Trust Co., 192 Md. 472, 64 A.2d 704 (1949);   Estate of Lawrence, 136 Pa. 354, 20 A. 521 (1890).   See Simes & Smith § 1273 (2d ed. 1956).

the powers are exercisable beyond the period of the rule and are invalid.[59]

It is clear that if the donee of a special power or a general testamentary power is a person who is unborn at the time of the creation of the power, the power is void unless the time of exercise is expressly circumscribed in such a way as to limit the exercise to the period of the rule.

One more example of the invalid special or general testamentary power. Testator bequeaths in trust to pay the income to A for life, remainder to such persons as A shall by will appoint. A survives the testator, and at A's death he appoints in his will in trust to pay the income to B for life, remainder to such persons as B shall by will appoint. B was not alive at the testator's death, and B survives A. A's power was clearly valid. What about B's power? As we shall discuss shortly, the interests created by the exercise of a general testamentary power or a special power are read back into the donor's creating instrument, in this case the testator's will, and measured for perpetuities purposes from that time. If this is done, then testator's will provides for a life estate in A, life estate in B, and a general testamentary power in B. But B was not alive at the testator's death, and consequently his power may be exercised beyond the period of the rule. B's power is void.[60]

Now let us consider the general power exercisable by deed or will. Testator bequeaths in trust to pay the income to A for life, then to pay the income to the children of A for their lives, and upon the death of the last surviving child of A to pay over the corpus to such persons as the last surviving child of A shall appoint by deed or will. A is alive at the testator's death and has two children at that time. Must the power be acquired, or be exercisable, within the period of the rule? It seems not since A may have children after the testator's death, and the identity of the last surviving child, who is the donee, may not be determined until after the period of the rule. There is a condition precedent to the acquisition of the power, namely survivorship of all other children of A, and that condition precedent may not be satisfied within the limits of the rule. It cannot be said that the power must be acquired within the period of the rule, and consequently it is void.[61]

59. Burlington County Trust Co. v. Di Castelcicala, 2 N.J. 214, 66 A.2d 164 (1949). See Simes & Smith § 1272 (2d ed. 1956).

60. Wilmington Trust Co. v. Wilmington Trust Co., 21 Del.Ch. 102, 180 A. 597 (1935), modified 21 Del.Ch. 188, 186 A. 903 (1936); Gambrill v. Gambrill, 122 Md. 563, 89 A. 1094 (1914); In re Estate of Davis, 449 Pa. 505, 297 A.2d 451 (1972).

61. Simes & Smith § 1272 (2d ed. 1956).

Suppose testator bequeaths in trust to pay the income to A for life, remainder to such persons as A shall appoint by will. A survives the testator, and A appoints in trust for B for life, remainder to such persons as B shall appoint by deed or will. B survives A. B was not alive at the testator's death. Is B's presently exercisable general power valid? The period of perpetuities is measured from the testator's death. A is the measuring life, and the power was acquired by B at the time of A's death. Consequently B's power is valid, although he may not exercise the power within the period of the rule.[62] It should be emphasized that the valid presently exercisable general power may properly be exercised after the period of the rule.

It is unusual for an owner of property, a donor, to give a power of appointment to a person who is unborn; if a power is given to one who is alive at the time of the creation of the power, the power is necessarily valid. If a power is invalid, it is likely to happen in the situation in which a power is created in the exercise of a power, and in the discretionary trust situation which we shall now consider.

Suppose testator bequeaths in trust to pay the income to the children of A in such proportions as the trustee in its discretion determines from time to time, and upon the death of the last surviving child of A, to pay the principal to B. A is alive at the testator's death, and is, of course, presumed to be capable of having children after the death of the testator. This is a discretionary trust with respect to income. The power which the trustee has does not appear to be the conventional power of appointment, but for perpetuities purposes it is like a special power. The trustee from time to time may exercise his discretion as to the disposition of the income, and such exercise is like an exercise of a power of appointment. The power may be exercised after the period of the rule, and consequently it is void.[63]

However, this discretionary power may be upheld if it is determined that the discretion is personal to the trustee named by the testator if the trustee is a human being and not a corporation; if this is so, then the power cannot be exercised beyond the period of the rule since it must be exercised by that one trustee and the power dies with him.[64] Besides the personal discretionary power qualification, it has also been maintained that the discretionary trust constitutes a series of separate powers of appoint-

62. Simes & Smith § 1273 (2d ed. 1956). See In re Ransom's Estate, 89 N.J.Super. 224, 214 A.2d 521 (1965).

63. Andrews v. Lincoln, 95 Me. 541, 50 A. 898 (1901); Bundy v. United States Trust Co., 257 Mass. 72, 153 N.E. 337 (1926); Thomas v. Harrison, 24 Ohio Op.2d 148, 191 N.E.2d 862 (1962).

64. Simes & Smith § 1277 (2d ed. 1956). See Thomas v. Harrison, 24 Ohio Op.2d 148, 191 N.E.2d 862 (1962).

ment, and that consequently the discretionary powers exercisable within the period of the rule are valid; this results in the validity of the discretionary aspects of the trust for the lives of A and children of A alive at testator's death, plus 21 years.[65] The reasoning is that each discretionary disposition is an exercise of an independent power of appointment.

We have discussed the question of the validity of the power. Now we proceed to the question of the validity of the interests created by the exercise of the power. With respect to special powers of appointment and general testamentary powers of appointment, the appointment is read back into the instrument creating the power and the period of perpetuities is computed from the date of the creation of the power;[66] however, one is permitted to consider facts existing at the date the appointment is made for the purpose of determining the validity of the appointed interests.[67] With respect to the general power exercisable by deed or will, that is, the power which is presently exercisable, the period of perpetuities is computed from the date of the appointment.[68]

Testator bequeaths in trust to pay the income to A for life, remainder to such issue of A as A shall by will appoint. A survives the testator and at his death appoints in trust to pay the income to A's son, C, for life, remainder over to C's children. C was not alive at testator's death. A had a special testamentary power, and consequently the appointed interests are read back into the testator's will. This means that the donor's will, for our purposes, reads to A for life, then to C for life, then to the children of C in fee. The life interest of C is valid because it must vest in interest during A's life, but the class remainder to C's children is invalid because the interest of a member of the class may vest beyond the period of the rule.[69] In this case,

---

65. This position is adopted in Fla.Stat.Ann. § 689.22(3)(a)(4) and Ill.Ann.Stat.ch. 30, § 194(a)(4). See 6 American Law of Property § 24.32, at 96 (Casner ed. 1952); Simes & Smith § 1277 (2d ed. 1956).

66. United California Bank v. Bottler, 16 Cal.App.3d 610, 94 Cal.Rptr. 227 (1971); Second National Bank v. Harris Trust & Savings Bank, 29 Conn.Sup. 275, 283 A.2d 226 (1971); Fiduciary Trust Co. v. Mishou, 321 Mass. 615, 75 N.E.2d 3 (1947); Thomas v. Harrison, 24 Ohio Op.2d 148, 191 N.E.2d 862 (1962). See Simes & Smith §§ 1274, 1275 (2d ed. 1956).

A different position has been adopted in several states. In Industrial National Bank v. Barrett, 101 R.I. 89, 220 A.2d 517 (1966), it was held that the appointed interests in the exercise of a general testamentary power are measured from the time of the exercise. Wis.Stat.Ann. § 700.16 is to the same effect. Wisconsin has the rule against suspension of the power of alienation. Del.Code Ann.tit. 25, § 501 and Fla.Stat.Ann. § 689.22(2)(b), provide that appointed interests under special as well as general powers are measured from the time of exercise.

67. Simes & Smith § 1274 (2d ed. 1956).

68. Id.

69. United California Bank v. Bottler, 16 Cal.App.3d 610, 94 Cal.Rptr. 227 (1971); Graham v. Whitridge, 99 Md. 248, 57 A. 609 (1904); Boyd's Estate, 199 Pa. 487, 49 A. 297 (1901).

literally reading back the appointment to C into the donor's will is a bit strained because the interest could not have been given to C as such by the donor since he wasn't in existence at the donor's death, but for purposes of analyzing the validity of the appointed interests this bit of incongruity must be tolerated.

Suppose in the previous example C had been alive at the donor's death. Do we then have a different result? If C is a life in being at the time of the creation of the remainder interests of the children of C, then such remainder interests are valid since the interest of each member of the class must vest not later than the death of C.[70]

Suppose in this same example C was not alive at the testator's death, and predeceased A leaving two children who survived A. Are the remainder interests of the children of C valid? We are permitted to take into consideration the facts which are known at the time of the appointment, which is the date of A's death. At that time we know that the interests of C's children vest within the period of the rule—the measuring life is A and the interests vest immediately upon A's death. Under these circumstances, the interests of C's children are valid.[71]

Assume settlor irrevocably transfers inter vivos in trust to pay the income to A for life, remainder to such persons as A shall by will appoint. A appoints in trust for his children for their lives, and upon the death of the last surviving child, to pay the corpus to the grandchildren of A. All of A's children were alive at the date of the settlor's transfer in trust. A had a general testamentary power. Reading the appointment back into the donor's instrument of trust, the disposition is to A for life, then to A's children for their lives, then upon the death of the last surviving child of A, to the grandchildren of A. On its face, the remainder to grandchildren is invalid, but we are permitted to consider the fact that all of A's children were alive at the time of the creation of the grandchildren's interests; the children of A constitute measuring lives and the future interests in the grandchildren are valid because the interest of every member of the class must vest not later than the death of the last surviving child of A.[72]

---

70. Breault v. Feigenholtz, 358 F.2d 39 (7th Cir. 1966), cert. denied 385 U.S. 824, 87 S.Ct. 52, 17 L.Ed.2d 61 (1966); Equitable Trust Co. v. McComb, 19 Del.Ch. 387, 168 A. 203 (1933); Amerige v. Attorney General, 324 Mass. 648, 88 N.E.2d 126 (1949); Marx v. Rice, 3 N.J.Super. 581, 67 A.2d 918 (1949).

71. See Simes & Smith § 1274, at 212 (2d ed. 1956).

72. Legg's Estate v. Commissioner, 114 F.2d 760 (4th Cir. 1940); In re Bird's Estate, 225 Cal.App.2d 196, 37 Cal.Rptr. 288 (1964); De Charette v. De Charette, 264 Ky. 525, 94 S.W.2d 1018 (1936); In re Warren's Estate, 320 Pa. 112, 182 A. 396 (1936).

This consideration of the facts known at the time of the appointment is sometimes referred to as the "second look" doctrine. It should be stressed that only such facts as exist at the time of the appointment may be considered in determining the validity of the appointed interests under the rule against perpetuities; events relating to the appointed interests which occur subsequent to the appointment cannot be considered. There is also a case which held that the facts existing at the time of the expiration of an unexercised inter vivos special power could be considered for the purpose of determining the validity of gifts in default of appointment.[73] So to this limited extent we are permitted to substitute "what happened" for "what could have happened"; in Section 11 of this Chapter we shall consider the statutes in some jurisdictions which have extended the "what happened" approach to even more rational lengths.

Let us take a brief look at the interests created by the exercise of a presently exercisable general power. Testator bequeaths in trust to pay the income to A for life, remainder over to such persons as A shall by deed or will appoint. A survives the testator and appoints by will in trust for B for life, remainder to the children of B. B was not alive at the testator's death, but he was alive at A's death. We measure the period of perpetuities not from the testator's death but from A's appointment. Since B is the measuring life, the remainder interests of the children of B are valid.[74]

Suppose testator bequeaths in trust to pay the income to A for life, remainder over to such persons as A shall by deed or will appoint. A survives the testator and appoints by will in trust for B for life, remainder over to such persons as B shall by will appoint, and in default of appointment, in trust for the children of A for their lives, and upon the death of the last survivor of such children, to the grandchildren of A. B was not alive at the testator's death, but B survived A. However, A had a general power exercisable by deed or will; the interests created by A's exercise are measured from the time of the exercise. B's general testamentary power is valid because it can only be exercised at B's death and B is the measuring life.[75] The interests created in default are also valid since they are measured from the time of A's exercise; obviously the interests of A's children are valid, and the interests of A's grandchildren are valid because the interest of every grandchild must vest not later than

---

73. Sears v. Coolidge, 329 Mass. 340, 108 N.E.2d 563 (1952).

74. In re Estate of McMurtry, 68 Misc.2d 553, 326 N.Y.S.2d 965 (1971);

Appeal of Mifflin, 121 Pa. 205, 15 A. 525 (1888); Restatement, Second, Property, Donative Transfers § 1.2 (1983).

75. See supra pp. 199–200.

the death of the last surviving child of A, and the children of A are the measuring lives.[76]

The difference between the perpetuities treatment of appointed interests under the special power and the general testamentary power on the one hand, and the general power exercisable by deed or will on the other hand, makes sense. The former is in the nature of a delegation of the authority to create a future interest which is restricted as to time of appointment or objects or both, whereas the latter is tantamount to ownership in the donee of the property interest subject to the power. The former is in the nature of a deferred future interest controlled by the donor of the power which is appropriately measured from the time of the creation of the power, whereas the latter is ownership of the property interest which is the subject of the power (the donee can appoint to himself at any time), and accordingly the interests created should be measured as if the donee were transferring his own property. Similar reasoning supports the difference in perpetuities treatment of these different types of powers with respect to the validity of the power itself, if one thinks of the exercisability of the power as in the nature of a future interest.

SECTION 7.   INTERESTS SUBJECT TO THE RULE

The contingent remainder and the executory interest are subject to the rule against perpetuities, but the possibility of reverter and the right of entry are not subject to the rule in this country.[77] Both the possibility of reverter and the right of entry are by their nature contingent future interests; their becoming possessory necessarily is conditional upon an event which may or may not occur. They impair the marketability of land and inhibit the use and development of land at least as much as a remote contingent remainder or executory interest. But the rule against perpetuities was an ad hoc common law development and these future interests just didn't get caught in the net, although in modern times they have been made subject to the rule in England.[78] In this country there has been legislation in several states which has limited the life of the possibility of reverter and the right of entry to a specific number of years from their creation, such as 30 years, but these statutory limitations may be only prospective in application.[79] In most jurisdictions today these interests are valid in perpetuity.

76.   See supra p. 182.

77.   See cases cited supra note 6.

78.   Simes & Smith §§ 1238, 1239 (2d ed. 1956).

79.   E.g., Conn.Gen.Stat.Ann. § 45–97;   Ky.Rev.Stat.Ann.   §§ 381.218, 381.219; Neb.Rev.Stat. § 76–2,102; R.I. Gen.Laws §§ 34–4–19, 34–4–20.

The reversion subject to divestment is not subject to the rule against perpetuities although its becoming possessory is also conditional upon an event which may or may not occur. The conceptual reason is that it is viewed as a vested interest. But more convincingly, if the divesting contingency is within the rule, then the reversion must be divested or not within the period of the rule; if the divesting contingency violates the rule, then we are left with the reversion which for obvious reasons is not subject to the rule. If a disposition is incomplete, the property must return to the transferor.

It should be pointed out that there is a problem as to whether all executory interests in land or only "contingent" executory interests in land are subject to the rule. Originally the executory interest was considered to be a non-vested interest for all purposes, regardless of the nature of the event which would cause it to become possessory; it is unusual that an executory interest will be subject to an event which is certain to happen, but it is possible. A conveys to B in fee to become possessory 25 years after the date of the conveyance. This is an executory interest in B which is not subject to any condition precedent. There is no reason why such an interest should be deemed to violate the rule.[80]

The issue has arisen concerning the application of the rule against perpetuities to certain types of life insurance settlements which provide for payments to beneficiaries extending into the future. It is possible that an individual carrying insurance on his life in a substantial amount would select a settlement option which would provide for the payment of certain sums to his descendants over a period of time which would violate the rule against perpetuities if it were applicable. Could the insured circumvent the rule by this means? The rule is concerned with future interests in specific real and personal property, and is not concerned with contract rights extending into the future which do not create interests in specific property. The insurance policy and settlement constitute a contract which creates no interests in specific property. It follows that the rule does not apply to the insurance settlement. This is a neat syllogism, but it does not necessarily furnish us a satisfactory answer.

How does the insurance settlement differ from the modern trust of stocks and bonds? When the settlor in the case of the living trust or executor in the case of the testamentary trust transfers certain stocks and bonds to the trustee, the trustee

---

80. Restatement, Second, Property, Donative Transfers § 1.4 comments *b* and *m* (1983); 6 American Law of Property § 24.20 (Casner ed. 1952); Simes & Smith § 1236 (2d ed. 1956). Contra, Gray, The Rule Against Perpetuities § 201 n.3 (4th ed. 1942). The analogous vested personal property gift with enjoyment postponed to a certain age is treated as "vested" for purposes of the rule.

holds legal title to this specific personal property and the beneficiaries of the trust hold the equitable title to this specific personal property. However, the trustee invariably is given the power to sell the stocks and bonds which are delivered to him and to reinvest the proceeds in other property to which the respective legal and equitable titles attach. So the modern trust is like a fund whose components are subject to frequent change. The insurance settlement, on the other hand, is in the nature of a contract, and the insurance company is a debtor whose obligation is to pay certain sums to the insurance beneficiaries in the future. The trustee, of course, is a fiduciary and not a debtor. The insurance company collects premiums and invests the money in real estate mortgages and stocks and bonds. There is no specific fund which represents a particular policy, as contrasted with the individual trust. Both insurance companies and trustees must invest their funds conservatively. The insurance company usually binds itself to pay certain fixed sums of money, whereas the trustee is not responsible for losses unless it has been guilty of mismanagement, and, of course, the trustee does not gain from appreciation in investments, as the insurance company does.

There are significant legal differences between the insurance settlement and the trust, but it seems that the benefit of donative wealth is controlled, or tied up, just as much in the case of the insurance settlement as it is in the case of the trust, and the manner in which the funds are invested and the consequent effect on the economy are similar. However, the rule has not been applied to the insurance settlement.[81] The incidence of insurance settlements which approach the limits of the rule against perpetuities is probably very small.

It should be pointed out that although a contract claim does not create an interest in specific property and therefore is not subject to the rule against perpetuities, it is itself considered specific property if it is divided into different legal or equitable interests.[82] For example, a government bond is a contract claim for money, and does not create an interest in specific property. However, if the bond is placed in trust to pay the income to A for life, then to pay the income to A's children for their lives, and then to pay the principal to A's grandchildren, the equitable future interests in the bond are subject to the rule against perpetuities. In the same fashion, life insurance contracts are often

---

81. Doyle v. Massachusetts Mutual Life Insurance Co., 377 F.2d 19 (6th Cir. 1967); First National Bank & Trust Co. v. Purcell, 244 S.W.2d 458 (Ky.1951); Holmes v. John Hancock Mutual Life Insurance Co., 288 N.Y. 106, 41 N.E.2d 909 (1942).

82. See discussion in Simes & Smith § 1246 (2d ed. 1956).

placed in trust, and the equitable future interests in the contract are subject to the rule.   Indeed, most trust assets are contract rights, e.g., bonds, stocks, certificates of deposit, life insurance policies.

The corporate pension trust maintained by corporate and employee contributions is a fund of indefinite duration for innumerable beneficiaries, some of whom may be unknown or unborn; this type of trust is cleary sui generis and has been exempted by statute in many jurisdictions from the rule against perpetuities and other property rules in order to permit it to operate.[83]

Problems have arisen with respect to the application of the rule against perpetuities to the commercial transaction in land. Normally the rule has no application to contract rights, but the option to purchase specific land is a contract which creates something in the nature of an equitable contingent interest in the property since the option contract is usually specifically enforceable.   It has been held that the option to purchase in gross is violative of the rule if the option is capable of being exercised beyond the period of perpetuities.[84]   The option in gross is one in which the optionee does not own any other interest in the land which is the subject of the option.   However, the option to purchase in which the optionee is also the lessee of the land has been held to be exempt from the rule.[85]   The distinction is that the option in gross tends to discourage the development of the land by the holder of the possessory interest, whereas the option held by one who is also lessee tends to encourage the development of the land by the lessee-optionee.   It has also been held for similar reasons that the option in the lessee to renew a lease is exempt from the rule.[86]   It should also be noted that options to purchase land held by persons who own only mineral rights in the land have been treated in the same manner as options in gross.[87]

There is certainly good reason to limit the option in gross to a relatively short period of time, but the rule against perpetuities is

83. E.g., Cal.Civ.Code § 715.3; Fla.Stat.Ann. § 41.01; N.C.Gen.Stat. § 36A–6; Ohio Rev.Code Ann. § 2131.09.

84. Atchison v. City of Englewood, 170 Colo. 295, 463 P.2d 297 (1970); Thomas v. Murrow, 245 Ga. 38, 262 S.E.2d 802 (1980); Three Rivers Rock Co. v. Reed Crushed Stone Co., 530 S.W.2d 202 (Ky.1975); Emerson v. King, 118 N.H. 684, 394 A.2d 51 (1978).

85. Wing, Inc. v. Arnold, 107 So.2d 765 (Fla.App.1959); St. Regis Paper Co. v. Brown, 247 Ga. 361, 276 S.E.2d 24 (1981); Producers Oil Co. v. Gore, 610 P.2d 772 (Okl.1980); W.Va.Code § 36–1–24.

86. Lonergan v. Connecticut Food Store, Inc., 168 Conn. 122, 357 A.2d 910 (1975); Ehrhart v. Spencer, 175 Kan. 227, 263 P.2d 246 (1953); Wallace v. Williams, 313 P.2d 784 (Okl.1957); Pechenik v. Baltimore & Ohio Railroad Co., 157 W.Va. 895, 205 S.E.2d 813 (1974).

87. Middleton v. Western Coal & Mining Co., 241 F.Supp. 407 (W.D.Ark.1965), affirmed 362 F.2d 48 (8th Cir. 1966); Rocky Mountain Fuel Co. v. Heflin, 148 Colo. 415, 366 P.2d 577 (1961); West Virginia-Pittsburgh Coal Co. v. Strong, 129 W.Va. 832, 42 S.E.2d 46 (1947).   See Quarto Mining Co. v. Litman, 42 Ohio St.2d 73, 326 N.E.2d 676 (1975), cert. denied 423 U.S. 866, 96 S.Ct. 128, 46 L.Ed.2d 96 (1975).

obviously not suited to the commercial transaction. The rule against perpetuities was formulated in the context of donative transfers of family wealth. Lives in being plus 21 years has no purpose in the commercial field. It seems that a limit of a specific number of years is called for, and there are a couple of statutes to this effect.[88]

SECTION 8. REVOCABLE TRUSTS AND OTHER SPECIAL MEASUREMENT SITUATIONS

If a settlor creates a revocable living trust, the period of perpetuities does not begin to run with respect to the future interests created by such trust until the termination of the power of revocation, usually the death of the settlor.[89] The reasoning behind this result is that the settlor's control is tantamount to ownership, and the property in the trust is not tied up so long as this control exists.

Similarly, if testator bequeaths in trust to pay the income to A for life, then to the children of A for their lives, and upon the death of the survivor of A's children, to pay the corpus to A's grandchildren, and A is given an unrestricted power to take principal of the trust during his lifetime, the future interests of the grandchildren of A are valid since the period of perpetuities does not begin to run until A's death.[90] By virtue of A's unrestricted power to invade corpus, the trust property is not in any sense tied up; A's power is tantamount to ownership. For the same reason the period of perpetuities does not begin to run as long as a person holds a presently exercisable general power of appointment.[91]

Restatement (Second) of Property, Donative Transfers § 1.2 adopts the positions stated above:

> The period of the rule against perpetuities begins to run in a donative transfer with respect to a non-vested interest in property as of the date when no person, acting alone, has a power currently exercisable to become the unqualified beneficial owner of all beneficial rights in the property in which the non-vested interest exists.

SECTION 9. EFFECT OF A VIOLATION; INFECTIOUS INVALIDITY

The general principle is that when a future interest violates the rule against perpetuities, the invalid interest is stricken and the rest of the disposition remains as if the invalid interest had

---

88. Fla.Stat.Ann. § 689.22(3)(a)(7); Ill.Ann.Stat.ch. 30, § 194(a)(7).

89. Cook v. Horn, 214 Ga. 289, 104 S.E.2d 461 (1958); Nelson v. Mercantile Trust Co., 335 S.W.2d 167 (Mo.1960); N.Y.Est.Powers & Trust Law § 10–8.1; Ohio Rev.Code Ann. § 2131.08(B);

Va.Code § 55–13.2; Wash.Rev.Code Ann. § 11.98.040.

90. 6 American Law of Property § 24.59, case 93 (Casner ed. 1952).

91. Simes & Smith § 1252 (2d ed. 1956).

never been created.[92]   So, if testator devises to A for life, remainder to such children of A as live to age 25, the remainder interest is excised, leaving a life estate in A and a reversion in residuary devisees or heirs of the testator.

The question has arisen as to the validity of a subsequent interest which does not violate the rule where a prior interest in the same property does violate the rule.   Testator bequeaths in trust to pay the income to A for life, then to pay the income to the children of A for their lives, then upon the death of the last surviving child of A, to pay the income to the grandchildren of A for their lives, and upon the death of the last surviving grandchild, to pay the corpus over to St. Luke's Hospital.   The future interests in the grandchildren of A are invalid and stricken from the disposition, but the ultimate remainder to the hospital was vested from the beginning.   There does not appear to be any reason to invalidate the interest of the hospital because a prior interest is invalid.[93]

There is a cute problem concerning the effect of a violation which involves the future interest which will vest if either of two events occurs, one of which is remote and the other of which is within the period.   Testator bequeaths in trust to pay the income to A for life, principal over to such surviving children of A as live to age 25, but if A shall have no surviving children, or if A shall have no surviving children who live to age 25, then to B. The first condition, that A have no children who survive him, is one which is within the period of the rule, but the second condition, that A have no surviving children who live to age 25, is one which is violative of the rule.   So the second condition is stricken, as well as the remainder interests in the children of A, and we are left with a life estate in A, remainder in B if A has no surviving children.[94]

But suppose this last disposition is changed so that the two conditions are not separately stated: Testator bequeaths in trust to pay the income to A for life, principal over to such surviving children of A as shall live to age 25, or on the failure thereof, to B. Here the condition to B's taking includes both the situation of A's not having any children who survive him, and A's having children who survive him but do not survive to age 25.   The two separate conditions have not been separately stated;   there is

92. In re Freeman's Estate, 195 Kan. 190, 404 P.2d 222 (1965); Davis v. Davis, 449 Pa. 505, 297 A.2d 451 (1972); Sellers v. Powers, 426 S.W.2d 533 (Tex.1978); Hagemann v. National Bank & Trust Co., 218 Va. 333, 237 S.E.2d 388 (1977).

93. Restatement, Property § 402 comment *d* (1944); Simes & Smith § 1264 (2d ed. 1956).   But see Gray, The Rule Against Perpetuities § 251 (4th ed. 1942).

94. Layton v. Black, 34 Del.Ch. 1, 99 A.2d 244 (1953); Monarski v. Greb, 407 Ill. 281, 95 N.E.2d 433 (1950); First Portland National Bank v. Rodrique, 157 Me. 277, 172 A.2d 107 (1961); Springfield Safe Deposit & Trust Co. v. Ireland, 268 Mass. 62, 167 N.E. 261 (1929).

authority that the interest of B fails completely in this situation.[95] Where, however, the valid and the invalid conditions have been separately and expressly stated, the valid condition remains effective and the invalid condition is stricken.

There is authority for the proposition that the invalidity of a portion of a will can cause the invalidation of other wholly separate gifts in the will. This result may follow if the excision of one provision of the will as a consequence of a perpetuities violation produces a distorted distribution of the testator's wealth among his family. For example: Testator bequeaths and devises one-half his estate outright to C1, a child of testator, and one-half his estate in trust to pay the income to C2, another child of the testator, for life, principal over to the children of C2 who live to age 25. C1 and C2 survive the testator and are the testator's only children and only intestate takers. The remainder interests for C2's children are invalid under the rule, and consequently on C2's death one-fourth of the estate will pass to C1 and one-fourth to C2's estate; this results in three-fourths of the estate going to C1 and one-fourth going to C2's successors, subject, of course, to C2's life interest. In view of this unequal distribution, which obviously was not intended by the testator, some courts have taken the rather extreme but sensible step of striking the gifts to C1 and C2 and ordering the entire estate to pass by intestacy to C1 and C2 equally.[96] In effect, the court has written a new will for the testator because of this violation of the rule, but this is certainly justified under the circumstances.

This invalidation of a property interest which itself does not violate the rule, because of the fact that another property interest does violate the rule, is sometimes referred to as "infectious invalidity".

SECTION 10. CONSTRUCTIONAL DEVICES

Future interests can sometimes be saved from destruction by the rule by constructional ingenuity. Let us take the classic example of the testamentary trust to pay income to A for life, then to pay income to A's children for their lives, and upon the death of the survivor of A's children, to pay over the corpus to the grandchildren of A. A survives the testator. The remainder interests in the grandchildren of A violate the rule because A's children cannot constitute the measuring lives since A may have children after the testator's death. But what if A is 65 at the time of the execution of the will and has two children ages

95. Easton v. Hall, 323 Ill. 397, 154 N.E. 216 (1926). See 6 American Law of Property § 24.54 (Casner ed. 1952); Simes & Smith § 1257 (2d ed. 1956).

96. Connecticut Bank and Trust Co. v. Brody, 174 Conn. 616, 392 A.2d 445 (1978);

Taylor v. Dooley, 297 S.W.2d 905 (Ky. 1956); New England Trust Co. v. Sanger, 337 Mass. 342, 149 N.E.2d 598 (1958); In re Morton's Estate, 454 Pa. 385, 312 A.2d 26 (1973); In re Edwards' Will, 407 Pa. 512, 180 A.2d 590 (1962).

42 and 37? In most states for perpetuities purposes we still have the conclusive presumption of fertility.[97] But it certainly is arguable that the testator was not thinking of afterborn children when he gave the remainder interests to the children of A; he was probably thinking only of the children of A whom he knew and did not consider that there would be any other children. If we so limit the meaning of the term "children", then such children are the measuring lives and the remainder interests in the grandchildren are valid. This is not an unreasonable construction of the meaning of "children" where A is well along in years at the time the will is executed.[98] In any event, this construction has been adopted in order to save the remainder interests where the facts warrant it; it is a most sensible method of sidestepping the absurd conclusive presumption of fertility.

Another application of this constructional technique involves the bequest to such children of A who live to age 30. At the time of the execution of the will A was 50 and had three children ages 24, 22, and 18. Two years later the testator dies, survived by A and those three children. It certainly is arguable that the testator intended the term "children" to mean the three children of A whom the testator knew. If the class term is so limited, then the gift is valid since the three children of A are the measuring lives.[99]

Another unfortunate result, the "unborn widow" aberration, has been avoided by constructional ingenuity. Settlor irrevocably transfers inter vivos in trust for A for life, then to A's widow for life, principal over to A's children then living. A is 45 and married at the creation of the trust. Since A's widow may turn out to be someone who was not alive at the time of the transfer in trust and A may have children after the transfer, the remainder to children "then living" is violative of the rule. But if the court construes the term "widow" to mean the woman to whom A was married at the time of the transfer in trust, the gift to the children of A is valid.[1] This construction seems to make a good deal more sense than the invalidation of the remainder interest on the extremely remote possibility that A may remarry and be survived by a woman who wasn't alive at the time of the transfer in trust, particularly if at the time of the

---

97. See discussion infra p. 221, and accompanying notes 18 and 19.

98. Bankers Trust Co. v. Pearson, 140 Conn. 332, 99 A.2d 224 (1953); Worcester County Trust Co. v. Marble, 316 Mass. 294, 55 N.E.2d 446 (1944); Wright's Estate, 284 Pa. 334, 131 A. 188 (1925).

99. See Snyder's Estate v. Denit, 195 Md. 81, 72 A.2d 757 (1950); Bank of New York v. Kaufman, 26 N.Y.S.2d 474 (Sup.Ct.1940), affirmed 261 A.D. 818, 25 N.Y.S.2d 408 (1941); Joyner v. Duncan, 299 N.C. 565, 264 S.E.2d 76 (1980).

1. Willis v. Hendry, 127 Conn. 653, 20 A.2d 375 (1940); In re Will of Friend, 283 N.Y. 200, 28 N.E.2d 377 (1940); In re Chemical Bank, 90 Misc.2d 727, 395 N.Y.S.2d 917 (1977). See supra p. 189 for a more detailed discussion of the "unborn widow" problem.

judicial determination A is dead and is not survived by a widow, or if he is, the woman was his one and only wife. Whether such construction is appropriate to save the remainder interest where A is 22 and recently married at the time of the creation of the trust is something else again.[2]

It is obvious that the problems in the two previous examples would be avoided by naming specific individuals instead of using class or generic designations, if in fact specific individuals are intended.

Another unfortunate victim of the rule against perpetuities can be saved by constructional common sense. We have previously discussed the gift to the issue of the testator living at the time of the final settlement of the estate of the testator, which has been held to be violative of the rule. But it has been held that there is an obligation imposed upon the executor to administer the estate expeditiously, and consequently the rule is not violated by the contingent gift.[3] It doesn't take 21 years to complete the administration of a decedent's estate. There are also statutes in several states which have the effect of validating interests which are contingent in this manner.[4]

We have seen that there is a preference in the law of property for the vested construction over the contingent construction. This necessarily works in favor of saving future interests from destruction by the rule. In view of the fact that the distinction between contingent and vested subject to condition subsequent, or vested with payment postponed, is one of language, the court has considerable latitude if the validity of the gift under the rule turns upon this distinction.

Let us assume a bequest to the children of A when they reach age 25. At the testator's death A is alive and has two children ages 12 and 10. The bequest violates the rule if it is construed as contingent upon reaching the designated age, rather than vested with payment postponed to age 25. The traditional construction of this specific wording is that it creates a contingent interest, but the words are sufficiently ambiguous that a court could find the gift vested without much difficulty in order to save it from destruction by the rule.

Suppose testator bequeaths in trust to pay the income to A for life, remainder to such persons as A shall by will appoint.

2. There are statutes in several states which validate the interest in the children by presuming that A's widow was intended to be a person who was living at the testator's death. Cal.Civ.Code § 715.7; Fla.Stat.Ann. § 689.22(5)(b); Ill.Ann. Stat. ch. 30, § 194(c)(1); N.Y.Est.Powers & Trusts Law § 9–1.3(c).

3. Belfield v. Booth, 63 Conn. 299, 27 A. 585 (1893); Asche v. Asche, 42 Del.Ch. 545, 216 A.2d 272 (1966). See supra p. 188 for discussion of the "administrative contingency."

4. Fla.Stat.Ann. § 689.22(5)(c); Ill.Ann.Stat. ch. 30, § 194(c); N.Y. Est.Powers & Trusts Law § 9–1.3(d).

A appoints to continue in trust for B for life, principal over to B's son C if he survives B, but if C shall predecease B, to D. B and C survive A but neither was alive at the testator's death. If C's interest is a contingent remainder, it violates the rule, as does D's alternative contingent remainder.   However, if C's interest is construed as a vested remainder subject to divestment, then C's interest is within the rule and only D's interest, which would be in the nature of an executory interest, violates the rule.[5] The result is an indefeasibly vested remainder in C.   As we have seen in the chapter on conditions of survivorship, the vested subject to divestment construction has been applied in this situation.   This is a reflection of the common law bias in favor of a vested construction, and it can be useful as protection from the destructive force of the rule against perpetuities.   Several states have legislated a preference for that construction of language which produces validity under the rule.[5a]

SECTION 11. MODERN REFORM OF THE RULE

In the past several decades there has been considerable legislative and limited judicial modification of the rule against perpetuities.   One modification has been the so-called "wait-and-see" principle, in which the determination of the validity of a contingent future interest is made on the basis of whether it in fact does vest within the period of the rule as actual events unfold, rather than on the basis of whether it must of logical necessity vest, if it ever does vest, within the period of the rule viewed from the time the period begins to run.   The other major modification is the cy pres, or reformation, principle, in which the contingent future interest which violates the rule is reformed to make it conform to the rule and approximate the intent of the donor.   In 1979, Restatement (Second) of Property, Donative Transfers §§ 1.1 through 2.2 were adopted which, among other things, include wait-and-see and reformation principles.

First, let us examine the wait-and-see principle.   Some states have enacted broad wait-and-see statutes,[6] of which the Pennsylvania statute is an example:

Upon the expiration of the period allowed by the common law rule against perpetuities as measured by actual rather

---

5. See 6 American Law of Property § 24.19, at 60–61, case 22 (Casner ed. 1952).

5a. Cal.Civ.Code § 715.5; Fla. Stat.Ann. § 689.22(5)(a); Ill. Ann.Stat. ch. 30, § 194(c)(1)(A); N.Y.Est.Powers & Trusts Law § 9–1.3(b); Okla.Stat.Ann. tit. 60, § 75; Tex.Rev.Civ.Stat.Ann. art. 1291b.

6. Alaska Stat. § 34.27.010; Iowa Code Ann. § 558.68; Ky.Rev.Stat.Ann. § 381.216; Nev.Rev.Stat. § 111.103; N.M.Stat. § 47–1–17.1; Ohio Rev.Code Ann. § 2131.08(c); Pa.Stat.Ann. tit. 20, § 6104; R.I.Gen.Laws § 34–11–38; Vt.Stat.Ann. tit. 27, § 501; Va.Code § 55–13.3; Wash.Rev.Code Ann. §§ 11.98.010, 11.98.050.

than possible events, any interest not then vested and any interest in members of a class the membership of which is then subject to increase shall be void.

Several states have enacted limited wait-and-see statutes,[7] of which the Massachusetts statute is an example:

In applying the rule against perpetuities to an interest in real or personal property limited to take effect at or after the termination of one or more life estates in, or lives of, persons in being when the period of said rule commences to run, the validity of the interest shall be determined on the basis of facts existing at the termination of such one or more life estates or lives. In this section an interest which must terminate not later than the death of one or more persons is a 'life estate' even though it may terminate at an earlier time.

Under the broad wait-and-see statute one waits to see for the entire period of the rule, if necessary, whereas under the limited wait-and-see statute one waits to see only up to the expiration of life estates of individuals who were lives in being.

The wait-and-see provision of the new Restatement (Second) of Property, Donative Transfers is as follows:

1.4 . . . a donative transfer of an interest in property fails, if the interest does not vest within the period of the rule against perpetuities.

The wait-and-see principle is contained in the words "does not vest". The provision is not as explicit as the statutes, but the meaning is clear.

There have also been several cases which have employed the wait-and-see principle.[8]

It should be emphasized that if the contingent future interest is valid under the common law rule, there is no need to wait. If the interest must vest, if it ever does, within the period of the rule, then obviously it is valid if one waits. It is only if it is invalid under the traditional rule that there is any need to wait to determine validity. That then raises the question of what lives may be used as measuring lives under wait-and-see. The lives that would customarily be used to validate different but similar contingent future interests under the common law rule

7. Conn.Gen.Stat.Ann. § 45–95; Fla.Stat.Ann. § 689.22(2)(a); Me.Rev.Stat.Ann. tit. 33, § 101; Md.Est. & Trusts Code Ann. § 11–103(a); Mass.Gen.Laws Ann.ch. 184A, § 1.

8. Merchants National Bank v. Curtis, 98 N.H. 225, 97 A.2d 207 (1953). See Grynberg v. Amerada Hess Corp., 342 F.Supp. 1314 (D.Colo.1972); Story v. First National Bank & Trust Co., 115 Fla. 436, 156 So. 101 (1934); Warner v. Whitman, 353 Mass. 468, 233 N.E.2d 14 (1968); Phelps v. Shropshire, 254 Miss. 777, 183 So.2d 158 (1966); In re Frank, 480 Pa. 116, 389 A.2d 536 (1978).

may be used under wait-and-see, but if such lives are not sufficient to validate an interest under wait-and-see, what additional
lives, if any, are permissible?

Let us take a simple example to illustrate the problem.   Testator bequeaths in trust to pay the income to A for life, remainder
in fee to such children of A as reach age 25.   At testator's death
A is living and has no children.   Under the common law rule,
the remainder to the children of A is invalid.   Now, assume that
A has only one child after testator's death, and A dies when the
child is 5 years old.   Under the broad wait-and-see statutes, and
under the limited ones as well, the remainder is valid.   If the
child's interest vests, it will do so within A's life plus 21 years.
Here the measuring life under wait-and-see is the life that would
have been used to validate a similar interest under the common
law rule, i.e., a remainder to such children of A as reach age 21.

But suppose A's child was 2 at A's death.   A's life obviously
won't serve to validate the child's interest.   Under the limited
Massachusetts-type statute the child's interest is invalid because
there is no one in the world who was alive at testator's death
and was also alive at A's death who must be alive when the child
reaches age 4.   Under the broad wait-and-see statutes, if the
child reaches 25 it will be necessary to identify a person who was
living at the testator's death and survived until A's child reached
age 4, which was two years after A's death.   The world is full
of people who answer that description, but can we use them?
Many of the broad wait-and-see statutes literally seem to permit
the use of any person in the world as a measuring life, but no
proponent of wait-and-see contends that they should be inter-
preted in this way.

Let us take a ridiculous example to illustrate the point further.
Testator bequeaths in trust to pay the income to Duke University
for 150 years, and at the end of that period, to pay the principal
to the testator's issue then living.   It is possible that there will
be a person alive at the testator's death who dies not less than
129 years thereafter; the only problem is to locate her.   If any
person in the world can serve as a measuring life, the future
interest in the issue may be valid under wait-and-see.   No one
supports this result.

Under wait-and-see certainly the lives that are used in traditional perpetuities analysis to validate similar interests can be
used as measuring lives, but beyond these who may be used?
The Kentucky statute makes an effort to define the lives:

> . . .   In determining whether an interest would violate
> the rule against perpetuities the period of perpetuities shall
> be measured by actual rather than possible events; pro-

vided, however, the period shall not be measured by any lives whose continuance does not have a causal relationship to the vesting or failure of the interest. . . .[9]

What does "causal relationship" mean? Assume testator bequeaths in trust to pay $100,000 to the grandchildren of A who reach age 21. At testator's death, A, two children of A, and five grandchildren of A, are living, but no grandchild is 21 at that time. The gift to grandchildren is invalid under the common law rule because of the possibility of after-born children of A who could have children. It has been maintained that under the Kentucky statute the lives having a causal relationship to the vesting or failure of the gift are A and the children and grandchildren of A who were living at the testator's death. A is a measuring life because he can have a child who can have a child who may take; A's children because they may have children who may take; A's grandchildren because they may take.[10]

The causal relationship test is vague, but it certainly includes the types of lives which are customarily used in traditional perpetuities analysis. It is likely that a broad wait-and-see statute which does not have the "causal relationship" restriction includes other beneficiaries of the trust whose lives are not "causally related" as well as those lives that are. In the above example of A for life, remainder to A's children who reach 25 (A is alive at testator's death, has no child at the time, has one child later who is 2 years old at A's death), it appears that under any wait-and-see statute the remainder fails; A is the only possible measuring life and he can't validate it.

Restatement (Second) of Property, Donative Transfers § 1.3 deals with the problem of the measuring lives under wait-and-see by stating precisely who qualify:

(2) . . .   the measuring lives for purposes of the rule against perpetuities . . . are:

a. The transferor if the period of the rule begins to run in the transferor's lifetime; and

b. Those individuals alive when the period of the rule begins to run, if reasonable in number, who have beneficial interests vested or contingent in the property in which the non-vested interest in question exists and the parents and grandparents alive when the period of the rule begins to

9. Ky.Rev.Stat.Ann. § 381.216. The measuring lives are defined in the same manner in Alaska Stat. § 34.27.010, Nev.Rev.Stat. § 111.103; N.M.Stat. § 47–1–17.1; R.I.Gen.Laws § 34–11–38.

10. See Dukeminier and Johanson, Wills, Trusts, and Estates 848 (3d ed. 1984).

run of all beneficiaries of the property in which the non-vested interest exists; and

c. The donee of a nonfiduciary power of appointment alive when the period of the rule begins to run if the exercise of such power could affect the non-vested interest in question.

Subsection (1) of § 1.3 of the Restatement, which precedes the subsection quoted above, provides that if at the time the period of the rule begins to run the contingent future interest must vest, if it ever does, within the period of the rule, as under the common law rule, the future interest is valid.[10a]

Let us take a couple of additional examples to see how wait-and-see deals with them. Testator bequeaths in trust to pay the income to A for life, then to pay the income to the children of A for their lives, and upon the death of the survivor of A's children, to pay over the principal to the grandchildren of A. A and a child of A, C1, are alive at testator's death, and no grandchildren of A are alive at testator's death. A has a second child, C2, five years after testator's death. C1 and C2 have children. Then A dies, and C1 dies thereafter. C2 dies 20 years after C1 dies. Under the broad wait-and-see statutes, and under the Restatement, the remainder to grandchildren is valid. Under the limited Massachusetts-type statute the remainder to grandchildren is invalid, because at C1's death there is no life which can serve to validate the remainder to the grandchildren. The remainder is, of course, invalid under the common law rule against perpetuities because A could have after-born children who could have children.

Let us examine the sub-class situation under wait-and-see. Testator bequeaths in trust to pay the income to A for life, then to pay the income to the children of A for their respective lives, and upon the death of each child of A, to pay to the children of such child a percentage of the principal equal to the percentage of the income which the parent was receiving. At the testator's death A is alive and one child of A, C1, is alive, and there are no grandchildren. Five years later C2 is born to A. A then dies, and 25 years thereafter C2 dies leaving children surviving him. C1 is alive at C2's death. Under broad wait-and-see statutes (except possibly the "causal relationship" statutes) and the Restatement the remainder to the issue of C2 is valid since C1 is a measuring life. Under the "causal relationship" statutes the remainder is causally related to C1 only in the sense that C1's existence determines the size of the remainder interest;

10a. Iowa has enacted a perpetuities reform statute patterned after the Restatement but broader in the respect that the measuring lives include grandparents of a beneficiary and the issue of such grandparents. Iowa Code Ann. § 558.68.

whether this satisfies the statute is not clear. The remainder is invalid under the limited Massachusetts-type statute because at A's death there is no life which can serve to validate the remainder. The remainder is, of course, invalid under the common law rule because it is a remainder in children of an after-born child of A.

Suppose a person who is alive at the time the period of perpetuities begins to run becomes an adopted child after the period begins, and that prior to adoption she does not qualify as a measuring life but in her status as an adopted child she qualifies as a measuring life. Is she deemed to have been "born" at the time of adoption, or is her actual date of birth determinative? The Restatement provides that she is a measuring life.[11]

There have been two basic objections to wait-and-see. One is the problem of the measuring lives. The other is the uncertainty of the title. Under the common law rule the contingent future interest is valid or invalid from the beginning; in theory all one has to do is apply logic to find the answer. This certainty, however, is often more apparent than real when one considers the constructional problems that frequently arise in connection with perpetuities questions, and the doctrine of infectious invalidity.[12] Under wait-and-see, of course, it may take a while to determine if the contingent future interest is valid. Uncertainty of a similar nature, however, seems to inhere in the contingent future interest which complies with the common law rule in the sense that one doesn't know if the condition will be satisfied.[13]

Now let us examine the reformation principle. A group of states have enacted broad cy pres, or reformation, statutes,[14] of which the Vermont statute is an example:

> Any interest in real or personal property which would violate the rule against perpetuities shall be reformed, within the limits of the rule, to approximate most closely the in-

---

11. Restatement, Second, Property, Donative Transfers § 1.3, illustration 6 (1983).

12. See supra Section 9. Courts may decline to resolve questions of validity of future interests years before the time of possession.

13. For discussions of wait-and-see and the measuring lives problem, see Fetters, Perpetuities: The Wait-and-See Disaster—A Brief Reply to Professor Maudsley, With a Few Asides to Professors Leach, Simes, Wade, Dr. Morris, et al., 60 Cornell L.Rev. 380 (1975); Jones, Measuring Lives Under the Pennsylvania

Statutory Rule Against Perpetuities, 109 U.Pa.L.Rev. 54 (1960); Maudsley, Perpetuities: Reforming the Common Law Rule—How To Wait and See, 60 Cornell L.Rev. 355 (1975).

14. Alaska Stat. § 34.27.010; Cal.Civ.Code § 715.5; Idaho Code § 55–111; Iowa Code Ann. § 558.68; Ky.Rev.Stat.Ann. § 381.216; Mo.Ann. Stat. § 442.555; Nev.Rev.Stat. § 111.103; N.M.Stat. § 47-1-17.1; Ohio Rev.Code Ann. § 2131.08; Okla.Stat.Ann. tit. 60, § 75–78; R.I. Gen.Laws § 34-11-38; Tex.Rev.Civ.Stat.Ann. art. 1291(b); Vt.Stat.Ann.tit. 27, § 501; Va.Code § 55–13.3; Wash.Rev.Code Ann. § 11.98.030.

tention of the creator of the interest. In determining whether an interest would violate said rule and in reforming an interest the period of perpetuities shall be measured by actual rather than possible events.

It should be noted that this statute provides for wait-and-see as well as reformation, and that reformation may be employed only after invalidity is determined under wait-and-see. In those states which have adopted cy pres but not wait-and-see, reformation may be done at the time of the creation of the invalid future interest or at some time thereafter, depending upon the time suit is brought. A court may be inclined to defer reformation until close to the time the invalid future interest would become possessory in order to have the benefit of all relevant facts with respect to the situation.

Several states have enacted limited reformation statutes that provide for the reduction of an age contingency to 21 in situations in which there is an age contingency in excess of 21 which renders an interest invalid.[15] The Illinois statute is an example:

> . . . where any interest . . . would be invalid because it is made to depend upon any person attaining or failing to attain an age in excess of 21 years, the age specified shall be reduced to 21 years as to every person to whom the age contingency applies . . .

Restatement (Second) of Property, Donative Transfers § 1.5 provides for reformation as follows:

> If under a donative transfer an interest in property fails because it does not vest or cannot vest within the period of the rule against perpetuities, the transferred property shall be disposed of in the manner which most closely effectuates the transferor's manifested plan of distribution, and which is within the limits of the rule against perpetuities.

Several cases have employed the reformation principle in the absence of statute to reduce age or time contingencies to 21 years to make valid a future interest which was invalid in its original form.[16]

Let us examine how the broad reformation statutes may be applied to several situations. In this analysis it is assumed that

---

15. Conn.Gen.Stat.Ann. § 45–96; Fla.Stat.Ann. § 689.22(4); Ill.Ann. Stat. ch. 30, § 194(c); Me.Rev.Stat.Ann. tit. 33, § 102; Md.Est. & Trusts Code Ann. § 11–103; Mass.Gen.Laws Ann. ch. 184A, § 2; N.Y.Est.Powers & Trusts Law § 9–1.2.

16. In re Chun Quan Yee Hop, 52 Hawaii 40, 469 P.2d 183 (1970); Carter v. Berry, 243 Miss. 321, 140 So.2d 843 (1962); Edgerly v. Barker, 66 N.H. 434, 31 A. 900 (1891); Berry v. Union National Bank, — W.Va. —, 262 S.E.2d 766 (1980). See In re Estate of Kelly, 193 So.2d 575 (Miss.1967).

the common law rule against perpetuities is in effect, without the wait-and-see modification. Testator bequeaths in trust to pay the income to A for life, remainder to such of A's children as reach age 25. A is living and has no children at the testator's death. The remainder interest is invalid under the traditional rule. The obvious way of making the remainder valid by reformation is to reduce the age contingency to 21. But probably a better way of reforming the interest is to add a clause that would read something like this: "provided that if the trust has not terminated within 21 years following the death of A, it shall terminate at that time and the principal remaining in trust shall then be distributed to the children of A then living who have not reached age 25". This is a so-called "saving clause" that a draftsman could have incuded in the will. If the draftsman doesn't do it, the court can do it by reformation.[16a] In all likelihood under this clause the trust will run its intended course, using the 25 year contingency, within the period of the rule; the only way it may not would be if A had a child under 4 years of age at his death. If the trust does not run its intended course, the principal may be distributed within the period of the rule to a child or children who are at least 21 years old.

Let us take the example of the testamentary trust to pay the income to A for life, then to pay the income to the children of A for their lives, and upon the death of the survivor of A's children, to pay the principal to the issue of A then living per stirpes. A is alive at testator's death and has two children living at that time. The ultimate remainder to the issue of A is invalid under the common law rule. The remainder could be saved by reforming the will to provide that in the event the trust has not terminated in accordance with its terms within 21 years following the death of the survivor of A and the two children alive at the testator's death, it shall terminate at that time and the principal shall be distributed to the issue of A living at that time per stirpes.

Let us take the sub-class situation. Testator bequeaths in trust to pay the income to A for life, then to pay the income to the children of A for their respective lives, and upon the death of each child of A, to pay over the percentage of the principal equal to the percentage of the income the child was receiving, to the issue then living of such child per stirpes. At the testator's death A is alive and one child of A, C1, is also alive. Remainders to the issue of after-born children of A are invalid

---

16a. Illinois has "saving clause" legislation which provides for the modification of trusts in this manner in order to make them valid under the rule against perpetuities. Ill.Ann.Stat. ch. 30, § 195. See Browder, Construction, Reformation, and the Rule Against Perpetuities, 62 Mich.L.Rev. 1 (1963).

under the common law rule. The will may be reformed to provide that in the event the trust has not terminated in accordance with its terms within 21 years following the death of the survivor of A and C1, it shall terminate at that time and the principal shall be distributed to those children of A who are receiving the income. The will could, of course, be reformed more restrictively by providing that the shares of the children of A who were not living at the testator's death are to be distributed to such children upon A's death.

It should be noted that the statutory reforms being discussed are usually prospective in their application; future interests which antedate the statutes are likely to be subject to the common law rule. It may be, however, that the courts will be inclined to apply the statutory principles to previously created interests.[17]

A word about the presumption of fertility. We have seen that the traditional conclusive presumption of fertility causes interests to be invalid under the common law rule that would not be if the presumption were rebuttable.[17a] Several states have enacted statutes which permit the introduction of evidence to establish that a person is incapable of having children, and a couple of them provide that it shall be presumed that a person over a certain age such as 65, or 55 in the case of a woman, is incapable of having children.[18] There have also been some cases that do away with the conclusive presumption of fertility for property purposes, including a case in the perpetuities area.[19] The conclusive presumption is probably still with us in most states. It should be stressed that under broad wait-and-see statutes the presumption of fertility is usually irrelevant.

The relationship between the presumption of fertility and adoption should be noted. Today an adopted child is likely to be deemed to be included in a class gift to children, grandchildren, descendants, and the like. An elderly person, incapable of hav-

---

17. The Iowa statute (Iowa Code Ann. § 558.68) and recently the Pennsylvania statute (Pa.Stat.Ann.tit. 20, § 6104) have been made expressly retroactive in application. The Virginia statute (Va.Code § 55–13.3) is expressly retroactive unless injury or reliance on the common law rule can be shown. Legislative retroactivity may present a constitutional issue. Warner v. Whitman, 353 Mass. 468, 233 N.E.2d 14 (1968), and In re Frank, 480 Pa. 116, 389 A.2d 536 (1978), are cases in which the courts applied wait-and-see, after the enactment of the statute, to interests created before the statute and to which the statute therefore did not apply.

17a. See discussion infra p. 188.

18. Fla.Stat.Ann. § 689.22(5)(d); Idaho Code § 55–111; Ill.Ann.Stat.ch. 30, § 194(c)(3); N.Y.Est.Powers & Trusts Law § 9–1.3(e); Tenn.Code Ann. § 24-5-112.

19. In re Lattouf's Will, 87 N.J.Super. 137, 208 A.2d 411 (1965) (perpetuities). Other contexts: Fletcher v. Hurdle, 259 Ark. 640, 536 S.W.2d 109 (1976); Citizens National Bank v. Longshore, 304 So.2d 287 (Miss.1974); In re Bassett's Estate, 104 N.H. 504, 190 A.2d 415 (1963); In re Estate of Weeks, 485 Pa. 329, 402 A.2d 657 (1979). See 4 Scott, The Law of Trusts § 340.1 (3d ed. 1967).

ing children, may adopt a child. Assuming fertility is rebuttable, does the inclusion of adopted children within designated classes of offspring have the effect of reinstating the conclusive presumption of fertility? It appears to, but the Florida, Illinois and New York statutes provide that for perpetuities purposes the possibility that a person may have a child by adoption is to be disregarded.[20] It should be reiterated that discussion of the presumption of fertility is premised on the applicability of the common law rule, without wait-and-see.

We have previously considered statutory reforms dealing with interests which are contingent upon surviving the completion of administration of the estate,[21] or upon surviving the after-born widow,[22] two traps for the unsuspecting draftsman.

SECTION 12. ACCUMULATIONS

At common law a direction or authorization in a dispositive instrument for the accumulation of income for a period which does not exceed the period of the rule against perpetuities is valid.[23] If a dispositive instrument provides for the accumulation of income for a period which may exceed the period of the rule against perpetuities, in some states the provision for accumulation is invalid in toto, i.e., the trustee may not accumulate income for any period.[24] There is also authority that the accumulation is valid for the period of the rule, and void as to the period in excess of the rule.[25] If there is an invalid direction for accumulation in a will, the released income will usually be distributed to the residuary legatees if the accumulation is not with respect to the residuary estate, or if it is with respect to the residuary estate, then to the intestate takers.[26] It should be emphasized that this rule is separate from the rule against

20. See supra immediately preceding note 18.

21. See supra notes 36 and immediately preceding 4, and accompanying text.

22. See supra notes 38 and immediately preceding 2, and accompanying text.

23. Gertman v. Burdick, 75 U.S.App.D.C. 48, 123 F.2d 924 (1941), cert. denied 315 U.S. 824, 62 S.Ct. 917, 86 L.Ed. 1220 (1942); Gaess v. Gaess, 132 Conn. 96, 42 A.2d 796 (1945); In re Freeman's Estate, 195 Kan. 190, 404 P.2d 222 (1965); Vinson v. First Trust & Savings Bank, 44 Ohio Misc. 97, 73 Ohio Op.2d 489, 339 N.E.2d 670 (C.P.1974); Rentz v. Polk, 267 S.C. 359, 228 S.E.2d 106 (1976).

24. Pelton v. First Savings & Trust Co.,

98 Fla. 748, 124 So. 169 (1929); In re Foster's Estate, 190 Kan. 498, 376 P.2d 784 (1962); Kimball v. Crocker, 53 Me. 263 (1865). See Gertman v. Burdick, 75 U.S.App.D.C. 48, 123 F.2d 924 (1941), cert. denied 315 U.S. 824, 62 S.Ct. 917, 86 L.Ed. 1220 (1942).

25. Gaess v. Gaess, 132 Conn. 96, 42 A.2d 796 (1945); Walliser v. Northern Trust Co., 338 Ill.App. 263, 87 N.E.2d 129 (1949). See In re Lieberman's Will, 2 Misc.2d 833, 147 N.Y.S.2d 815 (1955).

26. Wilson v. D'Atro, 109 Conn. 563, 145 A. 161 (1929); Pelton v. First Savings & Trust Co., 98 Fla. 748, 124 So. 169 (1929); Murphy v. Northern Trust Co., 17 Ill.2d 518, 162 N.E.2d 428 (1959); In re Castner's Estate, 412 Pa. 232, 194 A.2d 330 (1963).

perpetuities; it has to do with the duration of the accumulation of income rather than remoteness of vesting.

There are statutes in some states which limit accumulations to the period of the rule against perpetuities.[27] These statutes usually provide that the invalid provision for accumulation does not invalidate the accumulation provision in toto, but rather only for the period in excess of the permissible period.[28]

Restatement (Second) of Property, Donative Transfers § 2.2 provides in part as follows:

> (1) An accumulation of trust income under a noncharitable trust created in a donative transfer is valid until the period of the rule against perpetuities expires with respect to such trust and any accumulation thereafter is invalid.

. . .

> (3) The trust income released by an invalid accumulation shall be paid to such recipients and in such shares and in such manner as most closely effectuates the transferor's manifested plan of distribution.

These provisions adopt the wait-and-see principle for the determination of the validity of the accumulation, invalidate only the accumulation which exceeds the permissible period, and apply the cy pres principle for the distribution of the released income.

SECTION 13. CHARITIES

A contingent future interest, legal or equitable, in a charity is subject to the rule against perpetuities just as a contingent future interest in an individual is, except that if the present interest and the future interest are both in charities, the remoteness of vesting of the contingent future interest does not invalidate it. If testator devises Blackacre to John Smith in fee, but if the property is ever used for commercial purposes, then to the First Baptist Church, the executory interest in the church is invalid as violative of the rule against perpetuities.[29] However, if testator devises Blackacre to Charity Hospital in fee, but if the property is ever used for non-hospital purposes, then

---

27. E.g., Cal.Civ.Code § 724; Ill.Ann.Stat.ch. 30, § 153; Ind.Code Ann. § 32–1–4–2; N.Y.Est.Powers & Trusts Law § 9–2.1.

28. E.g., Cal.Civ.Code § 725; Ind. Code Ann. § 32–1–4–4; N.Y.Est. Powers & Trusts Law § 9–2.1.

29. Colorado National Bank v. Mc-Cabe, 143 Colo. 21, 353 P.2d 385 (1960);

Talbot v. Riggs, 287 Mass. 144, 191 N.E. 360 (1934); Ledwith v. Hurst, 284 Pa. 94, 130 A. 315 (1925). Of course, if the first interest is charitable, and the second interest is private and remote, the second interest is void under the rule. Nelson v. Kring, 225 Kan. 499, 592 P.2d 438 (1979); City of Klamath Falls v. Bell, 7 Or.App. 330, 490 P.2d 515 (1971).

to the First Baptist Church, the executory interest in the church is valid although it may vest beyond the period of the rule.[30]

Restatement (Second) of Property, Donative Transfers § 1.6, provides as follows:

> If under a donative transfer an interest in property transferred to a charity does not vest within the period of the rule against perpetuities, it fails unless it would divest a valid interest in another charity, in which case it does not fail on the ground of the rule against perpetuities, even though the divestiture does not occur within the period of the rule.

The Restatement adopts the wait-and-see principle with respect to charitable gifts, but in other respects is consistent with the common law applicable to charitable gifts.

The common law rule prohibiting accumulations which may extend beyond the period of the rule against perpetuities has not been applied to accumulations for charitable purposes. Accumulations for charitable purposes are limited only by the standard of reasonableness.[31] If the court determines that the period of accumulation is unreasonable under the circumstances of the disposition, it will strike the invalid accumulation provision and modify the disposition in a manner which substantially achieves the donor's objective.[32]

The trust for exclusively charitable purposes, such as a trust to fund research leading to the discovery of a cure for cancer, is permitted to have indefinite duration.[33] The trust is subject to judicial modification if its purposes become obsolete or otherwise impractical of achievement.[34]

SECTION 14. DURATION OF TRUSTS

The common law rule against perpetuities is concerned with the remoteness of vesting of contingent future interests, and not

30. Dickenson v. City of Anna, 310 Ill. 222, 141 N.E. 754 (1923); City of Belfast v. Goodwill Farm, 150 Me. 17, 103 A.2d 517 (1954); Roxbury v. Roxbury Home for Aged Women, 244 Mass. 583, 139 N.E. 301 (1923).

31. Waterbury Trust Co. v. Porter, 131 Conn. 206, 38 A.2d 598 (1944); Frazier v. Merchants National Bank, 296 Mass. 298, 5 N.E.2d 550 (1936); In Trusts of Holdeen, 486 Pa. 1, 403 A.2d 978 (1979); Allaun v. First & Merchants National Bank, 190 Va. 104, 56 S.E.2d 83 (1949). See Restatement, Second, Property, Donative Transfers § 2.2(2) (1983).

32. Mercantile Trust Co. National Association v. Shriners' Hospital for Crippled Children, 551 S.W.2d 864 (Mo.App.1977); In re James' Estate, 414 Pa. 80, 199 A.2d 275 (1964). See 4 Scott, The Law of Trusts § 401.9 (3d ed. 1967); Restatement, Second, Property, Donative Transfers § 2.2(3) (1983); Annot., 6 A.L.R.4th 903 (1981).

33. Mitchell v. Reeves, 123 Conn. 549, 196 A. 785 (1938); In re Freshour's Estate, 185 Kan. 434, 345 P.2d 689 (1959); Boyd v. Frost National Bank, 145 Tex. 206, 196 S.W.2d 497 (1946).

34. See 4 Scott, The Law of Trusts § 399 (3d ed. 1967).

with the duration of trusts. It is generally accepted that a trust may last beyond the period of the rule if all the interests under the trust vest within the rule.[35] This leaves open the possibility of tying up property in a trust for a period of time which may not be consonant with sound public policy. This possibility raises the question of the power of all the beneficiaries by agreement among themselves to compel the termination of a trust and the distribution of the corpus to themselves. If this can be done, then the prospect of tying up property in a trust beyond the period of the rule is not as serious as it may appear.

Generally recognized in this country is the so-called "Claflin trust" principle,[36] to the effect that a trust may not be terminated by the beneficiaries if such termination would defeat a material purpose of the settlor in establishing the trust, unless, of course, the settlor is alive and consents. Trusts which are in this "Claflin" category are spendthrift trusts, support trusts, trusts in which distributions are made in the discretion of the trustee, and trusts in which the beneficiary is entitled to income until a certain age and principal at that age.[37] Probably most trusts are Claflin trusts. A trust which merely provides for successive enjoyment, i.e., income to A for life, principal at A's death to B, does not fall into the Claflin trust category and is generally terminable at any time if all beneficiaries choose to do so. If a Claflin trust lasts longer than the period of perpetuities, it appears that property may be tied up in trust for a period beyond that of the rule against perpetuities.

The Restatement (Second) of Property, Donative Transfers § 2.1, deals with this question as follows:

> 2.1 A trust created in a donative transfer, which has not terminated within the period of the rule against perpetuities as applied to such trust, shall continue until the trust terminates in accordance with its terms, except that a trust, other than a charitable trust, may be terminated at any time after the period of the rule against perpetuities expires by a written agreement of all of the beneficiaries of the trust delivered to the trustee, which agreement in-

---

35. Hill v. Birmingham, 131 Conn. 174, 38 A.2d 604 (1944); Dodge v. Bennett, 215 Mass. 545, 102 N.E. 916 (1913); Phelps v. Shropshire, 254 Miss. 777, 183 So.2d 158 (1966); Joyner v. Duncan, 299 N.C. 565, 264 S.E.2d 76 (1980); Rekdahl v. Long, 417 S.W.2d 387 (Tex.1967). There is sparse authority that a trust may not last beyond the perpetuities period. See Capers v. Camp, 244 Ga. 7, 257 S.E.2d 517 (1979); Throm's Estate, 378 Pa. 163, 106 A.2d 815 (1954); Howard's Estate, 54 Pa.D.&C. 312 (1943). Minn.Stat.Ann. § 501.11(6), and Okla.Stat.Ann.tit. 60, § 172 limit the duration of trusts. Nev.Rev.Stat. § 166.140 limits the duration of spendthrift trusts.

36. Claflin v. Claflin, 149 Mass. 19, 20 N.E. 454 (1889). See 4 Scott, The Law of Trusts § 337.1 (3d ed. 1967).

37. See 4 Scott, The Law of Trusts §§ 337–337.4 (3d ed. 1967).

forms the trustee that the trust is terminated and gives the trustee directions as to the distribution of the trust property.

California Civil Code § 771 also permits termination of trusts by agreement of all beneficiaries after the expiration of the perpetuities period.

The right of beneficiaries to terminate a trust after the expiration of the perpetuities period has been suggested by commentators in the past, although there is little judicial authority for it.[38] It should be emphasized that under this principle the trust which lasts beyond the perpetuities period is valid at its inception and remains valid after the expiration of the perpetuities period, subject to its being terminated by the beneficiaries at their option after the expiration of the perpetuities period. It should also be emphasized that this discussion is concerned only with private, as distinguished from charitable, trusts; trusts for charitable purposes may last in perpetuity and may be modified or terminated only by court order.

SECTION 15.   SUSPENSION OF THE POWER OF ALIENATION

In the nineteenth century New York enacted legislation which established the rule limiting suspension of the power of alienation, and a group of states subsequently enacted legislation of a similar nature.   This rule differed significantly from the common law rule against perpetuities.   The rule against suspension of the power of alienation is not concerned with when a contingent future interest vests, but rather with the ability of the owners of present and future interests to convey a fee simple absolute in possession to a third party.

If testator devises Blackacre to B in fee, but if the premises are ever used for commercial purposes, then to C in fee, clearly the executory interest in C violates the rule against perpetuities, but there is no violation of the rule against suspension of the power of alienation because B and C, or their successors, can get together at any time and convey a fee simple absolute to D.

A future interest in unascertained or unborn persons necessarily suspends the power of alienation.   Grantor conveys to A for life, remainder in fee to the children of A.   The class gift in remainder includes unborn persons and consequently a fee simple absolute cannot be transferred to another person; the power of alienation has been suspended.

---

38.   See 1 Scott, The Law of Trusts § 62.10 (3d ed. 1967); Simes & Smith § 1393 (2d ed. 1956).

The permissible period of suspension of the power of alienation often was different from the common law perpetuities period and varied among the states. In some states the period was two specific lives in being at the time of transfer plus minority of a person. In some states the period was multiple lives in being, as under the common law rule against perpetuities, plus the minority of a person. There were still different permissible periods in other states.

Some of the states which adopted the rule against suspension of the power of alienation have repealed the legislation and enacted the common law rule against perpetuities prospectively. New York currently has both the rule against suspension of the power of alienation and the rule against perpetuities. The rule against suspension of the power of alienation is now the law in only a handful of states, but in those states which have repealed it the rule still applies to dispositions made when it was in effect.[39]

SECTION 16. A COMMENT ON THE RULE AGAINST PERPETUITIES

The reader at this point may be asking herself whether all the complexity is necessary. The authors join in the query.

If legal future interests in unborn or unascertained persons are created in a particular parcel of land, extending many years into the future, clearly alienability is fettered. The original purpose of the rule was to impose limits upon dispositive provisions which made it difficult or impossible to convey a possessory fee and thereby effectively removed the land from commerce. However, if the donor places land or stocks and bonds in trust, the trustee having the power to sell at any time and reinvest the proceeds, with equitable future interests in unborn or unascertained persons, the alienability of the property involved has not been fettered in any way. What has been controlled by the proverbial "dead hand" is a changing fund. The donor has exercised control to the extent that a certain bundle of value is going to be channeled into conservative investment for an extended period of time, instead of being invested speculatively or consumed. Nothing is being taken out of commerce; rather, assets are being directed into a certain area of commerce. In addition, the donor has controlled who is to derive the benefit of the investment. Most future interests today are equitable

---

39. For treatment of this rule, see Browder and Waggoner, Family Property Transactions: Future Interests 479 (3d ed. 1980); Simes, Handbook of the Law of Future Interests 298 (2d ed. 1966); Restatement, Second, Property, Donative Transfers § 1.1, statutory note (1983).

interests in stocks and debt securities, with power of sale in the trustee.[39a]

What does "lives in being plus 21 years" accomplish? It seems that originally the 21 years was not in gross but was rather the actual minority of an infant, and that the rule was designed to enable a person to control his property for one generation and the infancy of a second. A skilled draftsman today can tie property up in trust for well over a century if he puts his mind to it. It is not easy to understand why the period should be "lives in being plus 21 years," or why the determining factor should be the "vesting in interest".

The modern reform movement which is concerned with wait-and-see and cy pres does not go to the heart of the matter which is the inherent abstruseness of the rule and the questionable appropriateness of the rule to modern circumstances. These changes are designed to make the rule somewhat easier to live with; they are in the nature of palliatives. But the experts quarrel about the meaning of the reform legislation. The very nature of the rule causes confusion.

Most people would agree that it is undesirable to permit an individual to control the benefit or the investment of wealth for too long a period of time after her death. Let the donor protect her family for a reasonable period of time, and thereafter let the current generation make the decisions as to the use of the wealth. Most would, or should, agree that a body of law dealing with this question which is scarcely understood by the bar and which is capable of producing erratic and occasionally absurd results, is a poor way of handling the matter.

This is not the place for a detailed proposal for change, but here are a couple of broad suggestions. First, the fee simple absolute must vest in possession (rather than vest in interest) within the period of the rule.[40] Second, the period of the rule should be a fixed number of years, such as 100 years,[41] with power in the court to extend the period or otherwise reform the disposition if necessary to avoid an inconvenient or undesirable result. Do we care all that much that the period is fairly long if

---

39a. Wisconsin and South Dakota, which have the rule against suspension of the power of alienation rather than the rule against perpetuities, exempt from the application of the rule interests in trusts in which the trustee has a power of sale. S.D.Comp.Laws Ann. § 43-5-4; Wis.Stat. Ann. § 700.16.

40. See Schuyler, Should the Rule Against Perpetuities Discard Its Vest?, 56 Mich.L.Rev. 683–726, 887–952 (1958).

41. California provides a period of 60 years for vesting in interest, as an alternative to the common law period which also obtains. Cal.Civ.Code §§ 715.2, 715.6.

in most cases the property is not removed from commerce? It is also suggested that the wait-and-see approach is to be preferred to the common law approach. These suggestions would simplify the rule without any compromise of its socio-economic purposes.

Chapter 9

MISCELLANEOUS CONSTRUCTIONAL PROBLEMS

SECTION 1. "HEIRS," "ISSUE," "CHILDREN"

The terms "heirs", "issue", and "children" are commonly used in dispositive instruments to designate a class of takers, and frequently the circumstances of their use call for some interpretation to determine precisely the individuals included within the class. Certain rules of construction have been developed to resolve these questions. The discussion in this section assumes that the doctrine of worthier title and the rule in Shelley's case are not applicable.

Heirs are those who take real property under the applicable intestacy statute. The terms "next of kin" and "distributees" describe those who take personal property under the applicable intestacy statute. In most jurisdictions today there is no distinction between the intestate takers of real and personal property, but in some states differences still exist. Frequently "heirs" is broadly used to describe those who inherit personal as well as real property. Suppose testator bequeaths $100,000 to the "heirs of John Smith;" assuming the jurisdiction passes intestate personalty differently from intestate realty, which set of intestate takers should receive this bequest? Even though the term "heirs" is used, the courts normally apply the personal property intestacy provisions; the nature of the gift determines the construction of the term "heirs".[1]

Heirs are determined at the date of the decedent's death. In other words, those who come within the terms of the intestacy statute and are living at the date of the decedent's death constitute the heirs. However, there sometimes are circumstances which call for a construction of the word "heirs", as used in a dispositive instrument, which results in a somewhat different meaning. The following discussion of constructional problems with respect to the use of "heirs" is also applicable to the use of "next of kin" or "distributees"; in view of the broader connotation of "heirs" and its more frequent use, most of the litigation in this area has concerned "heirs".

---

1. In re Estate of Pistor, 53 N.J.Super. 139, 146 A.2d 685 (1958), affirmed 30 N.J. 589, 154 A.2d 721 (1959); Quinn v. Hall, 37 R.I. 56, 91 A. 71 (1914); Spencer v. Stanton, 46 Tenn.App. 688, 333 S.W.2d 225 (1959). See Simes & Smith § 731 (2d ed. 1956).

Suppose testator bequeaths and devises his entire estate in trust to pay the income to his sons, C1 and C2, for their lives, and upon the death of the survivor, to pay over the principal to the "heirs" of the testator. C1 and C2 survive the testator and are the sole heirs and next of kin of the testator. Upon the death of the survivor of C1 and C2, does the corpus of the trust go to the estates of C1 and C2? It has been held that under these circumstances the testator did not intend the term "heirs" in its true sense; the term has been construed to mean the heirs of the testator to be determined as of the termination of the life interests—that is to say, as if the testator had died on that date.[2] Such an interpretation, of course, excludes C1 and C2; if they had children the property will go to them if they are living. There is also some support for the position that the heirs should be determined at the testator's death but excluding C1 and C2.[3] There is also authority that the word "heirs" is to be construed literally in these circumstances, and the corpus of the trust goes to the estates of C1 and C2.[4]

Suppose testator bequeaths $100,000 in trust to pay the income to his son C1 for life, remainder to testator's "heirs". The heirs are testator's widow, C1, and three other children. Should we distort the meaning of "heirs" in order to exclude C1? There is, of course, a strong presumption that words should mean what they appear to mean, and in this situation the courts usually have not disturbed the meaning of "heirs," thereby entitling C1's estate to a share of the remainder.[5] Here the prior interest is held by one of several heirs; in the previous problem the holders of the prior interest were the sole heirs and this may produce a different result. There is, however, contrary authority that the word "heirs" in this situation does not include C1.[6]

Suppose testator devises Blackacre to the "heirs of A". A was alive at the time of the execution of the will but A predeceased the testator, leaving as his heirs B and C. At the tes-

2. Abbott v. Continental National Bank, 169 Neb. 147, 98 N.W.2d 804 (1959); In re Will of Carlin, 6 A.D.2d 281, 176 N.Y.S.2d 112 (1958); In re Latimer's Will, 266 Wis. 158, 63 N.W.2d 65 (1954). See Restatement, Property § 308, comment *k* (1940).

3. South Norwalk Trust Co. v. White, 146 Conn. 391, 152 A.2d 319 (1959); In re Will of Iles, 17 Ohio Op.2d 451, 175 N.E.2d 781 (1960); In re Estate of Miller, 275 Pa. 30, 118 A. 549 (1922).

4. Hull v. Adams, 399 Ill. 347, 77 N.E.2d 706 (1948); Tyler v. City Bank Farmers Trust Co., 314 Mass. 528, 50 N.E.2d 778 (1943); Evans v. Rankin, 329 Mo. 411, 44 S.W.2d 644 (1931).

5. Bowman v. Phillips, 260 Ark. 496, 542 S.W.2d 740 (1976); In re Estate of McKenzie, 246 Cal.App.2d 740, 54 Cal.Rptr. 888 (1966); Robertson v. Eastern Long Island Hospital, 28 Ill.2d 483, 192 N.E.2d 895 (1963); Starrett v. Botsford, 64 R.I. 1, 9 A.2d 871 (1939).

6. Close v. Benham, 97 Conn. 102, 115 A. 626 (1921); In re Estate of Davis, 108 N.H. 163, 229 A.2d 694 (1967); Dean v. Lancaster, 233 S.C. 530, 105 S.E.2d 675 (1958).

tator's death, C was alive but B was not.   If the heirship of A is determined as of testator's death, C is the sole heir of A.   Who receives Blackacre?   It has been held that if a gift is made to the heirs of a person who predeceases the testator, the heirs will be determined as of the date of death of the testator—that is, as if the ancestor had died at the same time that the testator died.[7]   B's interest did not lapse here;   B was not a legatee.

Let us assume that testator bequeaths $100,000 to the heirs of C.   At testator's death, C is alive;   obviously C has no heirs. The bequest was intended to be an immediate one, and consequently it would not be appropriate for the executor to hold back the money until C dies.   In these circumstances "heirs" should mean those persons who would constitute C's heirs had C died at the same time as the testator.[8]

Sometimes "heirs" has been construed to mean children or descendants.   Suppose testator devises Blackacre to B for life, remainder to B's heirs, but if B has no heirs, to B's brothers and sisters.   Certainly the brothers and sisters of B can be heirs of B.   The word "heirs" was not used in its technical sense, but instead was intended to mean children or grandchildren.[9]

It should be reiterated that all the constructional questions discussed in this chapter can be, and should be, avoided by appropriate expression of intention in the dispositive instrument. These constructional rules fill the gaps left by the draftsman.

"Issue" means descendants;   a gift to the "issue of X" literally includes all his children, grandchildren and great grandchildren. However, our courts have usually given the term a more restricted meaning when it appears without qualification in a dispositive instrument.

Suppose testator bequeaths $50,000 to the "issue of B".   B predeceased the testator leaving two children, C1 and C2, and three grandchildren, the children of C1, all of whom survived the testator.   Is the bequest divided into five parts and distributed to all the descendants of B?   The courts have usually inferred that the testator did not intend the term "issue" in its basic or primary sense, but rather intended that the term include only descendants who would constitute the intestate takers of the

7. In re Estate of Austin, 236 Iowa 945, 20 N.W.2d 445 (1945); Boston Safe Deposit & Trust Co. v. Northey, 335 Mass. 201, 138 N.E.2d 613 (1956); Dunlap v. Lynn, 166 Neb. 342, 89 N.W.2d 58 (1958).

8. Hedrick v. Hedrick, 125 W.Va. 702, 25 S.E.2d 872 (1943). See Restatement, Property § 308, comment *h* (1940). There

is also support for the proposition that "heirs" means "children" in this circumstance.   See Simes & Smith § 733 (2d ed. 1956).

9. Dickson v. Renfro, 263 Ark. 718, 569 S.W.2d 66 (1978); West v. McLoughlin, 42 Mich.App. 180, 201 N.W.2d 336 (1972).

ancestor.[10] Intestacy statutes provide in this situation for a per stirpital distribution among the descendants who survive the ancestor; consequently, C1 and C2 would each receive one-half the bequest and the children of C1 would not receive anything, since in a per stirpital distribution the child receives nothing if the parent is alive.

Let us assume in the previous example that C1 predeceased B—who would be entitled to the bequest? If the property had been assets of B's estate, then under the intestacy statute C2 would receive one-half and each child of C1 would receive one-sixth, in accordance with the per stirpital principle that the children take the deceased parent's share; this same distribution would be called for by the use of the term "issue".

Suppose in this example we have been discussing, C1 survived B but predeceased the testator. It is likely that "issue" will be those who constitute the lineal heirs of B as determined at the testator's death.

The construction which the courts have given the gift to issue imposes a condition of survivorship of the ancestor, and this survivorship requirement may also be extended beyond the death of the ancestor to the time of distribution in the case of the gift of a future interest to issue. This is discussed in the chapter on conditions of survivorship.[11]

Questions have arisen as to whether a gift to "children" includes adopted children or illegitimate children. The traditional view has been that the adopted child is included in the gift to "children" where the adoptive parent is the testator or donor;[12] if, however, the gift is by one other than the adoptive parent, the adopted child is not included[13] unless the adoption existed and was known to the testator or donor at the time the will was executed or the gift was made, or there is other evidence of intention to include the adopted child.[14] The law, however, is in the process of change on this matter. The Uniform Probate Code § 2–611 provides that the adopted child is included in a

---

10. Clarke v. Clarke, 222 Md. 153, 159 A.2d 362 (1960); Merrimack Valley National Bank v. Grant, 353 Mass. 145, 228 N.E.2d 732 (1967); Mercantile Trust Co. v. Davis, 522 S.W.2d 798 (Mo.1975). See Simes & Smith §§ 774–776 (2d ed. 1956).

11. See supra p. 131.

12. Parker v. Mullen, 158 Conn. 1, 255 A.2d 851 (1969); Stewart v. Lafferty, 12 Ill.2d 224, 145 N.E.2d 640 (1957); Sewall v. Roberts, 115 Mass. 262 (1874); In re Chemical Bank, 90 Misc.2d 727, 395 N.Y.S.2d 917 (1977). See Simes & Smith § 724 (2d ed. 1956).

13. Morgan v. Keefe, 135 Conn. 254, 63 A.2d 148 (1948); Stewart v. Lafferty, 12 Ill.2d 224, 145 N.E.2d 640 (1957); Central Trust Co. v. Bovey, 25 Ohio St.2d 187, 267 N.E.2d 427 (1971); See Restatement, Property § 287 (1940).

14. In re Estate of Clancy, 159 Cal.App.2d 216, 323 P.2d 763 (1958); Whittle v. Speir, 235 Ga. 14, 218 S.E.2d 775 (1975); Mesecher v. Leir, 241 Iowa 818, 43 N.W.2d 149 (1950); Bullock v. Bullock, 251 N.C. 559, 111 S.E.2d 837 (1960); Estes v. Ruff, 267 S.C. 396, 228 S.E.2d 671 (1976); In re Estate of Breese, 7 Wis.2d 422, 96 N.W.2d 712 (1959).

class gift in a will if the adopted child is included in intestate succession, which she invariably is. The statutes of some states simply provide that the adopted child is a child for the purposes of dispositive instruments.[15] There are also a number of recent cases which presume that the adopted child is included in the class gift.[16]

There has been a traditional presumption in the law that the illegitimate child is not included in a gift to "children".[17] This presumption has been overcome in some cases by evidence that inclusion was intended.[18] There have also been some cases which have held that the illegitimate child would be considered to be one of the "children" of the mother for dispositive purposes because he was an heir of the mother.[19] In recent years the law has become more inclined to include the illegitimate child in the gift to "children". Uniform Probate Code § 2–611 provides that in a will the illegitimate child is included among the "children" of a person if he is an intestate taker of that person.[20] The illegitimate child is an intestate taker of the mother, and in some circumstances of the father.[21] There have also been recent decisions which do away with the presumption against inclusion of the illegitimate child in the class designation.[22] The presumption against inclusion possibly raises a constitutional issue in the light of the Supreme Court decision which held unconstitutional a statute which unreasonably discriminated against intestate inheritance by an illegitimate child from the father.[23]

15. E.g., Conn.Gen.Stat.Ann. § 45–64a; Ill.Ann.Stat. ch. 110½, § 2–4; N.J.Stat.Ann. § 9:3–30; N.Y.Est.Powers & Trusts Law § 2–1.3; N.C.Gen.Stat. § 48–23; Pa.Stat.Ann. tit. 20, § 2514(7).

16. McCaleb v. Brown, 344 So.2d 485 (Ala.1977); Estate of McCallen, 53 Cal.App.3d 142, 125 Cal.Rptr. 645 (1976); Elliott v. Hiddleson, 303 N.W.2d 140 (Iowa, 1981); In re Trusts of Harrington, 311 Minn. 403, 250 N.W.2d 163 (1977); Estate of Sykes, 477 Pa. 254, 383 A.2d 920 (1978); Wheeling Dollar Savings & Trust Co. v. Hanes, —— W.Va. ——, 237 S.E.2d 499 (1977).

17. Simes & Smith § 724 (2d ed. 1956); Restatement, Property § 286 (1940).

18. Meyer v. Rogers, 173 Kan. 124, 244 P.2d 1169 (1952); Old Colony Trust Co. v. Attorney General of United States, 326 Mass. 532, 95 N.E.2d 649 (1950); Fiduciary Trust Co. v. Michou, 73 R.I. 190, 54 A.2d 421 (1947); In re Kaufer's Will, 203 Wis. 299, 234 N.W. 504 (1931).

19. Eaton v. Eaton, 88 Conn. 269, 91 A. 191 (1914); Rhode Island Hospital Trust

Co. v. Hodgkin, 48 R.I. 459, 137 A. 381 (1927).

20. To be a "child" of the father, the section also requires that the child be openly treated as such by the father. See Alaska Stat. § 13.11.270; Fla.Stat.Ann. § 732.608; 18A Me.Rev.Stat. Ann. § 2–109; Pa.Stat.Ann. tit. 20, §§ 2514(8), 6114(5).

21. See Fellows, Simon & Rau, Public Attitudes About Distribution at Death and Intestate Succession Laws in the United States, 1978 Am. Bar Foundation Research J. 319, 371.

22. Walton v. Lindsey, 349 So.2d 41 (Ala.1977); Will of Hoffman, 53 A.D.2d 55, 385 N.Y.S.2d 49 (1976); Estate of Dulles, 494 Pa. 180, 431 A.2d 208 (1981); In re Trust of Parsons, 56 Wis.2d 613, 203 N.W.2d 40 (1973).

23. Trimble v. Gordon, 430 U.S. 762, 97 S.Ct. 1459, 52 L.Ed.2d 31 (1977). See Estate of Dulles, 494 Pa. 180, 431 A.2d 208 (1981). See also Lalli v. Lalli, 439 U.S. 259, 99 S.Ct. 518, 58 L.Ed.2d 503 (1978).

A stepchild is not included within the term "children" in a dispositive instrument unless there is evidence of intention to include her.[24]

The constructional rules concerning the inclusion or exclusion of adopted children, illegitimate children and stepchildren with respect to the class designation of "children" are also generally applicable with respect to class designations of "descendants," "issue," and "grandchildren".

SECTION 2.   RULE IN WILD'S CASE

In 1599, an English court said that if a testator devises to "A and his children", and at the time of the devise A has no children, A takes a fee tail.   This became known as the first resolution in Wild's case.   The court also said that if a testator devises to "A and his children", and at the time of the devise A has children, A and the children take as joint tenants for life.   This became known as the second resolution in Wild's case.[25]   These conclusions were certainly consistent with the various constructional rules and presumptions which obtained at that time.   It should be emphasized that Wild's case had to do with real property only.

It is not easy to explain why a decision of a sixteenth century English court concerning a constructional problem involving a sixteenth century devise should be relevant to the interpretation of a twentieth century disposition, but there is no doubt that the case has some precedential significance, and it is discussed in every textbook and casebook on future interests.   The courts would be well-advised to forget that Wild's case ever existed, and to construe the disposition to "A and his children" exclusively on the basis of what a twentieth century testator probably meant.

The first resolution in Wild's case makes little sense today. To construe a modern devise to "A and his children", where A has no children, as an attempt to create a fee tail seems rather far-fetched, but it has been done.[26]   In most states a fee tail cannot be created; if it is attempted, it is converted automatically into a fee simple or a life estate in the first tenant with a remainder to his issue in fee.[27]   It would seem a reasonable construction of the gift of real property to "A and his children" to give A a life estate with a remainder to his children, where

24.   Davis v. Mercantile Trust Co., 206 Md. 278, 111 A.2d 602 (1955);   In re Estate of Goetzinger, 12 Misc.2d 197, 176 N.Y.S.2d 899 (1958).   See Annot., 28 A.L.R.3d 1307 (1969).

25.   Wild's Case, 6 Co.Rep. 16b (K.B.1599).

26.   Gilchrist v. Butler, 214 Ala. 288, 107 So. 838 (1926);   Ewing v. Ewing, 198 Miss. 304, 22 So.2d 225 (1945);   Ziegler v. Love, 185 N.C. 40, 115 S.E. 887 (1923); Larew v. Larew, 146 Va. 134, 135 S.E. 819 (1926).

27.   See Simes & Smith § 313 (2d ed. 1956).

A has no children at the testator's death, and there is modern
authority for this view.[28]   In the case of a gift of personalty,
there is authority that A gets absolute ownership, and there is
also authority that A gets a life interest with remainder to his
children.[29]   Absolute ownership in A would follow from the construction that A and the children took an immediate gift as one
class.   A fee tail cannot be created in personalty.[30]

The second resolution in Wild's case makes sense today, provided it is updated by changing the joint tenancy for life to a
tenancy in common in fee.   It is consistent with the class gift
interpretation.   This is the prevailing construction of the gift to
"A and his children" if A has children at the date of the testator's
death, both with respect to realty and personalty.[31]   There is
some authority, however, to the effect that A gets a life estate
with a remainder in his children.[32]

SECTION 3.   GIFT OVER ON DEATH WITHOUT ISSUE

There has been considerable litigation during the past several
centuries over the meaning of a gift to "A and his heirs, but if
A shall die without issue, to B and his heirs".

First of all, what does "die without issue" mean?   The answer
appears simple—you look to the time of A's death to determine
whether or not he has any children or grandchildren.   But that
is not the way the English courts originally construed this language.   The English adopted the so-called "indefinite failure of
issue" construction—if at any time in the future A's line of descent should come to an end, then there was a gift over to B and
his heirs.   The effect of this was a fee tail in A and a remainder
in B.[33]   This seems a distortion of the language, and particularly
unsuited to American circumstances since the fee tail never found
a real home here.   Most of our jurisdictions, by judicial decision
or statute, adopted the so-called "definite failure of issue" construction—you look to the date of A's death to determine whether
he has issue, and to that time alone.   If A has issue at that time,

---

28.   Sewell v. Thrailkill, 209 Ark. 393,
194 S.W.2d 202 (1945);   Lacey's Executrix
v. Lacey, 170 Ky. 47, 185 S.W. 495 (1916);
Ellingrod v. Trombla, 168 Neb. 264, 95
N.W.2d 635 (1959).   See Restatement,
Property § 283 (1940).

29.   5 American Law of Property § 22.21
(Casner ed. 1952).

30.   Simes & Smith § 359 (2d ed. 1956).

31.   In re Parant's Will, 39 Misc.2d 285,
240 N.Y.S.2d 558 (1963);   Buckner v.

Maynard, 198 N.C. 802, 153 S.E. 458
(1930);   Rose v. Rose, 191 Va. 171, 60
S.E.2d 45 (1950).   See Simes & Smith
§ 698 (2d ed. 1956).

32.   Prewitt v. Prewitt's Executors, 303
Ky. 772, 199 S.W.2d 435 (1947);   Rum-
merfield v. Mason, 352 Mo. 865, 179 S.W.2d
732 (1944);   In re McCullough's Estate, 272
Pa. 509, 116 A. 477 (1922).

33.   Simes & Smith § 522 (2d ed. 1956).

then the gift over to B fails.[34] This seems to be the literal meaning of the words, and it is the only sensible conclusion in a system where the fee tail is virtually a dead letter. The English also struck down the constructional preference for indefinite failure by statute in the nineteenth century.

The remainder of our discussion then will be premised upon a definite failure of issue construction; the problems can arise in a gift of personalty as well as realty. Does A "die without issue" if A has a child who dies at the age of two days, and later A dies without any issue surviving him? Is the gift over destroyed the moment A has a child, regardless of survivorship of A? The prevailing view is that the clause means "die without issue surviving A"; there is a gift over to B if A is not survived by issue regardless of whether he had a child who predeceased him.[35]

Does B take if A dies after the testator without issue? That is what the words of the devise seem to say. But a number of courts have construed the language to mean that B takes only if A predeceases the testator without issue; if A survives the testator, A's interest then and there becomes absolute. This construction is sometimes called the substitutional construction.[36] Other courts have construed the language in accordance with its literal meaning and have held that B takes whenever A dies without issue. This construction is sometimes called the successive construction.[37] The substitutional construction clears the title to the land involved at the testator's death; if legal title to personal property is involved, it is also a practical result due to the awkwardness of legal future interests in personalty. Obviously the substitutional construction can have no application to the inter vivos gift.

Now suppose this same problem appears in a future interest: To X for life, remainder to A and his heirs, but if A dies without issue, to B and his heirs. Once again, the language seems to

---

34. E.g., Ga.Code Ann. § 44–6–25; Mass.Gen.Laws Ann. ch. 184, § 6; Neb.Rev.Stat. § 76–111; N.Y.Est.Powers & Trusts Law § 6–5.6; N.C.Gen.Stat. § 41–4; Va.Code § 55–13; Goldberger v. Goldberger, 34 Del.Ch. 237, 102 A.2d 338 (1954); Monroe v. Leckey, 4 Ohio Op.2d 208, 142 N.E.2d 314 (C.P.1956), affirmed 4 Ohio Op.2d 215, 143 N.E.2d 168 (Ct.App.1956). See Simes & Smith §§ 526, 527 (2d ed. 1956).

35. Massengill v. Abell, 192 N.C. 240, 134 S.E. 641 (1926); Briggs v. Hopkins, 103 Ohio St. 321, 132 N.E. 843 (1921); Drummond v. Drummond, 146 S.C. 194, 143 S.E. 818 (1928).

36. Roy v. McComb, 232 Ark. 769, 340 S.W.2d 381 (1960); Apple v. Methodist Hospital, 138 Ind.App. 420, 206 N.E.2d 625 (1965); Moore v. Hunter, 46 N.C.App. 449, 265 S.E.2d 884 (1980); Martin v. Taylor, 521 S.W.2d 581 (Tenn.1975).

37. Rushin v. Woodward, 230 Ga. 220, 196 S.E.2d 396 (1973); St. Joseph Hospital v. Dwertman, 268 S.W.2d 646 (Ky.1954); Hays v. Cole, 221 Miss. 459, 73 So.2d 258 (1954); Cook v. Crabill, 110 Ohio App. 45, 164 N.E.2d 425 (1959); Smith v. Bynum, 558 S.W.2d 99 (Tex.Civ. App.1977).

say that B takes whenever A dies without issue, and some courts have so held.[38] A few courts have applied the substitutional construction that we just discussed to this future interest situation—B takes only if A predeceases the testator without issue.[39] Probably the prevailing view, however, is that B takes only if A dies without issue prior to the termination of the preceding life estate in X; if A survives X, A's interest is absolute.[40]

If the future interest situation arises under a trust of personal property, then certainly the construction which gives A an absolute interest if he survives X makes good sense. An executory interest hanging over possessory title in personalty is very awkward and probably not intended.

38.   Vassar v. Vassar, 191 N.C. 332, 131 S.E. 647 (1926); Avery v. Avery, 107 Ohio App. 199, 157 N.E.2d 917 (1958); Vickers v. Vickers, 205 Tenn. 86, 325 S.W.2d 544 (1959).

39.   Richardson v. Chastain, 123 Ind.App. 444, 111 N.E.2d 831 (1953); Ballance v. Garner, 161 Kan. 371, 168 P.2d 533 (1946); Salem National Bank & Trust Co. v. Elkinton, 139 N.J.Eq. 429, 51 A.2d 889 (1947).

40.   In re Estate of Creekmore, 244 Ark. 1, 423 S.W.2d 548 (1968); Ashland Oil & Refining Co. v. Rice, 383 S.W.2d 369 (Ky.1964); Bowdle v. Hanks, 229 Md. 352, 182 A.2d 790 (1962); In re Estate of Carr, 173 Neb. 189, 112 N.E.2d 786 (1962).

TABLE OF CASES

References are to Pages

239

*

INDEX

†